"The Broaching Framework stands as one of the most influential contributions to culturally responsive practice across the helping professions in the past three decades. In this landmark book, Dr. Norma Day-Vines masterfully brings together the theory, research, and applied strategies that counselors, psychologists, social workers, and other helping professionals can use to broach issues of race, ethnicity, and culture with clarity, intentionality, and skill. Integrating compelling case illustrations with concrete guidance for practice, this text will shape how professionals facilitate meaningful cultural dialogue and how we prepare the next generation of practitioners. Pick it up and, as Dr. Day-Vines would say: 'You gon' learn today.'"

Joseph M. Williams, PhD, *NCC Professor, Program Director of the School Counseling Program, University of North Carolina at Chapel Hill, School of Education*

"Dr. Day-Vines draws readers in through the narrative of her personal journey into the field of counselor education. It is not often that we celebrate the panic that new professionals feel when they realize only five weeks remain to make a meaningful impact. Yet in this case, that moment of urgency became the catalyst for discovery, reflection, and professional agency. What unfolded during that fateful time-period ultimately led to the development of a powerful broaching paradigm; one that invites practitioners and counselors-in-training to see not only themselves, but also their clients and the broader worlds in which those clients live."

S. Kent Butler, PhD, *Past President and Fellow, American Counseling Association, Fellow, National Association of Diversity Officers in Higher Education, Professor of Counselor Education, University of Central Florida*

Broaching Race, Ethnicity, and Culture in the Counseling Process

Broaching Race, Ethnicity, and Culture in the Counseling Process identifies practical strategies and tools that help mental health providers facilitate discussions with their clients about the extent to which issues related to race, ethnicity, and culture impact their presenting concerns.

Broaching refers to a counseling approach in which the mental health provider discusses the contextual dimensions of race, ethnicity, and culture during the counseling process. This book provides a conceptual framework and an empirically supported set of strategies for helping mental health providers skillfully navigate conversations that support clients in their exploration and examination of how issues of race, ethnicity, and culture may intrude upon their sociocultural and sociopolitical realities. Each chapter provides a detailed discussion of a specific component of the broaching framework, a review of relevant research that provides evidentiary warrants supporting the model, guidance about implementing the broaching model, case examples to illustrate how the broaching process can unfold, and provider-client broaching dialogues, along with a set of discussion questions to support continued learning and skill development.

Drawing on the theoretical and empirical multicultural counseling literature, this groundbreaking text integrates and synthesizes the existing broaching literature in ways that render the process of discussing race, ethnicity, and culture more concrete.

Norma L. Day-Vines, PhD, is a professor at Johns Hopkins University and creator of the Broaching Framework, advancing culturally responsive counseling through research, training, and equity-centered counseling practice.

Broaching Race, Ethnicity, and Culture in the Counseling Process

Strategies for Facilitating Meaningful Dialogue with Clients

Norma L. Day-Vines

Routledge
Taylor & Francis Group
NEW YORK AND LONDON

Designed cover image: Getty Images

First published 2027
by Routledge
605 Third Avenue, New York, NY 10158

and by Routledge
4 Park Square, Milton Park, Abingdon, Oxon, OX14 4RN

Routledge is an imprint of the Taylor & Francis Group, an informa business

ISBN: 9781041092858 (hbk)
ISBN: 9781041092827 (pbk)
ISBN: 9781003649311 (ebk)

DOI: 10.4324/9781003649311

Typeset in Times New Roman
by codeMantra

This book is lovingly dedicated to the memory of my parents, the late Olivia and Norman E. Day, who were my first broachers. Long before I had language for broaching theory, they modeled the courage and care required to engage in honest conversations about race, ethnicity, and culture. They taught my sister and me that meaningful dialogue is both an act of love and a pathway to liberation.

I also dedicate this work to my late husband, J. Arthur Vines, who believed that the sun should never set on a disagreement without thoughtful conversation and genuine resolution. His commitment to dialogue, dignity, and repair continues to guide my work and my life.

Contents

Tables

Acknowledgments

An endeavor like developing a broaching framework that addresses the contextual dimensions of race, ethnicity, and culture does not happen in isolation. It evolves because multiple thought partners come together and help flesh out a substantive counseling model that centers clients' lived realities around race, ethnicity, and culture.

I stand on the shoulders of giants, including former professors, Don Locke, Herbert Exum, Norman Sprinthall, Edwin Gerler, as well as giants in the field such as William Cross and Janet Helms.

My first broaching partners in the academy were a group of doctoral students with whom I met weekly for a year as we refined what became the Continuum of Broaching Behavior. Many thanks to Laurie Craigen, Kylie Dotson-Blake, Marcy Douglass, Angela Holman, Tim Grothaus, and Susannah Wood. Our shared and different experiences, realities, and perspectives contributed to what has become a seminal article in the field.

Over the years, I've had many other collaborators, including Dana Griffin, Beverly Booker Ammah, Sam Steen, Kristy Arnold, Jennifer Brodar, Erica Fernandez-Korto, Carolina Garcia, Katelyn Jones, Mary Beth Cogan, Clio Franklin, Donna Sudak, Zane Sejdiu, Yas Patel, Hal Kronsberg, Anne Ruble, Robtrice Brawner, Zainab Jackson, Tongyao Ran, Nyki Caldwell, Michelle Muratori, Willmara Moye, Jonell McPherson, onsb Raymond Shorter Beth Day-Hairston, Anissa Howard, Hilde Depauw, Fallon Robinson, and Nick Highe, Richard Lofton, Anita Young, Yiying Xiong, Jodi Miller, Hsin-Ya Tang, Benny Hsieh, Betty Liu, Hsiang-Chen Yeh, Kristy Thedore. I am indebted to Erik Hines, Malik Henfield, and Ahmad Washington who included book chapters on the broaching framework in their edited collections. Many thanks to Anita Young for making the connection between school counseling leadership and broaching. More recently, I have collaborated with Dantavious Hicks, Fallon Cluxton-Keller, Courtney Agorsor, Sarah Gubara, Nana Otabil, Connie Jones, Tony Spann, and Dipika Daga. To Xie Zhang, whose brilliance in instrument development and linguistic refinement is incomparable. Four years ago, I received funding from the Provost's office to develop a predoctoral program

(Post-Baccalaureate/Graduate Research Edification and Preparedness for the Ph.D. [PREPPED]) designed to help prepare prospective doctoral students for doctoral study. Program participants engaged in a research project. In 2024, our research project investigated differences in African origin clients' perceptions of their counselors' broaching efforts. To my PREPPEd student colleagues who are aspiring PhD's, Bethann Mwombele, Miguel Austin, Caiya Hampton, Mikayla Henning, and Mide Pecku, thank you for your investment in our research project, Chipping Away at monolithic Blackness. Many thanks to the most recent pre-doctoral scholars who are expanding the notion of broaching in a global context - Arianna Asare, Dipika Daga, Emily Shipley, Sierra Campbell, Edgar Grajeda, and Selena Guthrie. More recently I've partnered with Hilde Depauw, Hsin-Ya Tang, Betty Liu, Hsiang-Chen Yeh, Benny Hsieh, and Kristy Theodore. To Hilde Depauw who literally crossed the pond so that we could collaborate on our mutual interest in the broaching framework, much obliged. I look forward to future collaborations.

Thirty years ago, it was a challenging feat for young, newly minted Black and African American female faculty members to navigate the academy. The most recent cohort of scholars engaged in a comparative analysis of African American and Afro-Caribbean clients' perceptions of their counselors' broaching efforts. Arianna Asare, Sierra Campbell, Dipika Daga, Edgar Grajeda, Selena Guthrie, and Emily Shipley, whether we're discussing the 19's or the 20's - you rock. Mentorship often felt elusive. For many of us, our survival depended on our ability to figure out how to develop a viable research agenda that cohered with our core personal and professional values. A small group of us decided to band together and support one another with regular meetings that helped us make sense of the idiosyncrasies of the academy and work on collaborative research projects. We called ourselves the SUPER Sister – Sisters United to Produce Excellent Research. I am eternally grateful for that meaningful start and to have had an opportunity to work with a remarkable set of Counselor Educators: Cheryl Holcomb-McCoy, Julia Bryan, Cheryl Moore-Thomas, and Natasha Mitchell.

Many thanks to Carla Adkison-Bradley who deemed it important to devote a special issue of the *Journal of Multicultural Counseling and Development* to the Broaching Framework. I moved forward with some trepidation, but I am eternally grateful for the opportunity to contribute to the profession.

To Isaac Burt who convinced me that the broaching construct is an emerging theory. To my JHU counselor education colleagues who incorporate the broaching framework in their classes I appreciate you. Many thanks to friends and colleagues who read early versions of this manuscript: Angie Coker, Kent Butler, Jordynn Connell, and Melissa Sweeney.

I've had several opportunities to present the broaching framework to a variety of audiences. Several years ago, Tony Spann introduced me to Kevin Dedner, who had recently founded Hurdle Health, a telemental health company dedicated to culturally intentional mental healthcare. Kevin invited me to spend the next two and a half years working with his team of experts to flesh out a training model for therapists. While at Hurdle, I had an opportunity to meet esteemed psychologist Woody Neighbors who found the broaching framework compelling.

I am especially indebted to my friend Lynn Friedman with whom I've had numerous broaching conversations. Lynn invited me to present the broaching framework at the Baltimore Washington Psychoanalytic Institute. From there I met Drs. Anne Ruble, Donna Sudak, and Mary Beth Cogan who invited me to assist with their training of second-year psychiatry residents in the broaching framework. I'm also appreciative of individuals who helped me think more broadly about the broaching framework. Dr. Valaida Wise insisted that the broaching framework is more than a counseling model; it is an organizational development model as well.

Feedback in the form of both praise and criticism from colleagues and students alike has been invaluable to the development of the Broaching Framework and ultimately to this book.

Friendship is the gift that binds the world. Without the Spring Water Lane Contingent, my world would surely have unraveled. They have been there for me more than 20 years through trials and triumphs. Many thanks to Sharon, Charles, Rochelle, Barry, and Maureen, who have helped with home projects, childcare, tutoring, meals, vacations, etc. I could not ask for a greater set of neighbors. When you work hard, you have to play hard – to members of the Black Self-Care Collective for our travel adventures. The most remarkable traveling buddies in the world – Jaelyn, Beth and Greg, Karen and Naja, Sierra and Melissa, Dantavious, Barry and Rochelle, Jeanette Joy, Felita, Tracey, Wallene, and Anissa.

To two of my closest friends—Karen Hall and Colleen. Karen, whom I met during my early years as a school counselor trainee, has inspired me in countless ways. She broadened my intellectual horizons, nurtured my love of reading, and challenged me to think more deeply about issues of equity, justice, and critical consciousness. Colleen, whom I have known since we were freshmen in college, has remained a steadfast source of friendship and support through every season of my life. She has celebrated my triumphs, helped me navigate life's challenges, and has always been there through every high and every low.

To my sister Beth who has been with me literally since day one thank you for always having my back from childhood to the present. We are twin tough!!! To my cousin Kim who has been a rock over the last several years. Most of all, to my daughter, Jaelyn, who knows more about broaching than she ever wanted to know, who has listened, to read, and even helped co-author a broaching article, thank you for joining me on this journey. Thank you for your love, encouragement, and for reminding me each day about what truly matters. May you always pursue oyur dreams with courage, compassion, and conviction. This book is lovingly dedicated to you.

About the Author

Dr. Norma L. Day-Vines is Professor of Counseling and Educational Studies at Johns Hopkins University's School of Education and a nationally recognized scholar in multicultural counseling. Over the past three decades, she has developed and advanced the Broaching Framework – a widely cited model that guides counselors and educators in intentionally addressing race, ethnicity, and culture within professional practice. Her scholarship has significantly shaped discourse on culturally responsive counseling, racial dialogue, and equity-centered practice. Dr. Day-Vines has published extensively in leading journals, including the *Journal of Counseling & Development* and the *Journal of Multicultural Counseling and Development*, and has served in editorial leadership roles that advance scholarship on broaching across disciplines. Currently, she serves as co-editor of the Review of Educational Research. Her research integrates conceptual as well as quantitative and qualitative methodologies to examine how culturally responsive engagement influences professional practice.

In addition to her scholarly contributions, Dr. Day-Vines is deeply committed to mentoring emerging scholars and strengthening the mental health workforce in under-resourced communities. Through her teaching, grant-funded initiatives, national and international trainings, she continues to equip professionals with practical strategies for facilitating meaningful dialogue about race, ethnicity, and culture in counseling and educational settings.

Chapter 1

Introduction

What Exactly Is Broaching and Why Is It Important?

Ordinarily, mental health providers experience little difficulty discussing clients' experiences of grief and loss, depression, anxiety, troubled relationships, substance use, etc. Providers experience far more difficulty broaching or discussing issues related to race, ethnicity, and culture; yet a growing body of research confirms that ethnic minority clients in particular attest to the value of mental health providers possessing and displaying a requisite set of culturally responsive counseling skills (Day-Vines et al., 2024; Eken et al., 2021; Lukowitsky et al., 2024). This book presents a conceptual framework for broaching or discussing clients' racial, ethnic, and cultural concerns, empirical evidence documenting the benefits that accrue when providers broach effectively, and a set of practical strategies for working more effectively with culturally and linguistically diverse clients.

Broaching reflects the mental health provider's consideration and open discussion about the way issues related to race, ethnicity, and culture may influence, shape, or even intrude upon the client's presenting concerns. The *Broaching* framework, as it is referred to in this book, represents the culmination of nearly 30 years of work as a counselor education scholar aimed at helping students and practicing professionals refine their ability to broach or discuss clients' concerns around race, ethnicity, and culture in ways that make clients feel heard, understood, and comfortable addressing these dimensions that shape their presenting concerns.

In my early years as a professor, I recognized that many of my students were reluctant to facilitate discussions with clients who were culturally and linguistically different from themselves. As an example, my first faculty appointment occurred in the late 1990s at a small liberal arts college. At that time, it was not unusual for me to be the only person of color in my classrooms. My regular teaching assignment included a course on multicultural counseling. The curriculum we used followed a tripartite multicultural counseling framework (awareness, knowledge, skills) designed to help students develop proficiency in working with clients across a range of cultural backgrounds. The conceptual model involved awareness competencies or recognition of one's own inner self

DOI: 10.4324/9781003649311-1

(e.g., attitudes, biases, and assumptions), as well as recognition of the sociopolitical challenges that clients confront (e.g., powerlessness, oppression). A second component of the model involved knowledge competencies or acquisition of factual information about people from culturally distinct groups. The third component of the model involved skills or the integration and synthesis of awareness and knowledge competencies.

The textbook I adopted for the course did a phenomenal job of addressing providers' awareness and knowledge competencies; however, as a brand-new first-semester assistant professor, I was unprepared for the fact that the skills component of the textbook contained very little clinical material I could translate into instructional strategies. In a panic, I had to decide how I was going to spend the last five weeks of the course. At that time, poor teaching evaluations in a class could make or break a faculty member, especially a faculty member of color. Given the limited number of strategies and interventions in the textbook, I had to rely on my own creative devices.

That same semester, I was also teaching a counseling practicum and internship course, and much to my chagrin, I noticed in reviewing students' tape-recorded counseling sessions with clients that when they were working with clients of color, they often dodged issues around race, ethnicity, and culture. As the instructor, it seemed patently obvious to me that this glaring omission was problematic. This was far less obvious, however, to my students. In an effort to help students surmount these challenges so they could engage in meaningful and substantive dialogues with clients, nurture the counseling relationship, and alleviate psychological distress, I developed a series of exercises to help students conceptualize the racial, ethnic, and cultural concerns with which both students and their clients seemed to grapple. My aim was to give students a frame of reference for subsequently discussing clients' cultural concerns with confidence. When senior faculty in the counseling clinic introduced my lesson plans to their supervisees, I realized that I was on to something. At the time, I referred to these classroom activities as *broaching* exercises, because broaching refers to one's effort to discuss a difficult topic. What started out as a lesson plan eventually became a series of journal articles and, subsequently, a viable research agenda that has gained traction in counselor education, psychology, and now psychiatry.

In subsequent semesters, I had students incorporate broaching exercises into their recorded counseling sessions with clients, regardless of the sociodemographic characteristics (e.g., race, gender, class, religion, sexual orientation, language, and national origin) of the client. In the practicum course, students would conduct audio- and video-recorded counseling sessions with their clients. During clinical supervision, I would meet with students and give them oral and later written feedback on their taped counseling sessions. One incident that I recall vividly involved a 25-year-old White female master's student in the counseling program who counseled a 19-year-old African American female matriculating as an undergraduate student at the same institution. Each week the counselor trainee would submit a tape, and her sessions would unfold in a fairly circuitous manner: "How are you? I am fine. How have things been since the last session?" To me, their sessions resembled chitchat, small talk, and coffee shop conversations versus actual counseling. To be clear, chitchat is definitely not counseling. Each week I would encourage the counselor trainee to achieve a greater level of depth and intimacy by exploring what it was like for her client to be one of the very few African American students on campus. I was guided by both the scholarly literature that described challenges students of color experienced as they matriculated at predominantly White institutions (Fleming, 1984) as well as my own intuition, clinical insights, and conceptual hypothesis that the client desired to talk in more depth about her racial, ethnic, and cultural concerns. It seemed to me the client was waiting for an invitation from her counselor trainee to explore these concerns; however, my White counselor trainee was reluctant to broach race, ethnicity, and culture with her client. For at least three consecutive supervision sessions, she submitted tapes that continued in the same circuitous pattern. Needless to say, her sessions remained flat and aimless.

I finally said to the counselor trainee, "If you do not ask this young African American client what it means to be one of very few students of color on this campus, you will not pass my class." Because students are addicted to A's, I'm convinced that got her attention. During the next supervision session, she submitted a tape where she did indeed broach with the client in a very substantive manner. The client went from talking superficially about college life, to an in-depth discussion about being the first in her family to go to college. She talked about feeling a sense of isolation and alienation on a predominantly White campus, moving to a college town from an urban community, not being invited to participate in study groups, and questioning whether she even belonged on a predominantly White college campus. The client confided that at one point she even contemplated leaving college. As the reader might surmise, my graduate student earned an A in the class because she was able to take my clinical feedback and move from having superficial conversations to discussing the client's existential angst. As a young professor, I felt vindicated, assured that I was helping students develop into competent providers.

The following semester, I had the same counselor trainee in my internship class. One day at the start of class she asked me if she could address her classmates. I said, "Of course." She told the class that I was her practicum professor during the previous semester, and I insisted that she broach. She shared that she didn't think broaching was necessary. She even had the gall to say that she approached a therapist in town to inquire about the appropriateness of having to discuss issues related to race, ethnicity, and culture with clients during treatment – as if clients' concerns around race, ethnicity, and culture are tangential to the counseling process. She told the class that I insisted that she broach and even threatened her chance of earning an A. Her comments were all accurate. She shared that she did indeed broach because she wanted to salvage her grade. She confided that once she broached the client's racial, ethnic, and cultural concerns, she came to the realization that she was the one who struggled to examine how issues of race and representation impacted the client. The client did not have any of these apprehensions. In fact, it seemed the client was waiting patiently, expectantly even, for the counselor trainee to initiate a dialogue about the embeddedness of race, ethnicity, and culture in her sociocultural and sociopolitical experience. By opening the door to some of the client's unstated concerns, the counselor trainee was able to make headways with the client and help her examine some of her most difficult intersectional challenges that were rooted in issues of race, gender, class, and oppression. That semester, the counselor trainee developed considerable confidence in her own ability to broach the client's racial, ethnic, and cultural concerns.

The silver lining in this story is that the client graduated from college and soon after matriculated in our counselor education program and is now a practicing counselor herself. This experience served as confirmation for me that teaching students to broach necessitated a strong theoretical and empirical rationale, a concrete set of strategies and techniques that students could implement with relative ease, support, and reassurance from those providing clinical supervision. Further, it set me on a path to writing and researching about what broaching is and how to broach effectively. Broaching is not a random act. It involves a deliberate and intentional set of cognitive processes that the provider conceptualizes before implementing a broaching statement.

In this book, the reader will develop essential tools for broaching the client's racial, ethnic, and cultural concerns. In particular, readers will learn about the benefits of broaching, the current broaching research literature, barriers to broaching, the potential for committing ruptures when broaching ineffectively, a conceptual framework, as well as a set of concrete strategies for facilitating meaningful broaching discussions with clients concerning the connection between their presenting concerns and race, ethnicity, and culture.

Who Will Benefit from Reading This Book?

Mental health students and providers are the target audience for this book. These professionals include but are not limited to counselors (e.g., school, clinical mental health, marriage and family, rehabilitation, addictions), psychologists, social workers, psychiatrists, clergy members, psychiatric nurses, nurse clinicians, allied mental health professionals, paraprofessionals, and any other personnel who work with clients in a helping capacity. Throughout this book, I use the term mental health provider and provider interchangeably to refer to these professionals collectively. Although the designation mental health provider does not capture the specific role function of each professional described above, it does serve as an appropriate umbrella term. Be that as it may, in each of these varied disciplines, providers will be called upon to work with clients who grapple with pressing personal challenges that may be connected to some aspect of their race, ethnicity, and/or culture. Many clients will likely expect providers to explore their sociocultural, sociopolitical, and sociohistorical realities with relative ease and without considerable prompting.

Because the provider wields the balance of power within the counseling dyad, the onus falls on the mental health provider to both initiate and respond to the client's need to explore the contextual dimensions of race, ethnicity, and culture during treatment (Cardemil & Battle, 2003; Chang & Yoon, 2011; Choi et al., 2015; Day-Vines et al., 2018). Given that by the time a client presents in counseling, they likely feel overwhelmed and even demoralized, the client should not have the added challenge of both experiencing a stressful life event and assuming the emotional burden of convincing the provider that issues of race, ethnicity, and culture are germane to their presenting problem. Much like the counselor trainee-client interaction described above, clients may withhold pertinent information about their racial, ethnic, and cultural concerns unless prompted specifically to explore these topics – primarily because they harbor apprehensions about provider reactions to issues of race and representation. Incidentally, a spate of previous research suggests that minoritized clients expect providers to have a basic understanding of their culture and to be able to skillfully process their concerns so that clients feel heard and understood (Eken, 2021; Lukowitsky et al., 2024). The inability to foster psychological safety and fruitful discussions about race, ethnicity, and culture may result in ruptures and subsequent premature termination (Brawner et al., 2025; Chang et al., 2020). Development of the relational skills to explore or broach clients' sociocultural and sociopolitical concerns becomes increasingly more relevant when considered in the context of the rapidly changing demographic landscape within the United States.

Demographic Trends in the United States

Demographic shifts in the population indicate that ethnic minorities are increasing at a rapid rate, compared to their non-Hispanic White counterparts. More specifically, the non-Hispanic White population decreased from 63.8% in 2010 to 58.9% in 2022 (USA Facts, 2023). According to the U. S. Census Bureau, in 2023, non-Hispanic Whites comprised 58.4% of the U.S. population, while Blacks, Asians, Hispanics, and those with two or more races made up 13.7%, 6.4%, 19.5%, and 3.1%, respectively. Demographers predict that by 2060, non-Hispanic Whites will become a numerical minority, dropping from 63.8% of the population in 2016 to less than 50% of the population. Collectively, Blacks, Asians, Hispanics, and individuals with two or more races will grow by 41%, 101%, 93%, and 197.8%, respectively, constituting a numerical majority (Vespa et al., 2020).

The population of mental healthcare providers does not resemble the demographic composition of the nation. Although the ethnic minority population is increasing rapidly, the mental health workforce has remained stagnant. To illustrate, only 10.4% of practicing psychiatrists are Hispanic, Black-African American, or Asian (Wyse et al., 2020). The psychology workforce has slightly more representation with 16.31% of providers comprising Hispanic, Black-African American, or Asian clinicians. Among mental health providers, Hispanic, Black-African American, and Asian clinicians make up 29% of the workforce (Career Explorer, 2024). Compared to other mental health providers, ethnic minority clinical social workers comprise 35.5% of the social work population, making them the most represented group of mental healthcare providers (Zippia, 2024). The majority of the mental health workforce is female and non-Hispanic White and may not be representative of the communities they serve. In addition to the underrepresentation of ethnic minority mental health providers, there are widespread shortages of providers overall (Health Resources and Services Administration, 2023).

Calculations, based on the 2020 U.S. Census Data, indicate that the chance two randomly chosen people will be from different racial and ethnic backgrounds stands at 61%, which represents a 6.1% increase since the 2010 census report (Jensen et al., 2021). These demographic findings imply a high probability that the race and/or sociodemographic characteristics of the provider will differ from the race and/or sociodemographic characteristics of the client, leading to a greater number of cross-racial and cross-cultural counseling dyads. Given the foregoing discussion, even when the provider and client share the same racial designation, there exists a high probability that the provider and client will differ ethnically. Differences in race, ethnicity, and culture between the provider and client may impact communication, trust, understandings, etc. (Sue et al., 2022). Consequently, providers must remain attuned to the sociocultural and sociopolitical complexities that clients experience. Providers will likely need to explore how clients' racial, ethnic, and cultural backgrounds intersect with their presenting concerns. Inattention to clients' racial, ethnic, and cultural concerns may result in cultural ruptures, client dissatisfaction with the counseling process, and high rates of premature termination (Chang & Berk, 2009). In fact, a large corpus of scholarship indicates that clients for whom race, ethnicity, and culture are important desire providers who can examine their REC concerns in a culturally adaptive and skillful manner (Alegria et al., 2020; Lukowitsky et al., 2024).

Demographic Shifts among Immigrant Populations

Prior to the Immigration and Nationality Act of 1965, immigrants to the United States originated primarily from European countries. Passage of the Hart-Celler Immigration Act of 1965 eliminated quotas in U.S. immigration policy, which contributed to an increasing number of immigrants entering the United States from destinations outside of western and northern Europe (Immigration and Nationality Act of 1965). These more equitable immigration policies have contributed to the diversity of countries from which immigrants originate (Passel et al., 2024). In 1970, immigrants accounted for 4.7% of the U.S. population, and by 2023, their share of the population rose to 14.3% (Moslimani & Passel, 2024). Mexico, India, the Philippines, Vietnam, and China are among the top countries of origin for immigrants to the United States (Migration Policy Institute, 2023). Demographers predict that by 2060 immigrants will account for 17% of the population, and 80% of U.S. immigrants will be members of an ethnic minority group (Vespa et al., 2020).

In January 2025, 53.3 million immigrants lived in the United States; yet, by June of 2025, that number decreased to 51.9 million, owing in large measure to immigration policy changes governing the rights of undocumented individuals and asylum seekers (Kramer & Passel, 2025). The arbitrary and capricious manner in which immigrants have been detained and deported has resulted in mental health consequences that stem from family separation, fear, uncertainty, loss of control over circumstances, and structural and physical violence. Even migrants who are in the United States lawfully have cause for alarm. In recognition of the enduring challenges immigrants face, the International Organization for Migration (IOM, 2011) requested that governments recognize migration as a social determinant of health by ensuring that migrants have equitable access to various forms of health and mental health care. Incidentally, social determinants of health involve non-medical factors such as immigration policies, housing, nutrition, and employment that directly impact health and wellness.

Immigrant communities work painstakingly hard to adjust to new communities. Factors that impact social resilience among foreign-born immigrants include family cohesion, neighborhood context, social support and/or exclusion, transnational ties to the homeland, fluency in the host language, discrimination, and acculturative stress. Incidentally, acculturative stress results from attempting to adapt to a new cultural milieu. The strain of acclimating to a new environment can have adverse effects on the experiences of immigrants in this country and include, but are not limited to, issues of race, gender, class, language, anti-immigrant sentiment, a sense of grief and loss of the homeland, cultural conflict, loneliness and isolation, and, depending upon the circumstances of migration, post-traumatic stress disorder. Scholars caution that acculturative stress, as well as sociodemographic characteristics such as race, ethnicity, national origin, gender, socioeconomic status, and language acquisition, varies considerably among immigrants. As such, providers should not regard the immigrant community as a monolith but consider how their ecological contexts affect their specific and unique circumstances (Alegria et al., 2017).

Scope of Mental Healthcare Disparities

The term mental health disparity is variously defined but refers broadly to differential mental health outcomes based on race, ethnicity, gender, socioeconomic status, etc., that are preventable and result from systemic factors that impact the incidence and prevalence of mental and physical disorders, access to and quality of care, and morbidity and mortality rates (Safran et al., 2009). These disparities have important implications for the delivery of culturally responsive mental health care. Although rates of depression are lower among ethnic minorities compared to their White counterparts, depression in Blacks and Hispanics tends to be more disabling and persistent (American Psychiatric Association, 2017a). Between 2013 and 2016, non-Hispanic Asians over age 20 had the lowest prevalence rates for depression (3.1%), followed by non-Hispanic Whites (7.9%), Hispanics (8.2%), and Blacks (9.2%); however, non-Hispanic White adults were more likely to receive mental health treatment (24.4%), compared to Hispanics (12.6%), non-Hispanic Blacks (15.3%), and 7.7% of Asians (Terlizzi & Norris, 2020). Published reports indicate that among those with serious mental illness, African Americans experience the highest lifetime prevalence of PTSD (8.7%) compared to their White (7.4%), Latino (7%), and Asian (4%) counterparts (Lu et al., 2023).

Among adults aged 18 or older who reported any mental illness in the past year, 35.2% were non-Hispanic Multiracial, 24.6% were non-Hispanic White, 21.4% were Hispanic, 19.7% were non-Hispanic Black, 19.6% were non-Hispanic AIAN, and 16.8% were non-Hispanic Asian (Substance Abuse and Mental Health Services Administration [SAMHSA], 2023). In 2022, 21.5% of adults received some form of mental health treatment; however, ethnic minorities were less likely to receive mental health care compared to Whites or multiracial adults (SAMHSA). More specifically, White individuals (56.1%) experienced the highest treatment rates, followed by individuals with two or more races (56%), Hispanics (39.6%), Blacks (37.9%), and 36.1% of Asians (SAMHSA). Immigrants who experience discrimination are at greater risk for depression, anxiety, and post-traumatic stress disorder (Derr, 2016). Immigrants from Asia, Latin America, and Africa underutilize mental health services compared to their U.S.-born counterparts, irrespective of the fact that they have equal or greater need, especially among men, the uninsured, and the undocumented (Derr).

Several studies have demonstrated connections between exposure to discrimination and diminished levels of psychological functioning. For instance, African American males experiencing severe depression are more likely to be misdiagnosed with schizophrenia. Mental health providers are more inclined to fixate on symptoms of psychosis and ignore symptoms associated with major depression, even when their symptomatology mirrors that of Whites (Metzl, 2011). To illustrate, in a study of patients in an outpatient treatment facility, Blacks diagnosed with schizophrenia were 8.2 times more likely to screen positively for major depression than White patients (Gara et al., 2019). The researchers attributed the diagnostic oversight to clinician bias. The Institute of Medicine (2003) has attributed the overdiagnosis of schizophrenia and underdiagnosis of affective disorders in Black men to clinician bias rather than prevalence rates.

A study surveying a sample of undocumented Mexican immigrants demonstrated that younger respondents, individuals residing in the United States for more than ten years, those who had experienced trauma, and those who experienced interpersonal discrimination were significantly more likely to be diagnosed with clinically significant levels of psychological distress (Garcini et al., 2018). The foregoing discussion implies that mental health providers must recognize the ethno-racial challenges clients confront around misdiagnosis in an effort to address mental health disparities and respond in culturally appropriate ways to the impact of discrimination and trauma on the psychological functioning of minoritized clients in order to enhance counseling outcomes.

Sexual Minorities

Nearly 5% of the U.S. population identifies as lesbian, gay, bisexual, and 39% of those individuals have reported a mental illness within the past year (Mental Health America, n.d.). Compared to their heterosexual counterparts, members of the LGBTQIA+ community are 2.5 times more likely to experience depression, anxiety, and substance misuse (Brenner, 2020). Regrettably, they have less social support, especially in areas of the country that have fewer sexual minorities. Moreover, members of the LGBTQIA+ community have difficulty accessing affirming mental health care and have reported insensitive treatment and microaggressions from mental health providers (Eliscu et al., 2023). Regrettably, this community struggles with stigma, homophobia, internalized homonegativity, and heteronormativity (American Psychiatric Association, 2017b).

Barriers to Mental Health Care

In addition to discrimination, scholars attribute underutilization of counseling services among minoritized groups to limited access to quality affordable mental health care, the dearth of providers of color, cost, language barriers, and stigma (American Psychiatric Association, 2017a). Misra et al. (2021) conducted a systematic review to examine cultural aspects of mental illness stigma among Asian Americans, Black Americans, and Latinx Americans. In general, racial and ethnic groups reported higher levels of public and self-stigma compared to White Americans. Findings indicated that stigma was associated with (a) structural barriers such as limited access to care; (b) affiliative care that contributed to concealment of mental illness stemming from concerns that the entire family may be stigmatized; (c) public stigma due to a lack of knowledge and cultural beliefs that interfere with pursuing treatment; and (d) self-stigma wherein individuals with mental illness attribute their disorders to personal weakness. Stigma may overlap with ethnicity, immigration status, and language.

Cultural miscommunication also emerges as a factor that impedes effective mental health care (Sue et al., 2022). I have always been puzzled by the term miscommunication because it implies that when the provider and client do not share the same background, they may not fully understand one another in ways that may adversely impact the counseling relationship. The term miscommunication is a euphemism that almost completely glosses over the level of abuse, pseudoscience, misdiagnosis, profiteering, etc., that has plagued African Americans and American Indians who needed mental health care, especially during the 19th and early 20th centuries (Guthrie, 2003; Summers, 2019), as well as other populations that were not White or male (Segrest, 2020). Regrettably, some of these same practices persist into the 21st century. Published reports document that many minoritized individuals continue to receive substandard mental health care (Alang, 2019; Metzl, 2011).

The past and present are inextricably bound, and counseling clients necessitates an understanding and consideration of how historical encounters with oppression influence clients' presenting concerns and distress levels. More specifically, the vestiges of the past intrude upon the present in ways that contribute to psychological distress (DeGruy, 2017). This is true for other marginalized group members as well, such as women, members of the LGBTQIA+ community, people with disabilities, low-wealth individuals, and immigrants. Treatment of these groups during both historical and contemporary times has led to an inability for some group members to consistently trust they would receive quality care.

Trust, Mistrust, and Distrust

Griffith et al. (2021) distinguished among the terms trust, mistrust, and distrust. They noted that trust presupposes that individuals believe they can count on their provider to deliver quality systems of care. Mistrust involves the client's intuitive sense that they may not receive an acceptable standard of care. Conversely, distrust involves a much stronger sense of suspicion and skepticism that quality care will not be forthcoming and is usually rooted in evidence resulting from prior traumas, both individual and collective. Thus, distrust contributes to what Grier and Cobbs (1968) defined as "healthy paranoia," or an adaptive response to perceived healthcare injustices that result in an individual's aversion to treatment. The vast history of health and mental healthcare inequities and abuses within marginalized communities has fueled distrust and aversion to help-seeking (Jones, 2022; Panchal et al., 2024; Washington, 2008). Spengler et al. (2023) argued that this level of mistrust of mental healthcare professionals may be especially prevalent among vulnerable populations such as the LGBTQIA+ community. To illustrate, early versions of the Diagnostic and Statistical Manual pathologized LGBTQIA+ people using heterosexist behavior, structural barriers that served as deterrents to help-seeking, etc. The next section of this chapter addresses foundational constructs regarding race, ethnicity, and culture that serve as a backdrop for the discussion and consideration of the provider's broaching efforts.

Defining the Constructs Race, Ethnicity, and Culture

As a precursor to our discussion about the broaching framework, it is important to operationalize terms that are foundational to this book. Throughout this book, I use the terms race, ethnicity, and culture. What exactly is meant by these three terms? In order to level set, I think it is important to define these terms so that the reader and writer are operating with the same set of assumptions. As an example, if I visit a car dealership and ask the salesperson for an inexpensive car, the salesperson may consider a $40,000 car inexpensive. Conversely, an inexpensive car to me may be $10,000 or less. In order for the car salesman and the purchaser to reconcile their expectations, there must be some agreement on what inexpensive means.

In the same vein, and in an effort to be as explicit as possible, I will define the terms race, ethnicity, and culture because they will be used consistently throughout this book. Further, the terms are sometimes used interchangeably because they are impossible to disentangle (Lewis et al., 2023). Separating these constructs would be like having salt and pepper in a single shaker and asking someone to divide the salt and pepper into two different piles – one salt, the other pepper. Such a task is just not practical. Similarly, mental health providers cannot merely focus on a singular aspect of the client's identity, to the exclusion of all other identity domains, because those identities are overlapping, intersecting, and integrally bound to one another. To reduce a client to a single aspect of their identity would be essentializing and problematic. As an African American woman, I can no more ferret out my race and address it as a separate and distinct entity from my gender, social class, religion, or age.

From this point forward, I will refer to the terms race, ethnicity, and culture or racial, ethnic, and cultural using the abbreviation REC. In the section that follows, a discussion ensues that differentiates between core terminology that is foundational to the broaching framework. Although the terms are used interchangeably, they represent similar but distinct constructs that constantly evolve yet have significant relevance given the specific contexts in which they are used.

Race

Originally, the term race was deemed a biological construct that referred primarily to people's phenotypic characteristics. People were classified based on their connection to a land mass (e.g., Africa, Asia, Europe). In the 1700s, Carl Linnaeus, who is considered the father of taxonomy, classified plants and animals. His research set the stage for what scholars now refer to as scientific racism because he later began classifying, ordering, and ranking human beings based on their skin color, geography, and presumed behavioral traits. Unsurprisingly, Europeans were listed at the top of the social hierarchy, and Africans were consigned to the bottom of the social and political hierarchy (Kenyon-Flatt, 2021).

These assumptions were promulgated under the guise of scientific fact to legitimize the oppression and subordination of various racial groups (Barkan, 1992). Using this classification system, the Caucasian race was deemed superior, and the colored races were regarded as inferior.

Historically, race was deemed a biological construct. People distinguished among groups based on their physical features (e.g., skin color, hair texture, and facial features), which were used to assign status and differential treatment to groups (Guthrie, 2003). Early anthropologist Johann Friedrich Blumenbach created a classification system that included five specific categories: Caucasian, Mongolian, Ethiopian, American, and Malayan (Lewis et al., 2023). These assumptions about subordinate groups were used as justification for slavery, medical experimentation, segregation, internment camps, the Indian Removal Act of the 1830s, the carceral state, etc.

Currently, race operates as a social construction that refers more to social and political interactions and dynamics that subordinate non-White groups rather than to skin color, genetic, or biological features (Smedley & Smedley, 2005). That is, race is used as a system of stratification that determines how people are treated, thus consigning minoritized individuals to subordinate status and treatment at both interpersonal and structural levels (Jones, 2000). Prevailing social hierarchies often determine treatment, access to resources, opportunity structures, legal justice, etc., associated with people of color. Pulitzer Prize–winning journalist Isabel Wilkerson (2020) described the system of human hierarchy as a caste system. According to Wilkerson:

> A caste system is an artificial construction, a fixed and embedded ranking of human value that sets the presumed supremacy of one group against the presumed inferiority of other groups based on ancestry and often immutable traits - traits that would be neutral in the abstract but are ascribed life-and-death meaning in a hierarchy favoring the dominant caste whose forebears designed it. A caste system uses "rigid, often arbitrary boundaries to keep the ranked groups apart, distinct from one another and in their assigned places".
>
> (p. 17)

What is notable about caste systems is that they confer dominance on powerful groups in ways that marginalize individuals with less power and status, consigning them to the bottom of the social hierarchy. Wilkerson (2020) noted that society has unwritten scripts that dictate treatment of specific groups depending upon their position within the hierarchy. She continued:

> We have been programmed to consign status, confer the benefit of the doubt, attribute value and virtue to dominant groups, based on race's unwritten ordering of groups, and to confer marginalized status to people occupying the bottom of the social and political hierarchy.

This is often done using colonizing narratives and controlling images that evoke automatic and often pejorative stereotypes and assumptions about specific group members that rob them of their dignity, humanity, and integrity (Lofton, 2024). For many clients, exposure to mistreatment and social hierarchies, negative tropes and stereotypes, as well as varying forms of structural racism, results in both direct trauma and/or vicarious trauma that has a cumulative negative impact on people's everyday lives in ways that create psychological distress and trauma. Critically conscious providers use therapy to help metabolize client stress. In any case, over time and given intermingling between gene pools through both voluntary and forced migration, as well as miscegenation, categorizing people by their physical attributes became imprecise. Eventually, race assumed social constructions and was used to create social hierarchies that dictate one's value, worth, dignity, and treatment in society. It is this very social construction that creates psychological distress and subsequent harm for many, though certainly not all, clients from minoritized groups, and thus warrants discussion during treatment.

The intergenerational effects of varying forms of inequality, manifested using structures of oppression that have existed during both historical and contemporary times, have disconnected people from their sense of self in ways that jeopardize mental health and well-being (Degruy, 2017; Lofton, 2024; Mullan, 2023). Far too many therapists regard discussions about historical trauma as unnecessary, gratuitous broaching conversations that seemingly have little to do with mental health and wellness. Yet, these experiences are inextricably bound to clients' psychological distress and functioning, especially given the nature of intergenerational trauma and the fact that trauma is stored in the body (Menakem, 2017; Neighbors & Day-Vines, 2021; van der Kolk, 2015).

Some providers regard broaching discussions as a discrete set of facts and/or experiences that have limited relevance to clients' mental health, without consideration that these historical traumas intrude upon clients' lives and render them emotionally inert. This text operates under the supposition that clients' REC concerns warrant discussion during treatment. Until recently, there have been limited opportunities to situate REC discussions within a sociopolitical framework. Mullan (2023) contends that we cannot treat clients without accessing their social, cultural, and historical contexts and traumas. Ignoring clients' REC concerns contributes to dissatisfaction, cultural concealment, less favorable counseling outcomes, and premature termination (Brawner et al., 2025; Day-Vines et al., 2024; Depauw et al., 2024; Drinane et al., 2018; Fuertes et al., 2002; Lukowitsky et al., 2024; Zhang & Burkard, 2008).

Ethnicity

Much like the term race, ethnicity is a social construct, not a scientific construct. Specifically, ethnicity refers to a shared cultural heritage that includes language, geography, religion, nationality, cuisine, ancestry, politics, and a sense of group solidarity (Baumann, 2004). Racial group categories comprise multiple ethnic groups. For instance, Asian refers to a racial group designation comprising at least 30 distinct ethnic groups and includes but is not limited to people with Chinese, Japanese, Taiwanese, Vietnamese, Korean, Hmong, and Indian heritage. Similarly, African refers to racial group members whose ancestral roots lie in continental Africa and comprise numerous ethnicities such as African American, Jamaican, Ghanaian, Bahamian, Black-British, and Afro-Latino. Although these groups share racial group membership on the basis of their common African ancestry, as well as related encounters with colonialism, each group represents a certain distinctiveness as evidenced by characteristics such as geopolitical history, linguistic diversity, ethnic pride, and customs. Very little scholarship has addressed the distinctiveness between say descendants of U.S. enslaved peoples, Caribbean émigrés, and African émigrés, even though an emerging body of evidence suggests that these groups have shared but distinctive experiences (Day-Vines et al., in press). These distinctions have important implications for counseling, lest providers confound ethnic groups in ways that may render counseling less meaningful and more problematic. That is, a U.S. descendant of enslaved African people may share African ancestry with a Somali refugee, yet the Somali person's experience with migration, civil unrest, acculturative stress may be radically different than the experience of African Americans (Brawner et al., 2025; Dutt et al., 2022; Isawi & Post, 2020). Providers who work effectively, ethically, and responsibly with clients will have a robust appreciation for the heterogeneity of varying racial, ethnic, and cultural groups. Many textbooks use formulations that essentialize clients by focusing on demographic information that makes sweeping yet inaccurate generalizations about specific groups. This book assists providers in assessing clients' REC concerns and needs using more complex formulations.

Culture

Culture is a complex construct that encompasses a shared set of attitudes, values, beliefs, norms, patterned ways of behaving, and symbol systems that provide groups with a sense of social meaning and a way of living and operating in the world. In the context of broaching, culture refers broadly to not only race and ethnicity but also shapes construals that clients perceive about their gender, socioeconomic status, religious identity, linguistic diversity, national origin, gender identity, sexual orientation, ability/disability, occupational status, etc., and the impact of these identity markers on their presenting concerns. It is important to note that culture is not static but ever-evolving. That is, discussions about REC should not focus exclusively on a client's race or ethnicity but incorporate the client's intersectional identities that engender power and oppression in ways that can impact the client's sense of self and well-being. To illustrate, it is not sufficient to acknowledge a client's refugee status, but consideration must also focus on the premigration, migration, and resettlement experience, as well as second language acquisition, loss, survival, torture, religion, acculturative stress, etc., and the way these identity domains likely reflect multiple oppressions, as appropriate (Mullan, 2023). Moreover, an astute provider would need to recognize not only stressors that clients encounter but also sources of resilience that help sustain clients.

To reiterate, broaching reflects the provider's effort to initiate or respond to the client's stated or implied concerns related to REC. The provider must translate the client's REC experiences into meaningful dialogue that helps clients feel heard and understood, facilitates self-understanding, alleviates distress, supports effective coping mechanisms, promotes client empowerment, and enhances resilience (Day-Vines et al., 2018). As such, the provider commits to accepting and understanding the client's REC frame of reference. This results from listening with empathic awareness and understanding, professional development, immersion in literature that helps the provider better understand the client's REC experience, a healthy acceptance and appreciation of the client's background, critical self-awareness, cultural humility, clinical supervision, journaling, personal counseling, etc.

No discussion about the contextual dimensions of race, ethnicity, and culture is complete without an understanding of racism and its impact on humanity during both historical and contemporary times. All too often, people oversimplify the reality of racism, reducing it to individual acts of meanness. The next section of this chapter explores more complex definitions of racism.

Racism

To fully understand constructs such as race, ethnicity, and culture in clinical practice, providers must consider the impact of varying forms of systemic oppression that intrude upon clients' lives, namely, racism and discrimination. Racism is a particular form of oppression that refers to the systematic process of enlisting institutional resources, not only to support and promote a belief in the inferiority of groups on the basis of skin color but also to deny opportunities to one group and subsequently grant them to a preferred group (Nieto, 2021; Sue et al., 2022; Tatum, 2017). According to Pinderhughes (1989), the insidious nature of racism prevails because "policies and institutions interlock and reinforce one another in their capacity to deprive and cripple many people while offering preparation, support, and opportunity …" to members of a dominant group (p. 89). Tatum noted that if racism victimizes one group of individuals, then, by default, another group profits from those preferential arrangements. Mental health providers equipped with this information have a better foundation for administering culturally responsive and appropriate services to clients from minoritized groups.

Jones (2000) identified three specific forms of racism: (a) institutional, (b) personally mediated, and (c) internalized. Institutional racism refers to the concomitant structural forms of racism that are embedded in policies, laws, and practices that undermine well-being and access to resources and opportunities, such as adequate schooling, housing, employment, voting rights, immigration law, due process, health, and mental health care. People from minoritized groups are disproportionately impacted by institutional racism. That is, resources are often funneled away from marginalized communities toward more privileged groups. The detrimental impact of racism and discrimination is often understated given the romanticized manner in which K–12 education portrays U.S. history, making it difficult for learners to recognize pernicious connections between atrocities of the past and realities of the present. Consider, if you will, for example, Christopher Columbus discovering America, Pilgrims inviting indigenous people to dinner, and slavery as unpaid labor with little connection to settler colonialism and its impact on the social, psychological, and economic well-being of those who were impacted by necropolitical efforts to determine what groups are worthy of living or dying (Mbembe, 2003). Textbook companies seldom connect westward expansion (e.g., Manifest Destiny) and the annihilation of indigenous people. Publishers devote even less attention to the way the slave economy helped thrust the United States into a world superpower, leaving school-age children to imbibe a colossal set of dehumanizing myths about individuals from minoritized groups (Wilder, 2014). Partial truths fuel gross misunderstandings of U.S. history and by extension perpetuate negative attributions that pathologize people from minoritized groups, characterizing them in the racial imagination as lazy, inferior, bellicose, and hypersexual (Litam, 2025). These colonizing images justify dehumanizing treatment, while falsely extolling the virtues of whiteness and reifying social dominance. Efforts at dismantling romanticized notions of U.S. history are regarded as un-American propaganda (Bryan & Gerald, 2020). In fact, groups have invested enormous effort into banning books in order to perpetuate these problematic narratives (Harris, 2024).

Personally mediated forms of racism refer to individual acts of meanness or varying forms of prejudice and discrimination such as lack of respect, suspicion, devaluation, scapegoating, and dehumanization. This includes assumptions that are made about people from minoritized groups that devalue their sense of worth, dignity, and well-being. Personally mediated forms of racism may be intentional or unintentional; however, they typically involve individual forms of disrespect, suspicion, avoidance, scapegoating, racial slurs, hate speech, hiring, etc. This contributes to psychological harm.

Internalized racism refers to the premise that over time, encounters with racism and discrimination, whether institutional or personally meditated, result in people enacting and believing the negative stereotypes perpetrated against them. Prolonged exposure to internalized racism can lead to self-doubt and self-deprecation (David & Derthick, 2017; Litam, 2025). In fact, noted scholar Carter

G. Woodson (1933/2006) stated very convincingly that over time, one's exposure to unrelenting forms of racism, may result in people acting against their own self-interest. More specifically, he said:

> When you control a man's thinking you do not have to worry about his actions. You do not have to tell him not to stand here or go yonder. He will find his 'proper place' and will stay in it. You do not need to send him to the back door. He will go without being told. In fact, if there is no back door, he will cut one for his special benefit. His education makes it necessary.
>
> (p. 84)

This quote suggests that domination and control are not just physical. They can be mental in that people exposed to racist assault are manipulated into believing negative assumptions about themselves. Consequently, they begin to enact some of those negative assumptions. For instance, Amara is a 25-year-old Pakistani American female who sought counseling. She feels depressed because she is dissatisfied with the way she looks. Although she is beautiful, she loathes the darkness of her skin. She confided to her mental health provider that several of her family members have encouraged her to use skin lighteners, and she has complied, believing that lighter skin will help her gain social acceptance. Amara's belief that lighter skin tones are superior to darker skin tones and that skin tones dictate a person's beauty, dignity, or worth reflects internalized racism (Joshi et al., 2017; Monroe & Hall, 2018). Amara's internalized racism has led her to purchase and apply skin-lightening products with great regularity. A provider who broaches these concerns with Amara would explore with Amara the feelings of shame, rejection, and unattractiveness she has internalized about her complexion, the psychological distress associated with accepting a problematic aesthetic ideal, the structural forces that perpetuate and reinforce Eurocentric standards of beauty, and help her gain a greater sense of self-assurance that allows Amara to establish her own beauty standards (Day-Vines et al., 2021).

Scheurich and Young (1997) propounded a related theory of racism. They too noted that within popular culture, racism is often relegated to individual acts of meanness. They asserted, however, that racism cannot be reduced to forms of prejudice and discrimination that are enacted by individuals who feel a sense of entitlement and superiority over people from disadvantaged groups. Instead, they proposed that racism undergirds numerous institutions, societies, and the world. Their work identified four specific categories of racism: (a) overt and covert racism, (b) institutional, (c) societal, and (d) civilizational racism.

Overt racism is an intentional and deliberate form of racism that is purposely enacted to inflict pain solely on the basis of race. *Covert racism* lacks the planned calculation of overt racism but results in similar consequences. For instance, a covert act of racism occurs when a child of color registers for class in a new school and it is assumed, on the basis of skin color, discourse style, and perhaps social class, that he or she requires a class for children with low abilities. In reality, this child may have a stellar academic record and may even be eligible for gifted education services.

Institutional racism refers to the establishment of institutionally sanctioned policies and practices that penalize members of a particular group on the basis of race, irrespective of the intentionality of such practices. More recently, government efforts to curb unlawful immigration have disproportionately targeted Latinx immigrants from Central and South America, with less attention directed toward immigrants from other areas of the world (Sanchez & Vargas, 2025). Societal racism occurs when the social and cultural assumptions of one group are favored over the norms and dictates of another. For instance, the definition of a "model" nuclear family includes two heterosexual parents and their offspring(s). Deviations from this dominant cultural dictate are frequently regarded as an aberration and, consequently, devalued.

Civilizational racism functions as a broad construct that is deeply embedded in how people think. Members within dominant groups or civilizations often take the liberty of assigning a subordinate status to the values and viewpoints of groups regarded as lower in the societal hierarchy. The values and viewpoints of dominant groups often prevail as superior forms of functioning and, subsequently, become deeply embedded in the fabric of our society such that these views are seldom questioned. Such beliefs are embedded in many forms of scientific thought and often assume prevalence in popular culture and behavior.

The most harmful aspect of racism is that it has an interlocking effect on minority groups and their experiences. Racism enacted at the civilizational level is supported and reinforced at lower levels (Scheurich & Young, 1997). For instance, the mistaken belief that people of color are intellectually inferior has been promulgated at numerous levels. This has been most damaging in the scientific community, given the credence placed on scientific inquiry. Furthermore, data generated in the scientific community contribute to subsequent policies, practices, and individual behaviors. As an example, if the scientific community advances a theory of racial inferiority at the civilizational level, these beliefs give way to popular thought about the intellectual capacity of individuals at the societal level. At the institutional level, officials may implement policies that make it more difficult for people from marginalized groups to gain access to resources and opportunities. At the individual level, gatekeepers may deem it their responsibility to deputize themselves and block opportunities for people from marginalized groups.

Structural Racism and the Differentiated Impact on Communities of Color

All too often, people assume that racism impacts racial groups similarly. Racism is a broad term that refers to the marshaling of resources and opportunities toward some groups and away from others on the basis of skin color. Most discussions of race do not account for the differential ways that racism impacts specific groups. That is, certain racial groups are predisposed to particular forms of racism and discrimination. Essentially, there are varied ways in which racial groups experience marginalization and systematic oppression. For instance, Asian people are often labeled "model minorities" due to their perceived economic and academic success (Chan et al., 2026). Society often weaponizes Asian success to negatively judge other minority group members. This results in pitting minority groups against one another. Such stereotypes ignore the historical experiences that Asians have endured in the United States such as the fact that for a period of time, Asians were not allowed to be citizens, gentlemen's agreements, restrictive immigration policies, internment camps that confined Asians during World War II, the hypersexualization of Asian women, the hyposexualization of Asian men, as well as the more recent resurgence in anti-Asian hate that scapegoated Asian communities during the COVID-19 pandemic (Litam, 2025). Whereas Asians are often positioned at the top of the racial and ethnic minority hierarchy, other groups occupy lower positions along this hierarchy. For instance, Hispanic people frequently encounter racism based on their linguistic differences and documentation status (Sanchez & Vargas, 2025). Many Latino people face deportation woes that jeopardize their sense of safety, security, and well-being. Federal policies ramping up border security and immigration enforcement disproportionately target the southern border to the exclusion of the northern border. Consequently, the Latino community experiences a disproportionate amount of hypersurveillance that disrupts psychological safety and well-being. As a result of U.S. immigration policies, a disproportionate number of Latino immigrants experience family separation, economic instability, reduced access to social service supports, and emotional distress (Sanchez & Pedroza, 2025).

Native Americans experience vast amounts of racism that is rooted in violations of sovereignty and land rights. Government actions include the seizure of large swaths of Native land that violates treaty rights, hazardous environmental impacts to water, crops, and animals, as well as the desecration of sacred lands such as the Keystone XL Pipeline (Native American Rights Fund (n.d.)). Published reports devote scant attention to the crisis of missing and murdered indigenous women in the United States and Canada (Urban Indian Health Institute, 2018). Many of these cases remain unsolved and are conspicuously absent from the news media.

African Americans experience disproportionate amounts of state-sanctioned police violence that far too often results in death (Alexander, 2020; Butler, 2018; Morris, 2018). Consider the unrelenting slew of unarmed Black men, women, and trans individuals who have been killed by the police (e.g., George Floyd, Ahmaud Arbery, Breonna Taylor, Natasha McKenna). Lawmakers have yet to enact legislation regarding H.R.1280, the George Floyd Justice in Policing Act of 2021 (2021). The bill passed the House but languishes in the Senate. Although White individuals experience state-sanctioned police violence (e.g., Alex Pretti and Renee Good), Black individuals experience such violence at disproportionately higher rates and within a historical systemic context of racialized state violence.

Additionally, many African American children and youth fall victim to the school-to-prison pipeline, which funnels children from educational settings into the criminal justice system. For far too many young people, whether they spend 30 days or 30 years in prison, the results are similar. They have effectively lost many of their civil rights including education, housing, voting, and employment (Alexander, 2020). Post-incarceration, they are often subjected to low-wage, low-skill, low-prestige jobs that limit their ability to earn a living wage. Improper access to employment contributes to high recidivism rates.

Racism manifests uniquely across different racial and ethnic groups, reinforcing a racial hierarchy that perpetuates systemic oppression. Although these experiences vary in form, ranging from stereotypes and legal exclusions to environmental violence and police brutality, they collectively reflect the pervasive and enduring nature of structural racism in society. The foregoing discussion implies that structural factors related to REC have a definite impact on clients' mental well-being and warrant attention within the counseling process (Chan & Westcott, 2025).

Oppression – Social Class Status, Religion, Sexual Orientation

Whereas racism refers to the manner in which people encounter obstacles on the basis of their racial designation oppression represents a far more broad and encompassing term. Reynolds and Pope (1991) contend that oppression operates as "a system that allows access to the services, rewards, benefits, and privileges of society based on membership in a particular group" (p. 174). The exercise of power is used to restrict access to resources. In general, oppression operates as an umbrella term that refers to all forms of domination and control, including racism, sexism, classism, and heterosexism. Frequently, people can experience single or even multiple forms of oppression, inequality, and unjust treatment.

Marilyn Frye (1983) referred to oppression as a network of forces and barriers that are systematically related in ways that immobilize targets. She identified five criteria to determine whether a group experiences oppression. She noted that such groups experience harmful limitations to their freedom, which are justified, imposed, and protected by social structure or institutionally. She noted that people also experience oppression based on their membership in a particular group, such as sexual, gender, racial, and religious minorities. Finally, a separate group must execute and benefit from the barriers and impositions experienced by the subordinate group's status. These racialized encounters often shape clients' sociopolitical realities and as a consequence – also when relevant – warrant consideration within the counseling process.

This book offers a culturally responsive framework that can assist providers in their effort to promote a more trusting therapeutic environment with their clients. The remainder of this chapter describes upcoming chapters that form the broaching framework. Chapter 2 introduces foundational concepts that support the Broaching framework. This chapter eschews the commonly used term multicultural counseling competence. In fact, this term is a misnomer because it suggests that providers achieve mastery in developing their repertoire of multicultural counseling skills, ignoring the fact that culture is not static. This chapter serves as a backdrop for enumerating factors that both promote and inhibit providers' broaching behaviors by presenting a budding framework referred to as multicultural orientation. Multicultural orientation reflects (a) the providers' demonstration of cultural humility, (b) cultural comfort discussing clients' REC concerns, and (c) the ability to engage in broaching discussions (Hook et al., 2017). I describe the importance of warmth, openness, critical self-awareness and attention to race, ethnicity, and culture and its impact on the client as a correlate of broaching effectiveness. On the contrary, cultural concealment, microaggressions, and therapeutic ruptures inhibit effective broaching behavior, subsequently leading to high rates of premature termination (Day-Vines et al., 2024).

This chapter also addresses previous research that serves as a base of support for the *Broaching* framework, including but not limited to racial identity theory as well as the Multicultural and Social Justice Counseling Competencies (Ratts et al., 2016). In this chapter, I also address the issue of who broaches with whom. For instance, is it necessary for White providers to broach with White clients, or providers of color to broach with clients of color? Many people contend that if the provider and client share similar identity dimensions (e.g., race, gender, and country of origin), then broaching is unnecessary (Day-Vines & Young, 2024). Several scholars, however, contend that any counseling interaction constitutes a multicultural interaction and warrants broaching.

Chapter 3 provides an overview of the *Continuum of Broaching Behavior,* a conceptual framework describing various orientations that providers can assume as they address the extent to which REC factors impact their clients' presenting concerns. Essentially, the *Continuum of Broaching Behavior* progresses from the provider's refusal to discuss the contextual dimensions of REC and advances toward an integrated and stylized ability to translate REC discussions into culturally relevant techniques and interventions (Day-Vines et al., 2007). Providers can assume five particular broaching orientations: (a) *Avoidant*, (b) *Isolating*, (c) *Continuing/Incongruent*, (d) *Integrated/Congruent*, and (e) *Infusing*. *Avoidant* providers ignore or minimize clients' REC concerns, opting instead to focus on more neutral dialogues. *Isolating* providers broach out of obligation so they can move on to other topics. *Continuing/Incongruent* providers have an openness toward broaching REC with clients but lack the accompanying skill set. *Integrated/Congruent* providers validate clients' REC concerns. *Infusing* providers broach as part of their professional identity and enlist social justice frameworks that tackle structural barriers clients confront as they work to surmount their mental health challenges. Day-Vines et al. (2013) operationalized the *Continuum of Broaching Behavior* using the Broaching Attitudes and Behavior Scale and found empirical support for a four-factor model of broaching. Readers will have an opportunity to take and score an abbreviated form of the instrument.

Chapter 4 focuses on the Multidimensional Model of Broaching Behavior (MMBB; Day-Vines et al., 2020), which serves as a conceptual tool that describes specific contexts in which providers explore clients' REC concerns. There are four specific components of the MMBB: (a) *Intra-counseling*, (b) *Intra-individual*, (c) *Intra-Racial, -Ethnic, -Cultural*, and (d) Inter-*Racial, -Ethnic, -Cultural* dimensions. *Intra-Counseling* dimensions address the provider-client relationship and reflect a kind of cultural immediacy wherein the provider invites the client to not only discuss salient REC concerns but also explore how the counseling process is unfolding given the differences and similarities between the provider and client. *Intra-individual* dimensions focus on the client's intersectional identities and the manner in which multiple identity dimensions may reflect multiple oppressions (e.g., race, gender, class, disability, and religion). The *Intra-Racial, -Ethnic, -Cultural* dimensions reflect the sources of intra-group support and stress that clients may experience from members of their own communities. The Inter-*Racial, -Ethnic, -Cultural* dimensions refer to the client's encounters with racism and discrimination. This chapter highlights the Intra-counseling broaching dimension.

Chapter 5 explores *Intra-Individual* broaching dimensions, which address providers' consideration of their clients' intersectional identities. Essentially, providers examine the confluence of identities that may impinge on the client's presenting concerns. By broaching the client's overlapping identity domains and sources of oppression, the provider avoids essentializing the client and addresses the way issues of power, oppression, and privilege pervade several of the client's identity statuses. That is, providers will consider how forces such as racism, classism, sexism, ableism, homophobia, xenophobia, etc. impact the client's presenting concerns in ways that promote a holistic consideration of the client's values, viewpoints, and experiences.

Chapter 6 covers *Intra-Racial, -Ethnic, -Cultural* broaching considerations for addressing the client's sense of connection or disconnection with people with whom they share a common racial, ethnic, or cultural designation. It explores the dual role that family and community members can play as a potential source of support or, conversely, as contributors to clients' psychological distress. This chapter addresses within-group challenges that can put a wedge between clients and their respective communities, such as differentials in social class status, education, income, immigration status, and age.

Chapter 7 addresses *Inter- Racial, -Ethnic, -Cultural* or the impact of racism and discrimination, as well as other sources of intergroup conflict that can impinge on the client's sense of psychological safety, security, and well-being. This can include the client's exposure to overt and covert acts of meanness and microaggressions, as well as varying forms of structural inequality. Many of these conflicts are rooted in pervasive forms of hostility and structural racism that are inextricably bound to historical encounters with colonialism and white supremacy.

Chapters 8 and 9 focus on the final component of the Broaching framework and involve a set of strategies that providers can use as they engage in several cognitive exercises to identify broaching statements with intentionality (Day-Vines et al., 2021). Although many scholars contend that exploring the client's REC concerns is important, very little scholarship provides specific guidance for facilitating REC conversations. These two chapters present a step-by-step guide to help mental health providers facilitate broaching discussions more comfortably (Day-Vines et al.). This four-step model involves (a) joining, (b) assessment, (c) preparation, and (d) delivery. Chapter 8 focuses on joining or establishing a trusting therapeutic relationship with the client and (b) assessment, or the provider's conceptual hypotheses about the client's racial identity and other intersectional identity domains, as well as client readiness to engage in a broaching conversation, the strength of the counseling relationship, and the provider's readiness to facilitate a broaching conversation.

Chapter 9 addresses the final two components of the strategies model: preparation and delivery. The preparation reflects the provider's effort to establish a set of intentions for broaching REC with the client by determining what, when, and how they are going to broach, as well as determining why certain broaching discussions may be helpful to the client. The delivery component refers to the execution of the actual broaching statement as well as the follow-up responses to help flesh out the client's REC concerns.

Chapter 10 addresses a set of strategies that providers can implement if and when a rupture or an impasse in the provider-client relationship occurs. Impasses are associated with microaggressions, premature termination, negative perceptions about the counseling process, and a weak therapeutic alliance or connection between the provider and the client (Brawner et al., 2025: Eubanks et al., 2018; Safran et al., 2011). Findings from previous research indicate that rupture-repair episodes or situations in which the provider works to mend the counseling conflict were positively associated with improvements in the therapeutic alliance and contributed to greater retention in treatment (Safran et al., 2011). This chapter features Chang et al.'s (2020) critical-cultural-relational approach to rupture resolution. Chapter 10 concludes with a case illustration demonstrating the appropriate implementation of rupture resolution strategies and reinforces the value of broaching clients' REC concerns in ways that help clients feel heard and understood, alleviate psychological distress, return for follow-up sessions, and engage in more effective problem-solving.

References

Alang, S.M. (2019). Mental health care among blacks in America: Confronting racism and constructing solutions. *Health Services Research, 54*, 346–355. https://doi.org/10.1111/1475-6773.13115

Alegria, M., Alvarez, K., & DiMarzio (2017). Immigration and mental health. *Current Epidemiology Reports, 4*, 145–155. https://doi.org/10.1007/s40471-017-0111-2

Alegria, M., Falgas-Bague, I., & Fong, H. (2020). Engagement of ethnic minorities in mental health care. *World Psychiatry, 19*, 35–36. https://doi-org.proxy1.library.jhu.edu/10.1002/wps.20695

Alexander, M. (2020). *The new Jim Crow: Mass incarceration in the age of colorblindness*. The New Press.

American Psychiatric Association. (2017a). *Mental health disparities: Diverse populations*. American Psychiatric Association. https://share.google/OSKSR6LvN4kbJFX15

American Psychiatric Association. (2017b). *Mental health disparities: LGBTQ*. American Psychiatric Association. https://share.google/fxKHMFXfX1C8MJwNI

Barkan, E. (1992). *The retreat of scientific racism: Changing concepts of race in Britain and the United States between the world wars*. Cambridge University Press.

Baumann, T. (September, 2004). Defining ethnicity. *SAA Archaeological Record.*

Brawner, R., Day-Vines, N.L., Gubara, S., Agorsor, C., Jackson, Z., & Ran, T., & Caldwell, N. (2025). Perceptions of racial, ethnic, and cultural ruptures in counseling: A qualitative case study of a client from a minoritized background. *Journal of Counseling and Development, 103*, 484–495. https://doi-org.proxy1.library.jhu.edu/10.1002/jcad.70004

Brenner, B. (2020). Understanding anxiety and depression for LGBTQ people. *Anxiety and Depression Association of America.* https://adaa.org/learn-from-us/from-the-experts/blog-posts/consumer/understanding-anxiety-and-depression-lgbtq

Bryan, K.C., & Gerald, J.P.B. (August, 17, 2020). The weaponization of English. *Language Magazine: Improving Literacy and Communication.* https://www.languagemagazine.com/2020/08/17/the-weaponization-of-english/

Butler, P. (2018). *Chokehold: Policing Black men.* The New Press.

Cardemil, E., & Battle, C. (2003). Guess who's coming to therapy? Getting comfortable with conversations about race and ethnicity in therapy. *Professional Psychology: Research and Practice, 34,* 278–286.

Career Explorer (2024). Mental health counselor demographics in the United States. *Career Explorer*. https://www.careerexplorer.com/careers/mental-health-counselor/demographics/

Chan, C.D., Anandavalli, S., Jones, C.T. (2026). Broaching as destigmatizing practice for anti-Asian oppression: An application of the Multidimensional Model of Broaching Behavior. *Journal of Multicultural Counseling and Development*, *54*(2), 77–84.

Chan, C.D., & Westcott, J.B. (2025). Structural vulnerability framework: An application to professional counselors. *Journal of Counseling and Development, 103,* 257–266. https://doi-org.proxy1.library.jhu.edu/10.1002/jcad.12558

Chang, D.F., & Berk, A. (2009). Making cross-racial therapy work: A phenomenal study of clients' experiences of cross-racial therapy. *Journal of Counseling Psychology, 56*, 521–536. doi: 10.1037/a0016905.

Chang, D.F., Dunn, J.J., & Omidi, M. (2020). A critical-cultural-relational approach to rupture resolution: A case illustration with a cross-racial dyad. *Journal of Clinical Psychology*, *77*(2), 369–383. https://doi.org/10.1002/jclp.23080

Chang, D.F., & Yoon, P. (2011). Ethnic minority clients' perceptions of the significance of race in cross-racial therapy relationships. *Psychotherapy Research, 21*, 567–582. https://doi-org.proxy1.library.jhu.edu/10.1080/10503307.2011.592549

Choi, G., Mallinckrodt, B., & Richardson, J.D. (2015). Effect of international student counselors' broaching statements about cultural and language differences on participants' perceptions of counselors. *Journal of Multicultural Counseling and Development,* 43, 25–37. https://doi-org.proxy1.library.jhu.edu/10.1002/j.2161-1912.2015.00062.x

David, E.J.R., & Derthick, A.O. (2017). *The psychology of oppression.* Springer.

Day-Vines, N.L., Booker Ammah, B., Steen, S., & Arnold, K.M. (2018). Getting comfortable with discomfort: Preparing counselor trainees to broach racial, ethnic, and cultural factors with clients during counseling. *International Journal for the Advancement of Counselling, 40*(2), 89–104. https://doi.org/10.1007/s10447-017-9308-9

Day-Vines, N.L., Bryan, J., & Griffin, D. (2013). The Broaching Attitudes and Behavior Survey (BABS): An exploratory assessment of its dimensionality. *Journal of Multicultural Counseling and Development, 41,* 210–223. https://doi.org/10.1002/j.2161-1912.2013.00037.x

Day-Vines, N.L., Cluxton-Keller, F., Agorsor, C., & Gubara, S. (2021). Strategies for broaching the subjects of race, ethnicity and culture. *Journal of Counseling and Development*, 99, 348–357. https://doi.org/10.1002/jcad.12380

Day-Vines, N.L., Cluxton-Keller, F., Agorsor, C., Gubara, S., & Otabil, N. (2020). The multidimensional model of broaching behavior. *Journal of Counseling and Development, 98,* 107–118. https://doi.org/10.1002/jcad.12304

Day-Vines, N.L., Wood, S., Grothaus, T., Craigen, L.,Holman, A., Dotson-Blake, K., & Douglass, M. (2007). Broaching the subjects of race, ethnicity, and culture during the counseling process. *Journal of Counseling and Development, 85,* 401–409. https://doi.org/10.1002/jcad.12069

Day-Vines, N.L., & Young, A. (2023). Broaching race and other cultural identities. In L. Summers (Ed.), *Multicultural counseling: Responding with cultural humility, empathy and advocacy* (pp. 466–477). Springer Publishing.

Day-Vines, N.L., Zhang, J., Cluxton-Keller, F., Hicks, D., Jones, C.T., Spann, T., Daga, D., & Agorsor, C., (2024). An investigation of the construct validation of the broaching attitudes and behavior scale – clients. *Journal of Multicultural Counseling and Development.* https://doi.org/10.1002/jmcd.12300

Day-Vines, N.L., Zhang, J., Cluxton-Keller, F., Hicks, D., Mwombele, B., Austin, M., Henderson, C., Henning, M., & Pecku, M. (2026). An Investigation of African origin clients' perceptions of their therapists' ability to broach racial, ethnic, and cultural concerns during the counseling process. *Unpublished Manuscript.*

Degruy, J. (2017). *Post traumatic slave syndrome: America's legacy of enduring injury and healing.* Joy Degruy Publications.

Depauw, H., & Van Hiel, A. (2024). Uncovering patterns in perceived therapist behaviour: A latent profile analysis of broaching experiences among ethnic minority group member clients. *Clinical Psychology and Psychotherapy*, 31, e3067. https://doi.org/10.1002/cpp.3067

Derr, A.S. (2016). Mental health service use among immigrants in the United States: A systematic review. *Psychiatric Services, 67*, 265–74. https://doi-org.proxy1.library.jhu.edu/10.1176/appi.ps.201500004

Drinane, J.M., Owen, J., & Tao, K.W. (2018). Cultural concealment and therapy outcomes. *Journal of Counseling Psychology, 65*, 239–246. https://doi.org/10.1037/cou0000246

Dutt, A., Jacquez, F., Kirkendall, A., Wright, B., & Alwan, R. (2022). Refugee experiences in Cincinnati, Ohio: A local case study in the context of global crisis. *Journal Social Issues, 78*, 126–145. https://doi.org/10.1111/josi.12471

Eken, H.N., Dee, E.C., Powers, A.R., 3rd, & Jordan, A. (2021). Racial and ethnic differences in perception of provider cultural competence among patients with depression and anxiety symptoms: A retrospective, population-based, cross-sectional analysis. *The Lancet. Psychiatry*, *8*, 957–968. https://doi.org/10.1016/S2215-0366(21)00285-6

Eliscu, A.H., Jamilkowski, J., Gonzalez, A., Higham, J.M., Kenny, L., & McGovern, M.M. (2023). Results from an LGBTQ+community health needs assessment in Nassau and Suffolk counties of New York State. *Community Mental Health Journal,* 59, 855–868. https://doi-org.proxy1.library.jhu.edu/10.1007/s10597-022-01069-8

Eubanks, C.F., Muran, J.C., & Safran, J. D. (2018). Alliance rupture repair: A meta-analysis. *Psychotherapy, 55*, 508–519. https://doi.org/10.1037/pst0000185

Fleming, J. (1984). *Blacks in college: A comparative study of students' success in Black and in White institutions*. Jossey-Bass.

Frye, M. (1983). *The politics of reality*. The Crossing Press.

Fuertes, J.N., Mueller, L.N., Chauhan, R.V., Walker, J.A., & Ladany, N. (2002). An investigation of European American therapists' approach to counseling African American clients. *The Counseling Psychologist, 30*(5), 763–788. https://doi.org/10.1177/0011000002305007

Gara, M.A., Minsky, S., Silverstein, S.M., Miskimen, T., & Strakowski, S.M. (2019). A naturalistic study of racial disparities in diagnoses at an outpatient behavioral health clinic. *Psychiatric Services*, *70*(2), 130 https://doi.org/10.1176/appi.ps.201800223

Garcini, L.M., Chen, M.A., Brown, R.L., Galvan, T., Saucedo, L., Berger Cardoso, J.A., & Fagundes, C.P. (2018). Kicks hurt less: Discrimination predicts distress beyond trauma among undocumented Mexican immigrants. *Psychology of Violence*, *8*(6), 692–701. https://doi.org/10.1037/vio0000205

George Floyd Justice in Policing Act of 2021, H.R. 1280, 117th Cong. (2021). https://www.congress.gov/bill/117th-congress/house-bill/1280

Grier, W.H., & Cobbs, P.M. (1968). *Black Rage*: Basic Books.

Griffith, D.M., Bergner, E.M., Fair, A.S., & Wilkins, C.H. (2021). Using mistrust, distrust, and low trust precisely in medical care and medical research advances health equity. *American Journal of Preventive Medicine*, *60*, 442–445. https://doi.org/10.1016/j.amepre.2020.08.019

Guthrie, R.V. (2003). *Even the rat was white: A historical view of psychology*. Allyn & Bacon.

Harris, E.A. (2024). Removing books from libraries often takes debate. But there's a quieter way. *New York Times*. https://www.nytimes.com/2024/10/08/books/book-ban-library-weeding.html

Health Resources and Services Administration. (2023). *Behavioral health workforce, 2023* (Brief). U.S. Department of Health and Human Services. https://bhw.hrsa.gov/sites/default/files/bureau-health-workforce/Behavioral-Health-Workforce-Brief-2023.pdf

Hook, J.N., Davis, D., & Owen, J. (2017). *Cultural humility: Engaging diverse identities in therapy*. American Psychological Association.

Immigration and Nationality Act of 1965, Pub. L. No. 89–236, 79 Stat. 911 (1965).

Institute of Medicine. (2003). *Unequal treatment: Confronting racial and ethnic disparities in health care*. The National Academic Press.International Organization for Migration. (2011). Governments should recognize migration as a social determinant of health, says IOM ahead of global conference. *International Organization for Migration*. https://www.iom.int/news/governments-should-recognize-migration-social-determinant-health-says-iom-ahead-global-conference

Isawi, D.T., & Post, P.B. (2020). Self-efficacy of counselors working with refugees. *Adultspan Journal, 10*(2), Article 4. https://mds.marshall.edu/adsp/vol19/iss2/4

Jensen, E., Jones, N., Rabe, M., Pratt, B., Medina, L., Orozco, K., & Spell, L. (2021). The chance that two people chosen at random are of different race or ethnicity groups has increased since 2010. *United States Census Bureau.* https://www.census.gov/library/stories/2021/08/improved-race-ethnicity-measures-reveal-united-states-population-much-more-multiracial.html

Jones, C. (2022). *The organ thieves: The shocking story of the first heart transplant in the segregated south.* Gallery/Jeter.

Jones, C.P. (2000), Levels of racism: A theoretic framework and a gardener's tale. *American Journal of Public Health, 90,* 1212–1215.

Joshi, S.N., Balaji, M., & Deshpande, P. (2017). De-hue-manizing them: Color and acculturation among second generation South Asians. In Monroe, C.R. (Ed.), *Race and colorism in education* (pp. 132–146). Routledge.

Kenyon-Flatt, B. (2021). How scientific Taxonomy constructed the myth of race. *Mindsets.* https://www.sapiens.org/biology/race-scientific-taxonomy/

Kramer, S., & Passel, J. (August 21, 2025). *What the data says about immigrants in the U.S.* Pew Research Center. https://www.pewresearch.org/short-reads/2025/08/21/key-findings-about-us-immigrants/

Lewis, C., Cohen, P.R., Bahl, D., Levine, E.M., & Khaliq, W. (2023). Race and ethnic categories: A brief review of global terms and nomenclature. *Cureus, 15,* e41253. https://doi:10.7759/cureus.41253

Lu, W., Silverstein, S.M., Mueser, K.T., Minsky, S., Bullock, D., Buchbinder, S., Chen, Q., Eubanks, R., & Guillaume-Salvant, A. (2023). Undocumented PTSD among African American clients with serious mental illness in a statewide mental health system. *Psychological Trauma: Theory, Research, Practice, and Policy, 15,* 781–790. https://doi.org/10.1037/tra0001243

Litam, S.D.A (2025). *Patterns that remain: A guide to healing for Asian children of immigrants.* Oxford University.

Lofton, R., Gamez, R., Nelson, N., & Smith-Onyewu, Z. (2024). Reviewing concentrated poverty literature through an antiblackness lens to reveal a concentrated debt. *Educational Researcher.* https://doi.org/10.3102/0013189X231193958

Lukowitsky, M.R., Winseman, J.S., Feld, E, Kam, S.M., & Balkoski, V.I. (2024). Patients' perceptions of their therapist: Effects of race, culture, and cultural competency on the working alliance. *American Journal of Psychotherapy.* https://doi-org.proxy1.library.jhu.edu/10.1176/appi.psychotherapy.20230056

Mbembe, A. (2003). Necropolitics. *Public Culture, 15,* 11–40.

Menakem, R. (2017). *My grandmother's hands: Racialized trauma and the pathway to mending our hearts and bodies.* Central Recovery Press.

Mental Health America (n.d.) *LGBTQ+ communities and mental health.* Mental Health America.

Metzl, J. (2011). *The protest psychosis: How schizophrenia became a Black disease.* Beacon.

Migration Policy Institute. (2023). *State immigration data profiles.* https://www.migrationpolicy.org/data/state-profiles/state/demographics/US

Misra, S., Jackson, V.W., Chong, J., Choe, K., Tay, C., Wong, J., & Yang, L.H. (2021). Systematic review of cultural aspects of stigma and mental illness among racial and ethnic minority groups in the United States: Implications for interventions. *American*

Journal of Community Psychology, 68, 486–512. https://doi-org.proxy1.library.jhu.edu/10.1002/ajcp.12516
Monroe, C.R., & Hall, R.E. (2018). Colorism and US immigration: Considerations for researchers. *American Behavioral Scientist, 62*(14), 2037–2054. https://doi.org/10.1177/0002764218810753
Morris, M.W. (2018). *Pushout: The criminalization of Black girls in School.* The New Press.
Moslimani, M., & Passel, J.S. (September 27, 2024). *What the data says about immigrants in the U.S.* Pew Research Center. https://www.pewresearch.org/short-reads/2024/09/27/key-findings-about-us-immigrants/
Mullan, J. (2023). *Decolonizing therapy: Oppression, historical trauma, and politicizing your practice.* W.W. Norton & Company.
Native American Rights Fund. (n.d.). *Keystone XL pipeline (Rosebud Sioux Tribe v. Trump).* https://narf.org/cases/keystone/
Neighbors, H., & Day-Vines, N.L. (2021). *Voices of a Collective Experience: Vicarious Racism and its Effects on Black Mental Health.* Hurdle Health.
Nieto, S. (2021). *Other people's children.* S&S/Marysue Rucci Books.
Panchal, N., Hill, L., Artiga, S., & Hamel, L. (May 23, 2024). Racial and ethnic disparities in mental health care: Findings from the KFF survey of racism, discrimination and health. *Kaiser Family Foundation.* https://www.kff.org/racial-equity-and-health-policy/issue-brief/racial-and-ethnic-disparities-in-mental-health-care-findings-from-the-kff-survey-of-racism-discrimination-and-health/
Passel, J.S., KKrogstad, J.M., & Moslimani, M.M. (July 22, 2024). *How the origins of America's immigrants have changed since 1850.* Pew Research Center. https://pewrsr.ch/1hqIRfk
Pinderhughes, E. (1989). *Understanding race, ethnicity and power: The key to efficacy on clinical practice.* Free Press.
Ratts, M.J., Singh, A.A., Nassar-McMillan, S., Butler, S.K., & McCullough, J.R. (2016). Multicultural and social justice counseling competencies: Guidelines for the counseling profession. *Journal of Multicultural Counseling and Development, 44*, 28–48. https://doi.org/10.1002/jmcd.12035
Reynolds, A.L., & Pope, R.L. (1991). The complexities of diversity: Exploring multiple oppressions. *Journal of Counseling and Development, 70*, 174–180.
Safran, M.A., Mays, Jr, R.A., Huang, L.N., McCuan, R., Pham, P.K., Fisher, S.K. McDuffie, K.Y., & Trachtenberg, A. (2009). Mental health disparities. *American Journal of Public Health, 99*, 1962–1966. https://doi-org.proxy1.library.jhu.edu/10.2105/AJPH.2009.167346
Safran, J.D., Muran, J.C., & Eubanks-Carter, C. (2011). Repairing alliance ruptures. *Psychotherapy, 48*, 80.
Sanchez, G.R., & Pedroza, A.A. (March 31, 2025). How immigration policy shifts are affecting Latino families. *Brookings.* https://www.brookings.edu/articles/how-immigration-policy-shifts-are-affecting-latino-families/?utm_source=chatgpt.com
Sanchez, G.R., & Vargas, E.D. (October 16, 2025). Racial profiling by ICE will have a marked impact on Latino communities. *Brookings.* https://www.brookings.edu/articles/racial-profiling-by-ice-will-have-a-marked-impact-on-latino-communities/
Scheurich, J., & Young, M. (1997). Coloring epistemologies: Are our research epistemologies racially biased? *Educational Researcher, 26*, 4–16.

Segrest, M. (2020). *Administrations of lunacy: Racism and the haunting of American psychiatry at the Milledgeville asylum*. The New Press.

Smedley, A., & Smedley, B.D. (2005). Race as biology is fiction, racism as a social problem is real: Anthropological and historical perspectives on the social construction of race. *American Psychologist, 60*, 16–26. https://doi.org/10.1037/0003-066X.60.1.16

Spengler, E.S., Tierney, D., Elledge, L.C., & Grzanka, P.R. (2023). Beyond the individual: Sexual minority help-seeking and the consequences of structural barriers. *Journal of Counseling Psychology, 70*(2), 133–145. https://doi.org/10.1037/cou0000657

Substance Abuse and Mental Health Services Administration. (2023). *Key substance use and mental health indicators in the United States: Results from the 2022 National Survey on Drug Use and Health* (HHS Publication No. PEP23–07-01–006, NSDUH Series H-58). Center for Behavioral Health Statistics and Quality, Substance Abuse and Mental Health Services Administration. https://www.samhsa.gov/data/report/2022-nsduh-annual-national-report

Sue, D.W., Sue, D., Neville, H.A., & Smith, L. (2022). *Counseling the culturally diverse: Theory and practice* (9th ed.). Wiley.

Summers, M. (2019). *Madness in the city of magnificent intentions: A history of race and mental illness in the nation's capital*. Oxford University.

Tatum, B.D. (2017). *Why Are All the Black Kids Sitting Together in the Cafeteria?: And Other Conversations About Race*. Basic Books.

Terlizzi, E.P., & Norris, T. (2020). *Mental health treatment among adults: United States*, NCHS Data Brief, no 419. Hyattsville, MD: National Center for Health Statistics. 2021. https://doi.org/10.15620/cdc:110593

Urban Indian Health Institute. (2018). Missing and murdered Indigenous women & girls: A snapshot of data from 71 urban cities in the United States. *Seattle Indian Health Board*. https://www.uihi.org/resources/missing-and-murdered-indigenous-women-girls/

USAFacts (2023). *Bureau of Labor Statistics data compiled by USAFacts*. Retrieved from https://usafacts.org/data/topics/people-society/population-and-demographics/our-changing-population/

van der Kolk (2015). *The body keeps the score: Brain, mind, and body in the healing of trauma*. Penguin.

Vespa, J., Medina, L., & Armstrong, D.M. (2020). *Demographic turning points for the United States: Population projects for 2020 to 2060. Current Population Reports, P25–1144,* U.S. Census Bureau. https://www.census.gov/library/publications/2020/demo/p25-1144.html

Washington, H. (2008). *Medical apartheid: The dark history of medical experimentation on Black Americans from colonial times to the present*. Vintage.

Wilkerson, I. (2020). *Caste: The origins of our discontents*. Random House.

Woodson, C.G. (1933/2006). *The miseducation of the Negro*. Dover.

Wyse, R., Hwang, W.T., Ahmed, A.A., Richards, E., & Deville, C. (2020). Diversity by Race, Ethnicity, and Sex within the US Psychiatry Physician Workforce. *Academic Psychiatry, 44*, 523–530.

Zhang, N., & Burkard, A. (2008). Client and counselor discussions of racial and ethnic differences in counselling: An exploratory investigation. *Journal of Multicultural Counselling and Development, 36*, 77–87. https://doi.org/10.1002/j.2161-1912.2008.tb00072.x

Zippia. (April 5, 2024). Licensed social worker demographics and statistics in the US. *Zippia*. https://www.zippia.com/licensed-social-worker-jobs/demographics/

Chapter 2

Foundational Concepts that Support the Broaching Framework

Multicultural Counseling Competence

At the turn of the 20th century, a number of seminal counseling theories emerged that centered around western European cultural thought, values, and norms almost exclusively. Theorists developed these counseling modalities primarily for elite members of society and not necessarily for nonwestern clients from the Global South. Be that as it may, nonwestern civilizations have existed and met their mental health needs for thousands of years prior to the emergence of Freud, Jung, and Adler. In any case, early theorists deemed people of color, women, the poor, the indigent, as well as people with intellectual disabilities unsuitable for treatment, positing that they lacked the necessary insight to benefit from mental health care (Segrest, 2020; Summers, 2019). Consequently, attention to the needs of individuals who did not belong to dominant groups (e.g., White, male, property owners) was ignored in the development of psychotherapeutic strategies and interventions (Guthrie, 2003). Consistent with this line of reasoning, scholars generated an acronym to describe the ideal mental health client using the moniker, YAVIS syndrome. Essentially, YAVIS refers to the provider's preference for "Young, Articulate, Verbal, Intelligent, and Successful" clients (Schofield, 1986; Sue et al., 2022).

Given the monocultural nature of counseling, the persistence of mental healthcare disparities among individuals from minoritized groups, as well as the disproportionate attention on white middle-class norms and value systems to the virtual exclusion of the culture-specific needs of people from minoritized groups, proponents of culturally responsive counseling approaches felt compelled to create guidelines that addressed the specific and unique mental health needs of individuals from minoritized groups. In response, the Association of Multicultural Counseling and Development published the Multicultural Counseling Competencies (MCCs), a set of multicultural counseling standards for mental health providers (Sue et al., 1992). These standards served as a clarion call to action for the profession and delineated the requisite attitudes, dispositions, and skills providers should possess in order to support clients from minoritized backgrounds.

DOI: 10.4324/9781003649311-2

Multiculturalism is now considered the fourth force in counseling, as it follows the psychological traditions of psychoanalysis, behaviorism, and humanism (Sue et al., 2022). The original MCC model focused on three specific counseling pillars: (a) awareness, (b) knowledge, and (c) skills (Sue et al., 1992). As discussed in the previous chapter, multicultural awareness competencies reflect the provider's consideration of their own attitudes, biases, and assumptions that potentially interfere with the delivery of culturally responsive counseling care for clients. The expectation is that providers engage in an earnest and critical self-examination of their personal dispositions and mindsets concerning specific populations. As we will discuss in Chapter 10, the provider's unaddressed personal biases are likely to leak out as countertransference, microaggressions, and indifference that can potentially erode the therapeutic alliance, leading to counseling ruptures (Foley & Gentile, 2010; Hill, 2020). Awareness competencies also involve the provider's consideration of those structural systems of oppression that negatively impact clients' lives, including but not limited to racism, sexism, classism, homophobism, ableism, xenophobia, raciolinguistics, Islamophobia, and Antisemitism.

Knowledge competencies refer to the acquisition of factual information regarding the cultural values, customs, history, migration stories (e.g., pre-, peri-, and post-), individual and collective experiences with oppression, and the compounded impact of those experiences on the client's mental health and wellness. Multicultural counseling skills competencies include but are not limited to the provider's effort to obtain multicultural training experiences, seek information about client groups, connect with communities outside the counseling dyad, communicate effectively with clients, assess clients' needs, and advocate on clients' behalf using institutional intervention skills, etc. (Sue et al., 1992).

Although an enormous contribution to the counseling profession, the original MCC models have operated under the premise that the provider was a privileged member of the counseling profession (e.g., usually white and male) who used clients' personal disclosures and insights to help them make important social, emotional, and psychological breakthroughs. Multicultural counseling models presumed that clients have marginalized identities and experiences, given their gratuitous encounters with varying forms of oppression. For this reason, early MCC models were less nuanced than more current models.

Multicultural and Social Justice Counseling Competencies

Since 2001, MCC models have undergone additional iterations. More recently, however, the Association for Multicultural Counseling and Development, a division of the American Counseling Association, commissioned the development of the Multicultural and Social Justice Counseling Competencies (MSJCC; Ratts et al., 2016). Much like early MCC models, the MSJCC identify competencies providers should possess. An important component of the MSJCC involves consideration of power dynamics governing the provider–client relationship, as well as the integration of social justice and advocacy interventions to eliminate structural barriers and inequities that clients confront (see Figure 2.1).

Historically, scholars presumed that providers occupied a privileged status, and clients occupied a marginalized status within the counseling dyad. Given explosive demographic shifts in the population, today more than any previous time in history, counselors may hail from privileged and/or marginalized groups. Similarly, clients may hail from privileged and/or marginalized groups. According to the MSJCC model, a privileged counselor might work with a privileged client or a marginalized client. Similarly, a marginalized counselor might work with a privileged or marginalized client. If not properly managed, the provider and client's sources of privilege and marginalization could potentially interact within the counseling dyad, invoking an unhealthy power dynamic that could potentially erode the counseling relationship.

The MSJCC contain four quadrants that address the impact of power, privilege, and oppression within the counseling relationship. These quadrants consider the nuanced interactions governing the social locations of the provider and

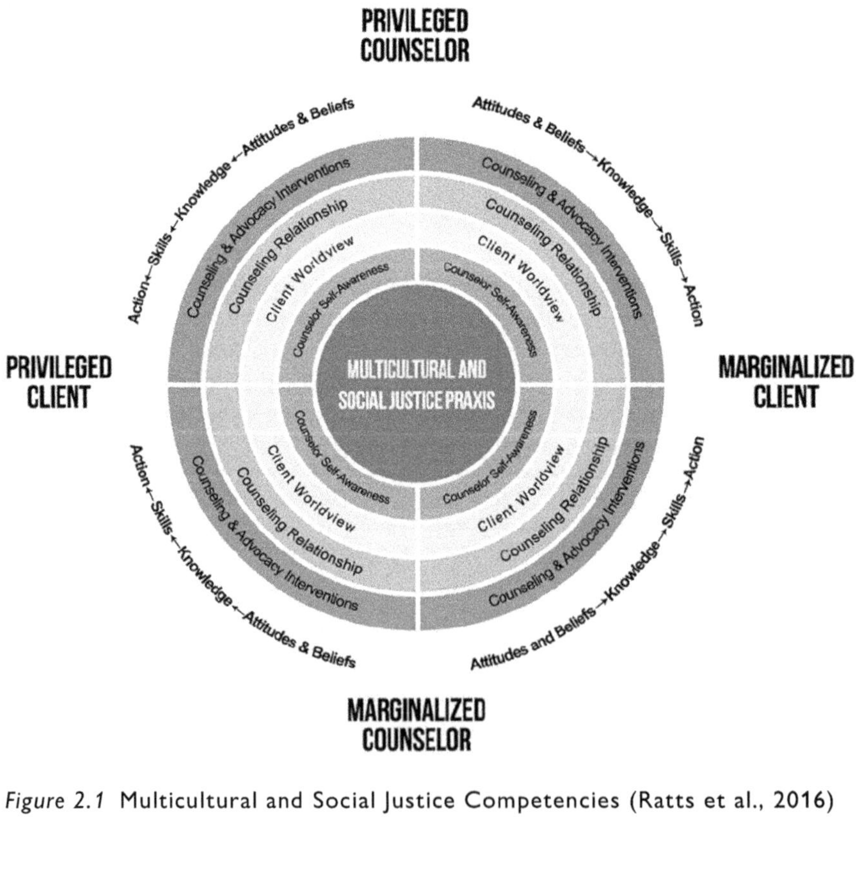

Figure 2.1 Multicultural and Social Justice Competencies (Ratts et al., 2016)

client. Incidentally, social locations refer to unique attributional characteristics, such as race, ethnicity, gender, religion, immigration status, sexual orientation, and linguistic diversity, that effect provider–client interactions. That is, a provider with privileged identities may exhibit social dominance by exhibiting an air of indifference, superiority, condescension, etc. (whether intentional or not), in ways that have the potential to marginalize clients. Conversely, a provider with marginalized identities may feel intimidated by clients based on the presumed power inversion in which a client from a more privileged group may exercise dominance toward a provider because of presumed deficits.

To illustrate, a counselor from a dominant group may harbor deficit perspectives about clients from minoritized groups, and a client from a dominant group may assume a provider from a minoritized group lacks the credentials, expertise, and/or social status to work with them. The MSJCC acknowledge the interacting social and cultural dynamics that shape the provider–client relationship and encourage providers to engage in critical consciousness in order to manage strong emotions that may undermine the counseling process.

The MSJCC contain four developmental domains that address the social locations of the provider and counselor: (a) counselor self-awareness or the provider's consideration of personal biases that may impede the counseling process; (b) client worldview or the provider's attention to the client's internal frame of reference, cultural norms, and values; (c) the counseling relationship or the therapeutic alliance developed between the provider and client; and (d) counseling and advocacy interventions, which refer to social justice advocacy interventions designed to eradicate sources of oppression (Ratts et al., 2016). Within each of these developmental domains, the MSJCC identify aspirational competencies: attitudes and beliefs, knowledge, skills, and action-oriented social justice strategies.

Askren (2022) suggested that although MCC models contain important counseling elements, they omit clinical interventions. She asserted that the application of tools for conversing with clients about their socially constructed REC contexts (e.g., broaching domains) should be used to operationalize MCC models. To that end, some scholars have shifted away from cultural competence models, asserting that the provider's presentation of self operates as a superior criterion for achieving counseling effectiveness. In fact, some scholars eschew competency models altogether, arguing that learning is never complete, and as such, providers can never really become competent given the evolving nature of culture (Hook et al., 2017; Liu et al., 2024). Additively, they contend that an awareness, knowledge, and skills framework is a necessary albeit insufficient criterion for working in meaningful ways with clients. Several scholars contend that MCC models emphasize counseling processes as opposed to counseling outcomes (Davis et al., 2018; Hicks, 2026). Given limitations associated with certain MCC models, psychologists in particular have devised counseling approaches such as the multicultural orientation (MCO) model that are empirically linked to more favorable counseling outcomes (Davis et al., 2018).

Multicultural Counseling Orientation

Several theorists have introduced MCO as a viable alternative to MCC models (Davis et al., 2018; Owen et al., 2011). Proponents of MCO models assert that MCC models emphasize counseling attitudes and beliefs that providers enlist as they deliver treatment approaches. In marked contrast, the MCO framework emphasizes the provider's presentation of self and orientation toward the client's REC factors as a basis for achieving favorable counseling outcomes (Davis et al., 2018; Owen et al., 2011).

The MCO model contains three specific components: (a) cultural humility, (b) cultural comfort, and (c) cultural opportunities (Owen et al., 2016). Cultural humility reflects the provider's unassuming nature, cultural presence, sense of curiosity about clients, and the willingness to admit mistakes. Cultural comfort refers to the provider's ease of manner in engaging with clients. Cultural opportunities emphasize the provider's ability to converse openly about the extent to which REC concerns influence the clients' sense of mental well-being. I contend that cultural opportunities cohere with the provider's efforts to broach clients' REC concerns. In fact, Jones and Branco (2020) have demonstrated a symbiotic relationship between MCO, MCC, and broaching behavior. More specifically, MCO represents a way of being with the client and functions as the foundation of multicultural competence. In turn, MCC has been defined as the behavioral manifestation of MCO, and broaching behaviors operate as a correlate of MCO. Be that as it may, the MCO framework has been linked to a number of counseling outcomes. For instance, studies show that the provider's cultural humility is associated with a stronger therapeutic alliance and symptom improvement (DeBlaere et al., 2023; Hicks, 2026; Hook et al., 2013).

In their study, Owen et al. (2016) concluded that clients who perceived that their providers missed opportunities to discuss their cultural concerns reported more negative counseling outcomes. Similarly, clients who reported that their providers missed opportunities to discuss their REC concerns rated their providers as less culturally humble; however, results demonstrated no relationship between favorable cultural humility ratings, openness to discussing clients' cultural concerns, and more favorable counseling outcomes. These results suggest that cultural humility and willingness to examine clients' salient REC identity structures and sociopolitical realities are necessary but insufficient criteria for promoting favorable counseling outcomes.

More recently, Hicks (2026) examined the relationship between chronically ill ethnic minority patients' self-reported experiences of discrimination in medical settings, internalized stigma, counselors' broaching efforts, and mental health outcomes. Findings indicted that chronic illness was significantly associated with depression and anxiety. Discrimination in medical settings partially mediated the association between chronic illness and mental health outcomes, and the counselor's effective broaching behavior buffered depression and anxiety.

The remainder of this book is devoted to helping clients develop a set of strategies and tools to facilitate meaningful and substantive discussions about their clients' REC concerns. I use the MSJCC and MCO models as points of departure for describing the broaching framework and identifying strategies that assist providers in their efforts to facilitate meaningful dialogue with clients about their REC concerns, but first, I review several factors that influence the provider's ability to engage openly, comfortably, and meaningfully with clients.

Against this historical backdrop of multicultural theories, we delve into the broaching framework, but first we address barriers to providers' ability to broach the client's REC-related concerns. These factors include social identity theory as well as values about one's access to privilege, imposter syndrome, colorblind racial attitudes, and microaggressions. This chapter closes with a set of mindsets that providers can enlist to enhance their ability to discuss clients' REC concerns, such as growth mindset and a broaching readiness model.

Factors That Inhibit or Promote Effective Broaching Behavior

Social Identity Theory

Social identity theory posits that membership in certain groups shapes how we construct our identities (e.g., nationality, religion, team affiliation, other social categories). Often as part of group membership people adopt the values, viewpoints, and sensibilities of these group affiliations. For instance, your undergraduate institution holds considerable sway over your allegiance or commitment to your college or university. In most instances, students and alumni members are loyal fans of their colleges and universities and develop a strong sense of pride based on their affiliation with the institution (e.g., Go Heels, Go Bulldogs, Go Pirates). Similarly, membership in religious, civic, and social organizations (e.g., fraternities and sororities), as well as families and communities, may result in our adoption of the values of larger communities or organizations. People often adopt the values, viewpoints, and ideologies based on their organizational affiliation, institutions, and communities to which they belong by virtue of their membership or association with certain groups. We are programmed to think and behave in particular ways about social phenomena. This social conditioning guides, directs, and influences our personal attitudes and allegiances to certain groups and/or ideologies (Harro, 2013). Without intervention or a conscious effort to challenge these messages, people often adopt messages they have internalized from the people around them (Harro). Their belief systems shape opinions and perceptions of other groups. For more detailed discussions, see research conducted by Henri Tajfel as well as Karen Wynn. Providers have an obligation to engage in critical self-awareness about how their own socialization experiences shape their orientation toward broaching in an effort to support clients who may be different from themselves (Day-Vines et al., 2018).

Defend, Deny, Distance, Dismantle

Shuman et al. (2024) extended social identity theory and asserted that people with advantaged backgrounds possess privilege and that questions or reminders about their privileged status can evoke a deep sense of emotional discomfort or cognitive dissonance. In order to minimize the internal conflict that may result from having privileges that are not available to others and to assuage possible feelings of guilt or shame, these individuals engage in identity management strategies. Shuman et al. identified a set of four possible stances or identity management strategies that individuals can assume. They can (a) defend or justify their privileged status, (b) deny their access to privilege by pretending that everyone has the same opportunity structure, (c) distance or separate themselves from their privileged identity by focusing on their individual identity, or (d) dismantle systems of inequality. The first three identity management strategies (e.g., defend, deny, distance) appear inconsistent with the provider's willingness to seize cultural opportunities to explore or discuss the contextual dimensions of REC with clients. The final identity management strategy seems consonant with providers who endorse social justice, advocacy, and systemic change in an effort to eliminate structural barriers for clients.

Shuman et al. (2025) assessed the identity management strategies across three samples and concluded that respondents in all four categories supported equality, although dismantlers reported the highest scores on preferences for equality. Individuals with high defend and deny profiles revealed stronger preferences for social hierarchies and meritocracy. Defenders, deniers, and distancers were opposed or moderately opposed to social change, while dismantlers demonstrated high preferences for social change. These findings imply that providers with defend, deny, and distance profiles may exhibit more difficulty having earnest conversations with clients from minoritized groups about their REC concerns. Providers who understand and demonstrate a willingness to confront their privileged status may be better positioned to engage clients empathically. Providers who find it difficult to confront their own privileged status may experience internal conflicts that interfere with their ability to engage in more effective broaching behavior.

For instance, a provider who assumes a defensive posture about their own privilege and does not consider structural factors as possible impediments to clients' difficulties may attribute clients' difficulties to their personal moral failings. This lack of empathic awareness may lead the provider to blame the client for challenges, recommend inappropriate interventions, or withdraw emotional support from the client. For instance, Tim, an experienced provider, believes fervently in the Protestant work ethic and that people are rewarded based on their effort. When his client disclosed that she applied for public assistance, he challenged her work ethic without considering how structural factors – such as low wages, limited access to affordable childcare, housing instability, and systemic barriers to employment – interfere with the client's ability to meet basic needs without some form of public assistance. He harbored subtle feelings of indifference toward the client that emerged in his treatment approaches. As we will see in the next section of this chapter, the manifestation of a privileged identity status may result from varying forms of imposter syndrome.

Years ago, when I first started teaching social and cultural diversity courses, I noticed that students had a range of emotions regarding course content. Some students would be really intrigued by the content and would engage with the material meaningfully, trying to make sense of what was going on in the world. They considered how their attitudes were shaped and contemplated what sort of mindsets they needed to extirpate. I had other students who were really resentful of the content they were studying in class. Consequently, they exhibited tremendous resistance toward the material. As I examine my encounters with students in the context of identity management theory, I believe my students who resisted course content were likely demonstrating a preference toward maintaining social dominance.

I would often say to them that it's one thing to have an oppositional mindset as you engage with course content. I would hold the textbook up in my hand and say, but what happens when the textbook becomes a client? How will you manage and navigate those strong reactive emotions toward the client? If you plan to work effectively with clients, you must sort through the attitudes you have about people who are poor, LGBTQIA+, immigrants, people who speak accented English, the elderly, disabled, etc. One of the things we know is that if you don't manage and navigate the attitudes that you have, they are likely to surface in the counseling arena as microaggressions, hostility, or subtle indifference toward the client. In class, I usually address the concept of nonverbal leakage (Foley & Gentile, 2010; Hill, 2020). That means that our internal impressions and reactions toward individuals are likely to manifest as we engage them within the counseling dyad. For instance, we may bristle when they talk and exhibit nonverbal expressions that communicate distaste and dislike. Conversely, we may distance ourselves emotionally in ways that are patently obvious to the client, such as fidgeting and refusing to engage clients in REC discussions that are relevant to their presenting concerns.

For many but certainly not all clients, particularly clients from minoritized backgrounds, the opportunity to explore their REC concerns provides catharsis (Sue et al., 2022). Regardless of the feelings and sentiments about clients that emerge within you, it is important to acknowledge those feelings (e.g., in supervision, personal counseling, journaling) because they are real. They are yours. Your bias may be conscious or unconscious. Whether clients recognize and/or verbalize their observations about your behavior or interaction with them, you can best believe they are very aware of the verbal and nonverbal signals you transmit, whether knowingly or unknowingly. People from minoritized groups find themselves having to be hypervigilant as a matter of psychological safety

(Grier & Cobbs, 1968). James Baldwin famously referenced the Ike and Tina lyrics, "I can't believe what you say, because I see what you do" (Baldwin, 1985, p. 339).

Imposter Syndrome

Imposter syndrome refers to the provider's feelings of self-doubt and concern about being exposed by clients as a fraud or as someone with limited understanding about social and cultural diversity. Imposter syndrome may result when people do not feel adequately prepared to address their client's concerns. Feelings of inadequacy may interfere with effective counseling efforts. For instance, Cynthia is a White provider who has just landed a job in a counseling facility that serves a large low-income immigrant and refugee population. She has an internalized sense of dread, concerned that she may lack the preparedness to work effectively with her clients. Even though she is fully credentialed and has demonstrated other measures of success as a mental health provider, she worries about being exposed as someone clients may experience as aloof, incompetent, and out of touch with their sociopolitical realities.

Sarah is a recently licensed 25-year-old White provider whose imposter syndrome shows up differently. Sarah was assigned to work with a 60-year-old Asian man who just lost his job with a federal government agency after more than 30 years of service. As the reader might imagine, Sarah harbors few concerns about the client's racial background or educational status but feels more preoccupied with the age differential between herself and her client, and the potential impact the age gap may have on the counseling process. Her trepidation about working with someone who is so much older than herself gives her a sense of fear and trepidation that she may say something wrong or that she lacks the life experience to work effectively with her client.

Jonathan is a White male provider who has very conservative values and viewpoints. He spends some of his leisure time combing right-wing websites, and although he will not admit it openly, he identifies as a White Christian nationalist. More recently, he has seen an uptick in his caseload of ethnic minority and sexual minority clients, many of whom do not identify as Christian or conservative.

Jonathan worries that his nativist views may seep out when he works with clients. His fear of exposure results in his reluctance to engage clients in discussions about their REC concerns. Providers like Jonathan disguise their strong views by spouting racial platitudes that only scratch the surface of racial consciousness (Liu et al., 2024).

Maria is a Peruvian national who immigrated to the United States to complete her doctorate in Counseling Psychology. She has completed her degree and is fully licensed and currently works in private practice. Because she has only been in the country since she started her degree program, she worries that she does not always have enough baseline knowledge about U.S. culture to understand the popular cultural references her clients make. She also worries about her accented English and whether or not she will be able to communicate effectively with clients. She has completely discounted her credentials and years of experience as a clinician in Peru.

Dr. Bhangi is a second-year psychiatry resident who sees patients in an outpatient clinic. She is a second-generation Indian American whose parents migrated to the United States from India on an employment visa in the 1980s. Her family is from the Dalit caste, which is considered part of the lowest stratum within the hierarchically structured Indian caste system. Her attending psychiatrist assigned her to work with Mehar, a 25-year-old Indian woman whose grandparents migrated to the United States to pursue careers in medicine. Mehar's family is from the Brahmin caste, which is considered the highest caste system within India. Mehar receives medication management in the outpatient clinic for an eating disorder. Given her status as a Dalit caste member, Dr. Bhangi worries that the prevailing social stratification system in India may be reinscribed within the provider-patient relationship. Her fear is that caste conflict may emerge, and she is uncertain about managing the cultural-relational dynamics that may surface during treatment. She also internalizes a sense of shame and guilt about the inverted caste hierarchy. She is treating someone from a higher caste and worries that her patient may not consider her capable, competent, or qualified to treat her. Dr. Bhangi believes that her attending physician assigned her this patient because they both shared Indian heritages, not realizing that Indian geopolitics may play out within the United States. Incidentally, caste discrimination has increased within the United States to such an extent that in certain jurisdictions, people from lower castes have challenged oppressive and discriminatory treatment such as verbal abuse, hostility, indifference, and employment denial in court. In fact, a study of caste discrimination in the workplace indicated that 67% of Dalits reported unfair employment practices, compared to 1% of Brahmins (Zwick-Maitre, 2018). Additively, 59% of Dalit members have experienced casteist jokes and slurs.

Each of these examples demonstrates how imposter syndrome can intrude upon the provider–client relationship in ways that may be detrimental to the treatment process, as well as treatment outcomes. Burnout is a possible consequence of imposter syndrome. Clark et al. (2022) examined the relationship between compassion satisfaction, burnout, and imposter syndrome in mental health professionals. Compassion satisfaction refers to the clinician's sense of accomplishment and satisfaction resulting from doing one's job effectively. In their study, lower levels of compassion satisfaction and higher levels of burnout were significantly related to the imposter phenomenon. The researchers concluded that imposter syndrome is a pathway through which clinicians could develop burnout. Further, without critical self-awareness, providers may do more damage than good to their clients. Imposter syndrome may inhibit the provider's ability to work effectively with clients. Focusing more on one's own shortcomings may remove focus from the client's needs. The fear of saying the wrong thing to the client or internalized feelings of inadequacy may lead to situations in which providers sidestep conversations that are crucial to client self-understanding. Providers who are preoccupied with their own inadequacies may be less attuned to clients' needs and not recognize the importance of considering clients' cultural needs. Similarly, colorblind attitudes, a related construct that involves one's effort to downplay the role of race by claiming not to see or recognize racial realities, may contribute to avoidant broaching behaviors by not exploring clients' REC concerns during the counseling process.

Colorblind Racial Attitudes

Colorblind racial ideology (CBRI) constitutes a form of racial insensitivity that involves an effort to ignore race and treat everyone equally. Essentially, CBRI assumes that issues of race and representation are inconsequential for people of color. Colorblind racial scholars argue, however, that efforts to ignore race operate as more nuanced, ultramodern forms of racism (Neville et al., 2013). Proponents of colorblindness presume that minimizing attention to race will somehow reduce racial prejudice. Although colorblindness seems desirable, it obscures the racial and ethnic disparities that are pervasive in this country. Because racism is presumed to be less acceptable, people often shield their racist intentions by rationalizing or avoiding racial topics.

Colorblindness can emerge in two distinct ways: color-evasion or power-evasion (Yi et al., 2022). Providers operating from a color-evasion stance deflect attention from racial differences and emphasize racial sameness due to beliefs that ignoring race may reduce or eliminate racial discrimination. A second form of CBRI involves power-evasion or efforts to deny institutional racism in ways that perpetuate racism and other forms of social dominance. An African American female client may share with her provider that she attributes the difficulties she's experiencing on her job primarily to race and racism. An untutored provider may respond by saying that the experiences that the client has described happen to women of all races. This type of nonfacilitative response invalidates the client's experience by reducing her concerns to gender without consideration of racial overtones. Such a stance renders the client less comfortable sharing her inner thoughts and feelings.

A provider operating from a power-evasion stance may respond by saying that racism is no longer as virulent as it used to be and that things are getting better for African American women – after all, we see many more African American women in positions of leadership. Look at Kamala Harris. Refusing to acknowledge race by focusing on the accomplishment of exemplars diminishes the role of race in the client's experience and may limit the client's willingness to disclose personal concerns.

Studies demonstrate that higher rates of CBRI are associated with lower empathy ratings as well as multicultural competence in predominantly White samples of psychologists and trainees (Neville et al., 2006; Spanierman et al.,

2008). A study of African American adults indicated that CRBI was associated with internalized oppression (Neville et al., 2005). These findings suggest that colorblind attitudes may result in dismissive narratives about the centrality of race and power and simultaneously interfere with providers' ability to delve into clients' REC concerns in ways that may undermine the therapeutic alliance and more favorable counseling outcomes.

Eduardo Bonilla-Silva (2021) studied the semantic tactics that people enlist in order to deflect attention from their racially biased proclivities. After engaging in politically charged conversations on topics such as affirmative action and interracial marriage, respondents in Bonilla-Silva's study spoke in nuanced ways that gave the appearance of being unbiased; however, Bonilla-Silva coded respondents' communication patterns as exhibiting CBRIs because their responses exuded racial resentment, revealed highly charged racial positions, and offered justification for racial inequities despite touting race-neutral attitudes and sentiments. After analyzing respondents' discourse styles, Bonilla-Silva concluded that people adopted several different stances for concealing their racial biases: (a) avoidance, (b) colorblindness, (c) projection, (d) diminutives, (e) rhetorical incoherence, and (f) attributing racialized behavior to anything but race.

Respondents in Bonilla-Silva's (2021) study who used avoidant discourse styles used innuendo and indirection to avoid talking negatively about racially charged issues. Respondents who adopted CBRIs maintained that they did not see color, were not prejudiced, or that they had friends from minoritized communities. They also responded using projections and assigning racial motivations to people of color. Respondents who used diminutives made comments, such as "I'm only a little against affirmative action or interracial relationships." Respondents categorized as engaging in rhetorical incoherence repeated themselves, paused, made grammatical errors, rambled, and exhibited anxiety when talking about race. A final rhetorical strategy that respondents employed involved the attribution of racialized dynamics to anything but race. In other words, when presented with topics that were undeniably racial in nature, respondents interpreted topics as completely unrelated to race.

Utsey et al.'s (2005) study examined counselor trainees' reactions to racially charged discussions that emerged in cross-racial counseling dyad simulations. Although some respondents engaged in racial self-awareness as a vehicle for understanding minoritized clients, several other respondents intellectualized the vignettes, denied and minimized racial dynamics that surfaced, exhibited heightened levels of anxiety and discomfort discussing racially charged incidents, experienced difficulty taking feedback from minority supervisors, used projection as a defense mechanism, evaluated cases absent a sociopolitical context, and avoided using terms such as race. Much like respondents in Bonilla-Silva's (2021) study, respondents in Utsey et al.'s study exhibited anxiety as evidenced by their trembling voices, pauses, hesitations, and flushed facial coloration when presented with racially provocative vignettes.

Providers who enlist colorblind rhetorical strategies with clients for whom race is salient may damage the therapeutic alliance and inflict harm. Walker (2024) cautioned providers who may be predisposed to ignoring issues of race when they are relevant to clients' counseling contexts. She noted that as a professor who trains clinicians, she has observed providers who practice cognitive behavioral therapy engage in premature problem-solving. She said providers often move immediately to the discussion of clients' distorted thought processes before comprehending the client's concerns. In some instances, providers do not consider the possibility that clients' concerns may actually have an REC component that warrants further discussion. Providers can undermine the counseling process when they ignore clients' REC contexts.

Liu et al. (2024) emphasized the importance of examining colorblind racism not just from an individual standpoint that considers the client's experience of racism but also highlighted the importance of deconstructing how broader sociopolitical forces shape clients' lived realities. Their analysis of the discussion patterns of providers who worked in a child welfare agency demonstrated that dismissing the contextual dimensions of REC can reinforce and perpetuate the very systems of inequality that providers claim they are trying to eradicate. A growing body of literature has indicated that the provider's inattention to the client's REC concerns constitutes a microaggression (Owen et al., 2014; Yeo & Harding, 2021).

Microaggressions

Microaggressions refer to slights and indignities that, whether conscious or unconscious, create psychological distress for the client. Usually, these insults occur based on one's race, gender, religion, sexual orientation, social class, language, immigration status, national origin, or other marginalized status. Previous research indicates that microaggressions are associated with weaker therapeutic alliances, lower levels of psychological well-being, limited satisfaction with counseling, and a diminished desire to return for therapy (Constantine, 2007; Drinane et al., 2018; Johnson et al., 2021; Nadal et al., 2012). One study, comprising more than 2000 racial/ethnic minoritized clients, found that 81% of clients reported experiencing at least one racial microaggression during treatment (Hook et al., 2016). Interestingly, the researchers concluded that the provider's avoidance of REC discussions constituted microaggressive behavior. Yeo and Torres-Harding (2021) examined the relationship between microaggressions, rupture repair, and working alliance in a sample of ethnic minority clients and concluded that microaggressions negatively impacted the therapeutic alliance. Ironically, providers are often not aware of their inappropriate statements.

Sue and Spanierman (2020) developed a taxonomy of racial microaggressions and identified three distinct categories: (a) microassaults, (b) microinsults, and (c) microinvalidations. Microinsults are derogatory statements or innuendos that are designed to humiliate and diminish a person's sense of self. For instance, a Latinx pre-med student schedules an appointment in the college counseling center. When he disclosed information about his current level of psychological distress, the provider asked if his career plans are too ambitious. Needless to say, the client felt humiliated and did not return for a follow-up session. Microinvalidations involve denial that a client has encountered some form of oppression. To illustrate, during the pandemic, an Asian national who worked for a major technology corporation sought counseling because he felt blamed by strangers in particular for the Coronavirus. He confided to his provider that he worried he might be placed in an internment camp, similar to the ones that Japanese Americans were confined to during World War II. The provider presumptuously stated that internment camps were a relic of the past, completely invalidating the client's sense of trepidation that he may encounter state-sanctioned punishments that would result in his confinement. In this instance, the provider was completely unaware that her dismissal of the client's intense feelings of dread contributed to his lack of confidence in the provider's ability to help him manage his heightened anxiety levels. Soon after, the client sought a new provider. The former provider remained oblivious to the emotional toll that the microaggressions imposed on the client.

More recently, Freeman and Stewart (2021) asserted that microaggressions as originally conceptualized focus on the behaviors and actions committed by the perpetrator. They maintained that an emphasis on the perpetrator's behavior camouflages the harm done to the target of the microaggression. Further, they asserted that the term "micro" is a misnomer because microassaults in particular are often not that subtle. In many instances, they are overt and emotionally violent. Freeman and Stewart argued that there is nothing micro about harming individuals.

Microaggressions that occur in therapy include avoidance of discussing the client's REC concerns, the provider's denial about having cultural biases or stereotypes, perceptions by the client that the provider harbors stereotypes, and lack of awareness about the reality of race in clients' lives (Hook et al., 2016). A spate of previous research indicates that racial microaggressions are closely linked to elevated levels of depression, anxiety, psychological distress, and other adverse consequences (Rudecindo et al., 2024). When microaggressions have been perpetrated by the provider, these behaviors contribute to ruptures, premature termination, and client dissatisfaction with the counseling process. The next section of this chapter addresses racial identity theory.

Racial Identity Theory

Racial identity functioning refers to an individual's perception of themself and others as racial beings. Those perceptions may range from stereotyped distortions about the self as well as others at the lower end of the continuum, to more complex and differentiated understandings of the self and others at the higher end. An individual's interaction with their social environment can help facilitate growth and maturation and new constructions of the self and others. Racial identity models reduce the tendency to essentialize individuals as monolithic entities. More specifically, racial identity functioning unfolds along a continuum from limited awareness of race and an adoption of stereotyped understandings of the self and others to more complex and differentiated ideas that culminate with a healthy appreciation for one's own racial heritage and the racial heritage of others who differ from themself.

William Cross (1971) developed the earliest racial identity model and documented the series of ideological transformations he observed in African Americans during the social consciousness period of the Civil Rights and Black Power Movements in the United States. This model is referred to as the Nigresence model because it articulated the process of becoming Black in a manner that helped shift segments of the African American community from internalizing oppression to developing a deepened sense of racial consciousness. Later, other scholars captured similar progressions in other racial and ethnic groups.

For instance, Sue et al. (2022) developed the Racial Cultural Identity Model for ethnic minority people. This model contains five distinct statuses: (a) conformity, (b) dissonance, (c) resistance and immersion, (d) introspection, and (e) integrative awareness. Individuals in the conformity category adhere to dominant cultural norms and more readily accept beliefs about white superiority and minority inferiority. During the dissonance stage, individuals begin to question previously held beliefs and attitudes about racial dominance and subordination. The resistance and immersion status reflects an individual's endorsement of minority-held viewpoints and rejection of societal values about white dominance. Individuals operating in the resistance and immersion status develop a strong aversion to cultural oppression, which results in a range of feelings including shame, guilt, and anger about having previously endorsed negative constructions of their racial-ethnic group, as well as pride in a newfound self-identity. The resulting emotional intensity required to maintain an anti-oppressive stance becomes unsustainable and ushers in the introspection status. Individuals operating in the introspection status experience discomfort about rigidly held values and viewpoints. During the integrative awareness category, people develop a more secure and healthy appreciation of their own culture and their acceptance of people from other cultures.

Janet Helms and Donelda Cook (1999) developed a companion framework referred to as the White Racial Identity Development model to track the racial identity trajectory that many White people experience. They identified six statuses: (a) contact, (b) disintegration, (c) reintegration, (d) pseudo-independence, (e) immersion-emersion, and (f) autonomy. Whites in the contact status are oblivious to their own racial identity. They harbor pernicious stereotypes about people of color and tend to operate from a colorblind racial stance. Many White people have had few opportunities or incentives to confront their own attitudes, biases, and assumptions, opting instead to endorse stereotypes about people of color. During the disintegration phase, Whites recognize contradictions between their previously held beliefs and behaviors and experience a sense of internal conflict. For instance, an individual may experience a sense of cognitive dissonance about believing in the importance of all people, yet resent the fact that a family member may decide to marry interracially. This involves choosing between group loyalty and respecting the humanity of others. During the reintegration phase, people revert to previously held biases toward a dominant white ideology, returning to beliefs about the superiority of Whites and the inferiority of people of color. This level of investment in challenging social dominance requires psychic energy that many White people are unwilling to expend. Individuals in the pseudo-independence phase have an intellectualized understanding of constructs such as racism, discrimination, power, and privilege. Pseudo-independent Whites begin to make overtures toward people from minoritized groups, especially those minorities who are quite similar to themselves. During the immersion status, people begin to engage in an honest appraisal of the significance of racism. They examine what it means to be White and how they have benefited from whiteness. They confront their own biases and engage others at a more experiential and affective level of awareness and understanding that have been absent in earlier stages of their development. In the autonomy status, White individuals have fewer feelings of guilt and acknowledge how they may benefit from and perpetuate racism. Autonomous Whites demonstrate a commitment toward eradicating racism and work to solidify an antiracist identity.

Previous research has demonstrated that school counselor trainees with higher levels of racial identity functioning were more open to broaching clients' REC-focused concerns (Day-Vines et al., 2022). As stated previously – not discussing clients' salient REC concerns constitutes microaggressive behavior that may lead to cultural impasses or fissures in the counseling relationship that contribute to clients withholding their cultural identity from the provider (Drinane et al., 2018).

In the final section of this chapter, we consider strategies that may help providers surmount some of the challenges and misgivings they have about working with clients who are culturally different from themselves. We start with a discussion of growth mindset and then the next section of this chapter addresses the importance of a growth mindset in developing broaching skills and strategies.

Growth Mindset

Psychologist and Stanford University professor Carol Dweck (2016) studies mindsets, or how people's thoughts and beliefs about their abilities impact their openness to learning new skill sets. Dweck identified two types of mindsets:

fixed and growth. Individuals with fixed mindsets believe that intelligence is static and cannot be enhanced through effort and hard work. They contend that either you have a particular skill set or you do not. Individuals with fixed mindsets believe that success is about demonstrating how smart you are. Often people with fixed mindsets harbor apprehensions about making mistakes and exposing deficiencies. They are preoccupied with success versus growth. In a counseling context, a fixed mindset may breed feelings of self-doubt in the provider that culminate in avoidance of working within clients' unique cultural contexts, reluctance to seek supervision, perfectionism, not seeking growth opportunities, and fear of exposure about being presumed incompetent. These dispositional states have problematic consequences for the client.

Conversely, a growth mindset reflects an orientation toward personal development. Individuals with a growth mindset believe that they can improve their performance by working hard and taking on challenges that stretch their capacity to learn. These individuals seize opportunities to learn and willingly make mistakes because they feel stimulated by new challenges. They recognize their potential for growth and development.

As a faculty member, I give students an opportunity to resubmit assignments, especially if they make a low grade, and I believe that they can enhance their multicultural understanding by having an additional opportunity to refine their skills and demonstrate their knowledge base. I personally believe that mastery involves a series of successive approximations. Trial and error helps improve performance. My students who are oriented toward a fixed mindset will often take the original grade they earned. Of course, there may be cogent reasons unrelated to the fixed mindset that interfere with students' ability to redo an assignment such as work, family obligations, and time constraints. In any case, my students who are oriented toward a growth mindset leap at the opportunity to make a subsequent attempt at learning in order to enhance their skill sets. Relatedly, a provider who maintains a fixed mindset might encounter some type of cultural challenge with a client and feel that they cannot help the client, that they must give up, or avoid talking about clients' cultural concerns. They may refer clients to other providers rather than commit to working through their own difficulties (Arnold, 2010). In marked contrast, a provider with a growth mindset would challenge themselves to learn more skills, delve deeper into their lack of understanding, figure out how to overcome barriers, and explore in more depth what they struggle to understand. To illustrate, providers with a growth mindset might read books like this one, *Broaching Race, Ethnicity, and Culture in the Counseling Process: Strategies for Facilitating Meaningful Dialogue with Clients*. Additively, they may engage in professional development through workshops, seminars, exposure (e.g., travel, volunteering), clinical supervision, mentorship, and engagement with professional communities. They would also embrace vulnerability by sharing their struggles with others, such as colleagues through peer mentoring, consultation, and clinical supervision to improve their approach to therapy. The foregoing discussion implies the importance of implementing systematic tools for developing the ego strength necessary to broach clients' REC concerns (Day-Vines et al., 2018, 2021). Consistent with several of the recommendations for consideration cited in this chapter (e.g., MSJCC), Newton and Steele (2025) identified a set of prerequisites that providers should consider, maintaining that providers cannot delve into meaningful broaching efforts without first engaging in the intrapersonal work that involves considerations such as critical self-examination, cognitive reframing, discomfort tolerance, and education.

In his heavily quoted *The New York Times* essay entitled "As Much Truth as One Can Bear," essayist and author James Baldwin (1962) implored literary artists as raconteurs of the culture to engage in honest truth and storytelling as a moral and ethical obligation. He noted that all too often people present the world as they wish it to be and, by doing so, evade important realities because they want to shield the truth. Baldwin concluded his essay by appealing to the reader and noting that circumstances "will not go away because we pretend they are not there." The same can be said of mental health processes. Sidestepping, minimizing, by-passing, or de-centering our clients' REC concerns will not alleviate problem situations. In fact, ignoring concerns may in fact exacerbate clients' difficulties. Baldwin continued by noting the importance of facing situations squarely when he said, "Not everything that is faced can be changed; but nothing can be changed until it is faced." Similarly, in counseling contexts, providers are not in a position to truly support a client unless they can see and understand the world as the client sees it; more specifically, from the client's internal frame of reference. Avoidant broaching behavior is a woefully inadequate means of forestalling necessary REC conversations that warrant further exploration. Meaningful dialogue about clients' REC concerns has the potential to stimulate catharsis. As providers, we are purveyors of clients' truths, and we must honor those truths and experiential realities in order to facilitate client growth, healing, and recovery, even if venturing into our clients' subjective REC realities creates cognitive dissonance for providers. It is in the spirit of a growth mindset and broaching readiness that we embark upon the important work of broaching clients' salient REC concerns.

Summary

This chapter addressed foundational broaching concepts that undergird the broaching framework. The chapter demonstrated the progression of theoretical underpinnings such as the early Multicultural Counseling Competencies, the Multicultural and Social Justice Counseling Competencies, and the Multicultural Orientation Framework. These models emphasize provider self-awareness, cultural humility, and openness to discussing the contextual dimensions of race, ethnicity, and culture with clients. The chapter also covered factors that inhibit broaching effectiveness such as social identity processes, imposter syndrome, colorblind racial attitudes, microaggressions, and racial identity functioning. The chapter closes with a discussion of growth mindset, noting that providers who believe that their capacity for broaching can be developed through practice and hard work are more inclined to invest the effort to learning how to engage clients in meaningful conversations about their REC concerns.

Discussion Questions

1 What category on Shuman's scale best reflects your orientation toward privilege?
2 How might your stance on privilege affect your counseling efforts with clients?
3 What are the counseling consequences of providers with CBRI orientations?
4 Given the different racial identity models presented in this chapter, what model and status best represent your level of racial identity functioning?
5 What seems most exciting or most unsettling about broaching clients' REC concerns?

References

Arnold, K.M.A. (2010). *A qualitative examination of African American counselors' experiences of addressing issues of race, ethnicity, and culture with clients of color* (Doctoral Dissertation). Virginia Tech.

Askren, K. (2022). *Integrated model for teaching multicultural competence: Incorporating broaching as a basic skill for counseling students* (Doctoral Dissertation). Liberty University https://digitalcommons.liberty.edu/doctoral/3662/

Baldwin, J. (1962, January 14). *As much truth as one can bear*. The New York Times Book Review.

Baldwin, J. (1985). A report from occupied territory. In *The price of the ticket: Collected nonfiction 1948–1985* (pp. 335–349). St. Martin's Press.

Bonilla-Silva, E. (2021). *Racism without racists: Color-blind racism and the persistence of racial inequality in America*. Rowman and Littlefield.

Clark, P., Holden, C., Russell, M., & Downs, H. (2022). The impostor phenomenon in mental health professionals: Relationships among compassion fatigue, burnout, and compassion satisfaction. *Contemporary Family Therapy*, *44*(2), 185–197. https://doi.org/10.1007/s10591-021-09580-y

Constantine, M.G. (2007). Racial microaggressions against African American Clients in Cross-Racial Counseling Relationships. *Journal of Counseling Psychology*, *54*, 1–16. https://doi-org.proxy1.library.jhu.edu/10.1002/j.1556-6678.2008.tb00519.x

Cross, W.E. (1971). Nego-to-black conversion experience. Toward a psychology of black liberation. *Black World*, *20*, 13–27.

Davis, D.E., DeBlaere, C., Owen, J., Hook, J.N., Rivera, D.P., Choe, E., Van Tongeren, D.R., Worthington, E. L., Jr., & Placeres, V. (2018). The multicultural orientation framework: A narrative review. *Psychotherapy*, *55*(1), 89–100. https://doi.org/10.1037/pst0000160

Day-Vines, N.L., Booker Ammah, B., Steen, S., & Arnold, K.M. (2018). Getting comfortable with discomfort: Preparing counselor trainees to broach racial, ethnic, and cultural factors with clients during counseling. *International Journal for the Advancement of Counselling, 40*(2), 89–104. https://doi.org/10.1007/s10447-017-9308-9

Day-Vines, N.L., Brodar, J.R., Hicks, D., Fernandez-Korto, E.B., Garcia, C., & Jones, K. (2022). An investigation of the relationship between school counselor trainees' broaching behavior and their racial identity attitudes. *Journal of Counseling and Development, 100*, 3–13. https://doi.org/10.1002/jcad.12406

Day-Vines, N.L., Cluxton-Keller, F., Agorsor, C., & Gubara, S. (2021). Strategies for broaching the subjects of race, ethnicity and culture. *Journal of Counseling and Development, 99*, 348–357. https://doi.org/10.1002/jcad.12380

DeBlaere, C., Zelaya, D.G., Dean, J.B., Chadwick, C.N., Davis, D.E, Hook, J.N., & Owen, J. (2023). Multiple microaggressions and therapy outcomes: The indirect effects of cultural humility and working alliance with Black, indigenous, women of color clients. *Professional Psychology: Research and Practice, 54*, 115–124. https://doi-org.proxy1.library.jhu.edu/10.1037/pro0000497

Drinane, J.M., Owen, J., & Tao, K.W. (2018). Cultural concealment and therapy outcomes. *Journal of Counseling Psychology, 65*, 239–246. https://doi.org/10.1037/cou0000246

Dweck, C.S. (2016). *Mindset: The new Psychology of success: How we can learn to fulfill our potential.* Random House.

Foley, G.N., & Gentile, J.P. (2010). Nonverbal communication in psychotherapy. *Psychiatry, 7*, 38–44.

Freeman, L., & Stewart, H. (2021). Toward a harm-based account of microaggressions. *Perspectives on Psychological Science, 16*(5), 1008–1023. https://doi.org/10.1177/17456916211017099

Grier, W.H., & Cobbs, P.M. (1968). *Black rage*: Basic Books.

Guthrie, R.V. (2003). *Even the rat was white: A historical view of psychology*. Allyn & Bacon.

Harro, B. (2013). The cycle of socialization. In M. Adams, W.J. Blumenfeld, C. Casteneda, H.W. Hackman, M.L. Peters, & X. Zuniga (Eds.), *Readings for diversity and social justice* (3rd ed., pp. 45–52). Routledge.

Helms, J.E., & Cook, D.A. (1999). *Using race and culture in counseling and psychotherapy: Theory and process*. Allyn & Bacon.

Hicks, D. (2026). *Counselors' broaching skills influence on the mental health outcomes of chronically ill racial and ethnic minoritized clients: A serial moderated mediation model* [Unpublished doctoral dissertation]. The Ohio State University.

Hill, C.E. (2020). *Helping skills: Facilitating exploration, insight, and action*. American Psychological Association.

Hook, J.N., Davis, D., & Owen, J. (2017). *Cultural humility: Engaging diverse identities in therapy*. American Psychological Association.

Hook, J.N., Davis, D.E., Owen, J., Worthington, E.L., Jr., & Utsey, S.O. (2013). Cultural humility: Measuring openness to culturally diverse clients. *Journal of Counseling Psychology, 60*(3), 353–366. https://doi.org/10.1037/a0032595

Hook, J.N., Farrell, J.E., Davis, D.E., DeBlaere, C., Van Tongeren, D.R., & Utsey, S. O. (2016). Cultural humility and racial microaggressions in counseling. *Journal of Counseling Psychology, 63*(3), 269–277. https://doi.org/10.1037/cou0000114

Johnson, V.E., Nadal, K.L., Sissoko, D.R.G., & King, R. (2021). "It's not in your head": Gaslighting, 'splaining, victim blaming, and other harmful reactions to microaggressions. *Perspectives on Psychological Science*, *16*, 1024–1036. https://doi.org/10.1177/17456916211011963

Jones, C.T., & Branco, S.F. (2020). The interconnectedness between cultural humility and broaching in clinical supervision: Working from the multicultural orientation framework. *The Clinical Supervisor*, *39*(2), 198–209. https://doi-org.proxy1.library.jhu.edu/10.1080/07325223.2020.1830327

Liu, W., Buckley, T.R., & Foldy, E.G. (2024). Colorblindness and race dismissiveness: Discursive racism and the limits of multicultural competence. *Journal of Social Issues*, *80*, 629–650. https://doi.org/10.1111/josi.12617

Nadal, K.L., Vigilia Escobar, K.M., Prado, G.T., David, E.J.R., & Haynes, K. (2012). Racial microaggressions and the Filipino American experience: Recommendations for counseling and development. *Journal of Multicultural Counseling and Development*, *40*(3), 156–173. https://doi.org/10.1002/j.2161-1912.2012.00015.x

Neville, H.A., Awad, G.H., Brooks, J.E., Flores, M.P., & Bluemel, J. (2013). Color-blind racial ideology: Theory, training, and measurement implications in psychology. *The American Psychologist*, *68*, 455–466. https://doi.org/10.1037/a0033282

Neville, H.A., Coleman, M.N., Falconer, J.W., & Holmes, D. (2005). Color-blind racial ideology and psychological false consciousness among African Americans. *Journal of Black Psychology*, *31*(1), 27–45. https://doi-org.proxy1.library.jhu.edu/10.1177/0095798404268287

Neville, H., Spanierman, L., & Doan, B. (2006). Exploring the association between color-blind racial ideology and multicultural counseling competence. *Cultural Diversity and Ethnic Minority Psychology*, *12*, 275–290. https://doi.org/10.1037/1099-9809.12.2.275

Newton, C., & Steele, J.M. (2025). The broaching readiness framework: A path for psychologists to embrace cultural opportunities. *Counselling Psychology Quarterly*, *38*, 1135–1152. https://doi-org.proxy1.library.jhu.edu/10.1080/09515070.2025.2458034

Owen, J., Tao, K.W., Drinane, J.M., Hook, J., Davis, D.E., & Kune, N.F. (2016). Client perceptions of therapists' multicultural orientation: Cultural (missed) opportunities and cultural humility. *Professional Psychology: Research and Practice*, *47*(1), 30–37. https://doi-org.proxy1.library.jhu.edu/10.1037/pro0000046

Owen, J., Tao, K.W., Imel, Z.E., Wampold, B.E., & Emil, R. (2014). Addressing racial and ethnic microaggressions in therapy. *Professional Psychology: Research and Practice*, *45*, 283–290. https://doi.org/10.1037/a0037420

Owen, J.J., Tao, K., Leach, M.M., & Rodolfa, E. (2011). Clients' perceptions of their psychotherapists' multicultural orientation. *Psychotherapy (Chicago, Ill.)*, *48*(3), 274–282. https://doi.org/10.1037/a0022065

Ratts, M.J., Singh, A.A., Nassar-McMillan, S., Butler, S.K., & McCullough, J.R. (2016). Multicultural and social justice counseling competencies: Guidelines for the counseling profession. *Journal of Multicultural Counseling and Development*, *44*, 28–48. https://doi.org/10.1002/jmcd.12035

Rudecindo, B., Imel, Z.E., Kuo, P.B., Smith, W.A., & Tao, K.W. (2024). Impact of racial microaggressions in psychotherapy vignettes with African American clients: An experimental analogue design. *Journal of Counseling Psychology*, *71*, 203–214. https://doi.org/10.1037/cou0000742

Schofield, W. (1986). *Psychotherapy: The purchase of friendship*. Routledge.
Segrest, M. (2020). *Administrations of lunacy: Racism and the haunting of American psychiatry at the Milledgeville asylum*. The New Press.
Shuman, E., Halperin, H., & Knowles, E. (2025). Advantaged identity management strategies differentiate five subgroups of white Americans. *Community Psychology, 3*, 58.
Shuman, E., van Zomeren, M., Saguy, T., Knowles, E., & Halperin, E. (2024). Defend, deny, distance, and dismantle: A new measure of advantaged identity management. *Personality & Social Psychology Bulletin*. https://doi.org/10.1177/01461672231216769
Spanierman, L.B., Poteat, V.P., Wang, Y.-F., & Oh, E. (2008). Psychosocial costs of racism to white counselors: Predicting various dimensions of multicultural counseling competence. *Journal of Counseling Psychology, 55*(1), 75–88. https://doi.org/10.1037/0022-0167.55.1.75
Sue, D.W., Arredondo, A., & McDavis, R.J. (1992). Multicultural counseling competencies and standards: A call to the profession. *Journal of Counseling and Development, 70*, 477–486.
Sue, D.W., & Spanierman, L. (2020). *Microaggressions in everyday life* (2nd ed.). Wiley.
Sue, D.W., Sue, D., Neville, H.A., & Smith, L. (2022). *Counseling the culturally diverse: Theory and practice* (9th ed.). Wiley.
Summers, M. (2019). *Madness in the city of magnificent intentions: A history of race and mental illness in the nation's capital*. Oxford University.
Utsey, S.O., Gernat, C.A., & Hammar, L. (2005). Examining White counselor trainees' reactions to racial issues in counseling and supervision dyads. *The Counseling Psychologist, 33*, 449–478. https://doi.org/10.1177/0011000004269058
Walker, R. (2024). *No racial elephants in the room: An unapologetic approach to providing culturally affirming mental health care to Black and African American clients*. PESI.
Yeo, E., & Torres-Harding, S.R. (2021). Rupture resolution strategies and the impact of rupture on the working alliance after racial microaggressions in therapy. *Psychotherapy, 58*, 460–471. https://doi.org/10.1037/pst0000372
Yi, J., Neville, H.A., Todd, N.R., & Mekawi, Y. (2023). Ignoring race and denying racism: A meta-analysis of the associations between colorblind racial ideology, anti-Blackness, and other variables antithetical to racial justice. *Journal of Counseling Psychology, 70*(3), 258–275. https://doi.org/10.1037/cou0000618
Zwick-Maitreyi, M., Soundararajan, T., Dar, N., Bheel, R.F., and Balakrishnan, P. (2018). *Caste in the United States. A survey of caste among South Asian Americans*. Equality Labs.

Chapter 3

Continuum of Broaching Behavior

Before reading this chapter, complete the Broaching Attitudes and Behavior Survey (BABS; Day-Vines et al., 2013). This survey is a brief instrument that provides you with some basic information about your openness to broaching or exploring clients' REC concerns. The survey is located at the end of this chapter. Please answer the questions as honestly and accurately as possible because there are no right or wrong answers. Once you finish the survey, calculate your score. You will receive a score for each subscale of the BABS. The subscale with the highest score represents your predominant mode of functioning. Regardless of which category your score falls along the broaching continuum, you will have opportunities for continued professional growth and development. Read the remainder of this chapter so that you can interpret your results as we discuss the broaching framework.

To reiterate, broaching refers to the provider's efforts to (a) initiate or respond to the client's REC concerns; (b) translate the client's sociocultural and sociopolitical realities into meaningful counseling practice; and (c) promote client empowerment, coping, problem-solving, resilience, and more effective functioning (Day-Vines et al., 2018). In this chapter, we will delve into the *Continuum of Broaching Behavior* which describes possible styles or orientations that providers can adopt as they help clients address their REC concerns (Day-Vines, 2007). The *Continuum of Broaching Behavior* contains five specific categories, and they proceed from less to more complex, adequate, and differentiated broaching styles: (a) *Avoidant*, (b) *Isolating*, (c) *Continuing/Incongruent*, (d) *Integrated/Congruent*, and (e) *Infusing*.

Avoidant Providers

Avoidant providers sidestep their clients' REC concerns, preferring instead to address clients' etic or universal concerns – those generic aspects of the client's experience that are relevant to all individuals irrespective of their cultural values and viewpoints. As a consequence, avoidant providers dismiss clients' emic or culture-specific concerns (Day-Vines et al., 2018). As REC concerns emerge,

DOI: 10.4324/9781003649311-3

avoidant providers are likely to redirect clients' attention to more generic topics. To illustrate, Bob is a gay, White male provider working with Hernando, a gay Latino client. Although Bob addresses Hernando's concerns about his sexuality with relative ease given his own experience as a gay male, he adopts an etic stance and neglects to consider Hernando's specific and unique concerns about how race and ethnicity shape Hernando's experience as a gay Latino man. Bob has not explored the extent to which Hernando has been impacted by pernicious stereotypes regarding the hyper-sexualization of Latino men, their marginalization within mainstream gay spaces, strong cultural and religious values that discourage same-sex attraction, the personal conundrum Hernando experiences as he works to reconcile his religious and personal convictions, cultural mores pertaining to the gay community, trauma that may result from denying an aspect of his gay identity, etc. Bob's inability to discuss the depth of Hernando's REC concerns inhibits Hernando from talking more freely and openly, exhibiting personal vulnerability, processing his innermost feelings, and initiating the healing process. Avoidant providers' inattention to clients' REC concerns impedes emotional expressiveness for clients who could likely benefit from opportunities to unpack the embeddedness of their REC realities within the safety of the counseling dyad. The following exchange illustrates the provider's avoidant broaching behavior with Hernando.

Provider: If our efforts together are successful, tell me what you would like to focus on specifically.

Client: Well, as a gay Latino man, I was hoping to talk about some of the challenges I'm having. I've known for a while that I'm gay, but I have struggled to come out to my family. I'm worried that they may not accept me completely. I listen to some of the comments and innuendos they make, and I'm concerned that my family will not be very supportive. My family is very important to me. In order to preserve peace in my family, I pretend to be someone I'm not and this is becoming way too exhausting for me. It's no longer sustainable. I'm tired of pretending that I plan to marry when I find the right woman or that my buddy is not my significant other. In my Latino family it's really unacceptable to be a gay man.

Provider: It sounds like you have concealed your gay identity because you're concerned about your family's reaction.

Client: Yes, I do believe that my family would have a hard time accepting me as a gay man. You know, for a lot of Latino families being gay is completely unacceptable. I couldn't bear to lose my family's love and support.

Provider: Yes, many families, not just Latino families, reject their gay family members.

Client: I agree, but in a lot of Latino families there is a certain stigma around gayness. My mother is very religious, and she would be mortified

> if she knew or even suspected that I was gay. My being gay might cause her tremendous stress, especially among her friends and church members.

Initially, the provider seemed curious about how he could support Hernando. As Hernando explained that he was tired of pretending not to be gay and described the corresponding psychological distress, the provider acknowledged Hernando's fear and trepidation about coming out to his family. As a result of feeling heard and understood, Hernando continued by emphasizing that the coming-out experience was especially challenging within Latino families. In response, the provider minimized Hernando's comments about the symbolic significance of being gay in the Latino community. Specifically, the provider noted that the coming-out process is challenging for all families, irrespective of their racial or ethnic background. This defensive response suggests that the Latino community is not the only community that problematizes sexual minorities. The provider adopted an etic response that minimized the client's culture-specific statement about the Latino community, insisting that families adopt a universal stance on same-sex relationships. Whether conscious or not, the provider invalidated Hernando's experience and revealed his own lack of REC self-awareness. In actuality, Hernando was not trying to deny or negate the reality of other racial and ethnic communities. He was merely emphasizing the significance of family and community attitudes about sexual minorities within his Latino community. He also communicated that Latino mores guide and direct his own personal and family functioning. Unfortunately, Hernando's sociocultural and sociopolitical realities were lost on the provider.

In that moment, Hernando shifted from talking openly about his personal experience of being Latino, gay, and male in a community where heterosexism prevailed, to having to defend Latino cultural values and norms. The provider's assertion that all communities may struggle with accepting a family member's sexual minority status revealed the provider's colorblind racial ideology and took the focus off Hernando's personal needs and experiences. In response, Hernando felt pressured to take a more defensive stance, insofar as having to educate the provider. The provider's dogmatism concerning the universality of attitudes toward sexual minorities contributed to a missed opportunity to use cultural humility to better understand Hernando's subjective frame of reference. Essentially, the provider took on an etic perspective, implying that the gay experience was universal or the same across cultures. By minimizing Hernando's culture-specific concerns, Hernando's avoidant provider perpetuated the notion that discussing REC is inappropriate and had the potential to alienate Hernando.

Because counseling functions as a microcosm of society, the counseling dyad often mirrors the outside world, such that providers reinscribe societal dynamics within the counseling dyad in ways that limit the client from feeling fully heard and understood. As such, Hernando's provider may have inadvertently evoked feelings of resentment that left Hernando with two monumental tasks – to protect himself outside the counseling session from the barrage of hostility, rejection, innuendo, and homophobic assault that runs rampant in the world and to simultaneously protect himself from similar dynamics that emerged within the counseling dyad. The consequence may result in Hernando's re-traumatization and disengagement from the therapeutic process.

As we discussed in Chapter 2, by dismissing Hernando's cultural concerns, the provider was committing a microaggression. Specifically, the research of Owen et al. (2014) demonstrated that not discussing clients' REC concerns serves as a microaggression. Further, the provider's inattention to Hernando's REC experience could ultimately erode any rapport that was built, resulting in Hernando experiencing frustration because he did not feel heard or understood. At the extreme, the provider's response could contribute to what Drinane et al. (2018) defined as cultural concealment or Hernando's effort to withhold information about his REC concerns. In the event that Hernando's provider does not recognize the verbal exchange as a possible rupture or breakdown in therapeutic communication, the consequence may contribute to a strained relationship or, at the extreme, premature termination (Brawner et al., 2025).

As we will see later in this chapter, the provider could easily have explored the intersection between Hernando's Latino, gay, and male identity; Hernando's relationship with his family; the connection between possible family rejection and Hernando's mental health functioning; the possibility that contrary to his belief Hernando's family may embrace him fully; internalized feelings around shame and guilt for clinging to a personal secret; Hernando's efforts to reconcile his belief systems with his sexual identity; relief that may result from relinquishing a secret; anticipation about how the community might react toward Hernando and his family once Hernando discloses his sexual orientation, etc.

In 1903, noted sociologist W.E.B. DuBois (1969) said that the problem of the 20th century would be the problem of the color line. He was referring to racial strife that people of color experienced at the dawn of the 20th century. The statement was prophetic, because we are now in the third decade of the 21st century and we have even more complexities around race, representation, and difference that have never been openly discussed or resolved. Because counseling is a microcosm of society, the counseling dyad often mirrors the outside world, such that providers reinscribe societal dynamics within the counseling dyad in ways that limit the client from feeling fully heard and understood (e.g., microaggressions).

Avoidant broaching is a woefully inadequate means of forestalling necessary REC conversations that warrant further exploration and that have the potential to help clients resolve some of their more deep-seated REC concerns. As providers, we are purveyors of clients' truths, and we must honor these truths in order to facilitate client growth, healing, and recovery, even if venturing into our clients' subjective REC realities creates cognitive dissonance for ourselves.

Burning Question

Norma, are there ever instances in which it may be more prudent not to engage in broaching behavior?

When clients have more immediate concerns such as a mental health crisis like suicidality or exhibiting signs of psychosis, it is important to attend to those concerns first prior to returning to the client's REC concerns. As we will discuss in subsequent chapters, the provider's broaching behavior is not a spontaneous act. It is a deliberate and intentional interaction requiring the provider's thoughtful consideration of the client's subjective realities prior to launching into a broaching event. In Chapters 8 and 9, we will review a conceptual framework for determining both what and how to broach the client's REC concerns. Without forethought about what, when, and how to broach effectively, the provider has the potential to harm the client by saying something inconsiderate or offensive, or by not responding at all. Such problematic statements can lead to ruptures within the therapeutic dyad, limiting the possibility for emotional connection between the provider and client that may ultimately forestall client growth, self-understanding, catharsis, healing, and the therapeutic alliance. In instances where the provider may have concerns about saying something inappropriate that derails the session, it is advisable to table the discussion and seek consultation, supervision, or, where appropriate, personal counseling.

If your highest score on the BABS (Day-Vines et al., 2013) was on the avoidant subscale, it is likely that you deemphasize clients' REC concerns and choose instead to address their etic experiences. As we discussed in Chapter 2, you may want to engage in critical self-awareness in order to explore what factors contribute to your reluctance to broach the client's REC concerns. The following section examines some reasons that may contribute to your reluctance to broach with clients who choose not to discuss how issues related to REC shape their experience.

Rationale for Providers' Inattention to Clients' REC Concerns

There are numerous reasons that providers may disregard clients' broaching concerns. For instance, some providers may lack the training and skill set to navigate REC discussions, worrying that once broaching conversations get underway, they may become unmanageable (Hemmings & Evans, 2018). For these providers, broaching clients' REC concerns may feel risky. In training sessions, my colleagues and I routinely ask participants whether they have had any formal training in broaching or in strategies for exploring clients' REC concerns. Ordinarily, participants report that both their training and feelings about their preparedness to discuss clients' REC concerns are limited. This finding is not in and of itself shocking. In fact, studies examining clients' perceptions of their providers' ability to explore the contextual dimensions of REC demonstrate that many clients perceive that their providers are poorly equipped to broach their REC concerns (Depauw & Ven Hiel, 2024). In their exploratory study, Hemmings and Evans (2018) found that 70.8% of providers reported working with clients who had encountered racialized stress, yet only 18.9% of respondents indicated they had received training in race-based trauma.

Some *avoidant* providers who lack the requisite skills to explore clients' REC concerns may opt instead to use an etic approach and focus on their clients' more generic concerns, much like Hernando's provider. Some providers may be reluctant to broach because they worry about offending the client. Other providers may view REC discussions as tangential to clients' presenting concerns and an effort on the part of clients to avoid taking responsibility for their behavior (Day-Vines et al., 2013). Still other providers may ignore or downplay clients' REC concerns because venturing into a broaching discussion may reveal the provider's hidden biases. In such cases, providers worry about being exposed as racially and culturally insensitive. Rather than risk exposure, *avoidant* providers may choose to ignore their clients' REC concerns because it seems safer. In actuality, their avoidant tactics may serve as a shield for concealing hidden biases. Unresolved biases may make it difficult for providers to offer genuine emotional support to clients. Be that as it may, providers' inability to engage clients in an exploration of their sociocultural, sociohistorical, and sociopolitical realities may limit clients' willingness to share their innermost REC thoughts and feelings. Denied the opportunity to be emotionally vulnerable within the counseling dyad, some clients exhibit cultural concealment by withholding important cultural content regarding the details of their lives (Drinane et al., 2018). Avoidant broaching effectively silences clients who see REC concerns as relevant to their presenting problems.

Relatedly, some providers may lack genuine concern about clients who encounter racial strife and other forms of marginalization (D'Andrea & Daniels, 2001). In some cases, providers may mistakenly believe that not broaching may represent a more appropriate response because most problem situations have little to do with REC influences. Sometimes, providers' personal struggles may be so raw and sensitive that it precludes them from exploring clients' REC concerns. Rather than leaning into clients' REC discussions, providers may distance themselves emotionally or blame the client for their problem situations in ways that suggest the provider is exhibiting varying forms of countertransference.

In some instances, providers may lack the historical and contextual knowledge base that sensitizes and allows them to comprehend the extent to which minoritized clients may be deeply impacted by their real-world encounters with oppression. More specifically, they may struggle to consider the symbiotic relationship between the historical factors associated with oppression and the eerily related contemporary dynamics that fuse the past and the present together (Mullan, 2023). For many clients, generational traumas of the past resulting from racism and varying oppressive forces may intrude upon their contemporary lives, both knowingly and unknowingly (Degruy, 2017; Menakem, 2017; Mullan, 2023). Clients' exposure to avoidant providers contributes to ruptures that may give way to premature termination (Brawner et al., 2025). Regrettably, some providers may adopt a colorblind racial orientation wherein they deny the salience of REC and its impact on the client's presenting concerns.

Inadequate clinical supervision has been attributed to the difficulties some providers experience in supporting their clients in REC discussions (Aydoğan et al., 2022). Yet a compelling body of research has identified benefits that accrue when supervisors broach REC concerns with their supervisees, such as the ability to discuss clients' concerns with more facility, development of a stronger working alliance, and a broader repertoire of skills (Jones & Welfare, 2019; White-Davis et al., 2016).

In other instances, providers may have experienced their own traumas that make it difficult for them to both empathize with and treat clients from marginalized backgrounds. To illustrate, as a newly minted professor nearly 30 years ago, I was teaching a social and cultural diversity class. I had a middle-aged White female student in class who struggled considerably with course content. She was often edgy, irritable, and unable to engage in perspective taking toward any of the client populations we studied. I was disturbed and dismayed by her behavior, so much so, that I invited her to my office to better understand the nature of her hostility. It turned out that her own personal trauma interfered with her ability to connect with course material. She was a housewife in her mid- to late 40s, and her husband announced that he wanted a divorce. He was liaising with a younger, prettier, more vibrant version of my student, which meant that she would soon become a single parent and need to return to the workforce after several years as a housewife. In preparation for the impending divorce, my student returned to school with students who were half her age. Compared to her peers, she often felt intimidated and underprepared. Drawing on social identity theory and advantaged identity management theory described in Chapter 2, I suspected she also had biases that made it difficult for her to empathize with people from marginalized groups, given that she defended against issues of racism, discrimination, and inequality. As she shared the unfortunate details regarding the dissolution of her marriage, I understood immediately that she was relatively incapable of attending to the pain and oppression of others given both her personal trauma and internalized biases. Her self-disclosure and my support and understanding helped her get through the remainder of the semester.

It might be tempting to assume that only White providers struggle with avoidant counseling behaviors, especially since some studies have documented that many White providers exhibit higher avoidant scores on broaching measures compared to their ethnic minority counterparts (Day-Vines et al., 2013, 2020). Be that as it may, providers of color may also struggle to explore clients' REC concerns. In fact, my colleagues and I conducted research demonstrating that school counselors of color maintained higher avoidant scores on a broaching measure compared to their White school counseling counterparts (Day-Vines et al., 2021). A secondary finding in this study indicated that racial identity served as a predictor of school counselors' openness to broaching. In a separate study, my colleagues and I found that Black and African American clients perceived that their same race providers were significantly more likely than non-Black and non-African American providers to exhibit more avoidant broaching behaviors and missed opportunities to discuss clients' REC concerns (Day-Vines et al., 2026). We surmised that providers' presumption of familiarity with clients who share racial and ethnic group membership may have rendered broaching discussions less necessary. It may also stand that clients may construe shared group membership between themselves and their providers as inattention to their REC concerns. As we discussed in Chapter 2, higher levels of racial self-awareness are associated with greater flexibility and willingness to broach clients' REC concerns (Day-Vines et al., 2020). Simply put, difficulty addressing issues concerning REC is not relegated to just White providers.

Years ago, I worked with a middle-aged African American female student from the deep south who was matriculating in my social and cultural diversity class. She seemed incredulous about a lot of the concepts that we reviewed in class, such as racialized stereotypes, racism, and discrimination. I was quite baffled because of her age and my assumption that her upbringing in the rural, segregated south might have sensitized her to certain racial realities. Like my White student described above, she too struggled to understand concepts in class that many of the younger White students understood with relative ease. My African American doctoral teaching assistant was quite annoyed with this student and encouraged me to "get her." I advised against that recommendation, noting that as counselor educators we were to lead with empathy, curiosity, and compassion. Because I too was stymied by the student's comments in class, I invited the student to my office to better understand how she made sense of course content. I inquired about personal factors that made it difficult for her to comprehend some of the concepts under review. This student informed me that she grew up in an abusive household, in a racially segregated southern community, with several siblings. She confided that her mother was unable to withstand her father's unrelenting physical and emotional abuse and ultimately abandoned the family, leaving the children to be cared for by their toxic father. The African American community held her family in contempt and ridiculed them, whereas the White community served as a source of support to her family and helped her complete high school and get her life on track. In that moment, I understood instantly that this student's difficulty connecting with the literature we were studying was the result of the trauma that she had experienced by members of her own community, whom she had fully expected to be a source of social support and not a source of derision. The student's effort to distance herself from the African American community, in particular, was an adaptive strategy that she continued to rely on even in adulthood. When providers are triggered by circumstances beyond their control, it makes sense to not only seek supervision but also to consider therapy in order that personal concerns do not undermine the counseling relationship, inflict harm, and derail the client's progress.

Burning Question

Norma, I think I struggle with broaching clients' REC concerns for some of the same reasons that your former students struggle. What should I do?

If you struggle with broaching, you should consider reading the remainder of this book, engaging in professional development training, examining literature that gives you greater understanding about people from a variety of cultural backgrounds, traveling, enrolling in workshops, seeking supervision and opportunities to connect with people and communities that are different from your own. You should also consider the extent to which the biases you harbor have the potential to perpetuate harm to clients. As stated previously, clients are far more cognizant of the biases we have, even those we don't admit. We often enact those biases through nonverbal leakage and microaggressions (Foley & Gentile, 2010; Hill, 2020). You should consider the complex interplay between your own worldview and the client's worldview, by considering the extent to which your similarities and differences with the client impact the counseling process. Further, consider how power shapes the counseling relationship, and identify a set of strategies for working through your cognitive dissonance. You are not a bad person because you struggle to broach; however, you should engage in the process of critical self-awareness as a prerequisite for enhancing your own ability to broach clients' REC concerns. Newton and Steele (2025) developed the broaching readiness framework to help providers examine and enhance their own intrapersonal processes that may interfere with the delivery of culturally responsive counseling services.

Isolating Providers

In our original framing of the broaching construct, my research team and I operationalized the *Continuum of Broaching Behavior* (Day-Vines et al., 2013). We developed five specific broaching categories but only found empirical support for four categories or subscales (e.g., *avoidant*, *continuing/incongruent*, *integrated/congruent*, *infusing*). Surprisingly, we did not find support for the *isolating* category of broaching behavior. As such, we maintained that there was considerable overlap between *avoidant* and *isolating* providers. We asserted that the two broaching categories were likely indistinguishable from one another. At conferences, however, counselor educators challenged our contention that *avoidant* and *isolating* categories overlapped. Conference attendees insisted that there are important distinctions between *avoidant* and *isolating* providers, exactly as we articulated within the original *Continuum of Broaching Behavior* model. Their encouragement has led our research team to revisit these distinctions conceptually and empirically.

Whereas *avoidant* providers do not broach at all, for many of the reasons described above, *isolating* providers only broach once or minimally and then move on to other more neutral topics. Frequently, they are inclined to restate the client's concerns and then quickly shift the focus of the session to more generic counseling topics. Their broaching efforts are superficial and often appear happenstance having little connection to the client's actual REC concerns. They miss opportunities to explore how sociocultural, sociopolitical, and sociohistorical factors impact clients' lived realities.

Much like my counselor education colleagues who report that their students broach at surface levels, I too have observed several of my own students who engage in what they deem a broaching event that in no way attends to their clients' REC concerns. Students may initially acknowledge their clients' REC concerns yet not explore those REC concerns in a substantive manner. Their broaching efforts are pro forma and emotionally detached, meaning providers broach out of a sense of obligation, and not as a deliberate and intentional counseling skill that has a particular purpose beyond checking off an obligatory requirement to broach. They parrot what they understand their clients to have said without being able to explore their clients' concerns at a deeper emotional level. Their broaching efforts are not integral to the client's REC concerns. The following dialogue epitomizes *isolating* broachers and continues with the case of Hernando.

Provider: If our efforts together are successful, tell me what you would like to focus on specifically.

Client: Well, as a gay Latino male, I was hoping to talk about some of the challenges I'm having. I've known for a while that I'm gay, but I have struggled to come out to my family. I'm worried that they may not accept me completely. I listen to some of the comments and innuendos they make, and I'm concerned that my family would not accept me. My family is very important to me. In order to preserve peace in the family, I pretend to be someone I'm not and this is becoming way too exhausting for me. I'm tired of pretending that I plan to marry when I find the right woman or that my buddy is not my significant other. In my Latino family it's really unacceptable to be a gay man.

Provider: You're stressed because you're not sure how your family will react once you come out to them. Well, before we go further into this session, I want to get something out the way. I want to make sure that you're okay working with me given the differences in our racial background. Although we're both gay we have different cultural backgrounds. Are you okay working with a therapist who is different from you?

Client: Your culture isn't a problem for me.

The above scenario unfolds exactly the way the *avoidant* scenario unfolded. Hernando explained his sense of fear and trepidation about disclosing his sexual identity to his family. Initially, the provider validated Hernando's feelings using an appropriate reflective statement. The provider's effort to acknowledge Hernando's concerns helped Hernando feel heard and understood; however, the provider shifted his focus abruptly and asked Hernando how he felt about working together given their different cultural backgrounds. This question seems premature, as well as poorly timed and sequenced. Ordinarily, the provider's broaching efforts should be deliberate, intentional, and purposeful. It's not clear why the provider asked this question in this particular moment and how the question is connected to the client's presenting concerns. It seems that Hernando's discussion of his culture prompted the provider to inquire about their shared and different identity dimensions; however, the abruptness of the question interrupted Hernando's train of thought.

Usually, providers ask specific and pointed questions because they want to elicit certain information from the client; however, it's not clear why the provider needs this information in this moment. The session is just unfolding, and the client may not have any inclination about how he feels about their work together. Unless the client gave some verbal or nonverbal indication that he objected to the therapist, it may be best to table this question until the client has an actual opportunity to observe the provider, get a sense of their relationship, and share in-depth, honest feedback about the nature of the counseling relationship. Asking such a question prematurely may signal to the client that the provider has some objection or bias about working with the client. It is helpful to note that at certain junctures during treatment, providers will have opportunities to discuss how the shared and different identity dimensions between themselves and their clients impact the counseling relationship (Day-Vines et al., 2020). This question might have been appropriate had Hernando given some verbal or nonverbal indication that he was put off by the provider or after several sessions to assess how shared and different identity dimensions impacted the counseling process.

Rather than process the relationship during the opening of the session, it would have been more appropriate for the provider to allow Hernando to explore his stated concerns in more detail. For instance, Hernando talked about his apprehension about coming out and his awareness that family members have signaled an objection to same-sex attraction. He also discussed how important his family is to him, described his intersectional identity as a gay Latino male, expressed his efforts to conceal his sexual identity, his deep desire to be accepted by his family, in spite of their objection to same-sex relationships, and the emotional exhaustion he feels pretending he's straight. Despite the opportunity to delve more fully into each of these concerns at a deeper emotional level, the provider completely glossed over Hernando's REC concerns and reduced his broaching efforts to a discussion of the differences between the provider and client. The provider operated as if he needed to check broaching off his to-do list so he could move on to more substantive counseling content, most likely the client's etic concerns. *Isolating* providers do not integrate and synthesize broaching discussions into their counseling efforts. Their broaching efforts are ancillary to the client's REC concerns; as such, they rush past the client's concerns, and as a consequence, inhibit meaningful and substantive client self-exploration. Instead of expounding upon his presenting concerns, the provider forced the client to shift gears and address the provider–client relationship prematurely. Essentially, the provider made the broaching moment about himself.

As the reader will recall, the provider wields the balance of power in the counseling relationship. By asking a question about the client's openness to working with a provider from a different background, the provider invokes a power dynamic that requires the client to respond to the provider before addressing his own personal concerns. The provider's misplaced question about how Hernando feels about working with someone from a different cultural background derails the session because the question is disconnected from the client's more salient concerns regarding his ambivalence about coming out. The provider should build a warm, trusting therapeutic relationship with the client before inquiring about provider–client differences. As we will discuss later in this book, the provider's broaching question was poorly timed, although it may be relevant at a later juncture within the counseling process.

Because we did not find empirical support for the *isolating* subscale on the BABS, we did not include isolating questions here.

Continuing/Incongruent Broaching Behaviors

Relative to their *avoidant* and *isolating* counterparts who address clients' REC concerns minimally or not at all, *continuing/incongruent* providers exhibit greater openness about exploring the contextual dimensions of REC with their clients (Day-Vines et al., 2013). They are not put off by the prospect of exploring clients' REC concerns. In fact, they are quite open to having these conversations; however, their desire to broach clients' REC concerns is not matched by their skill set. *Continuing/Incongruent* providers lack the verbal dexterity to broach or translate their clients' REC concerns into meaningful dialogue that both help clients feel supported and resolve their presenting concerns. That is, *continuing/incongruent* providers recognize the value of broaching, but they do not fully understand that broaching involves a deliberate and intentional set of skills designed to help the client explore their REC concerns. *Continuing/Incongruent* providers' broaching skills may come off as awkward, mechanical, superficial, unartful, and/or stereotypical. Clients may feel judged and misunderstood when providers do not implement culturally responsive counseling interventions effectively (Sadusky et al., 2024).

As we will address throughout this text, providers cannot merely delve into broaching discussions without considering the purpose of a broaching event, identifying what specific REC concerns warrant discussion, determining how broaching benefits the client, timing a broaching statement, generating appropriate broaching statements, etc. As the reader will recall from Chapter 1, there are three components of the broaching framework. The *Continuum of Broaching Behavior*, which identifies providers' openness toward engaging in broaching discussions; the Multidimensional Model of Broaching Behavior, which identifies specific broaching contexts; and a curated set of strategies and considerations that providers enlist as they prepare to broach clients' REC concerns. Although they do not exhibit reluctance to broach, *continuing/incongruent* providers have trouble exhibiting nuanced broaching behavior. They may lack in-depth knowledge about clients' REC background, such as historical context, information about clients' encounters with racism and discrimination, or clients' cultural values, as well as strategies for exploring how clients have been affected by their REC experiences. *Continuing/Incongruent* providers may regard clients as monolithic entities and draw on stereotypes about specific groups that can undermine the counseling process and lead to microaggressions. As the next provider–client dialogue demonstrates, *continuing/incongruent* providers have difficulty translating their broaching intentions into meaningful and impactful conversations that advance the therapeutic process. The *continuing/incongruent* provider broaches as follows:

Provider: If our efforts together are successful, tell me what you would like to focus on specifically.

Client: Well, as a gay Latino, I was hoping to talk about some of the challenges I'm having. I've known for a while that I'm gay, but I have struggled to come out to my family. I'm worried that they may not accept me completely. I listen to some of the comments and innuendos they make, and I'm concerned that my family would not accept me. My family is very important to me. In order to preserve peace in the family, I pretend to be someone I'm not and this is becoming way too exhausting for me. I'm tired of pretending that I plan to marry when I find the right woman or that my buddy is not my significant other. In my Latino family it's really unacceptable to be a gay man.

Provider: Determining whether or not to come out to your family is frightening.

Client: Yes, it's very frightening. Every day I go back and forth about what I should do.

Provider: Fernando, I can imagine that as a Mexican immigrant this is doubly difficult because of the objection that many of your people have to gay lifestyles.

Client: I'm not sure what you mean. My family is actually from Central America. My mother is Guatemalan, and my father is Costa Rican. They met once they arrived in the States. We're not Mexican. Also, I was born in the United States. I'm American just like you.

Provider: I'm sorry, that was an oversight on my part.

Client: No problem. That happens all the time. People often assume I am Mexican.

Provider: Okay. Let's shift gears and talk about the safest family members for you to come out to.

In this scenario, Hernando never mentioned his migration status or his specific ethnicity, yet the provider referred to Hernando as both Mexican and an immigrant. Essentially, the provider made problematic assumptions about Hernando that perpetuate stereotypes about members of the Latino community and call into question the provider's ability to respect his client's humanity. Referring to Hernando as Mexican is a form of ethnic misclassification that disregards Hernando's ancestry, drudges up antagonisms that characterize Latinos as immigrants irrespective of their national origin, exposes the provider's ignorance, reveals hidden biases, and diminishes Hernando's sense of personhood. In the current political climate where migrants are under unrelenting siege, the provider's comments are naïve and dangerous and may even contribute to the erosion of trust within the therapeutic relationship. These missteps speak to the importance of providers developing foundational knowledge about clients and their respective cultures. Moreover, they reinforce points made in Chapter 2 about the importance of critical reflexivity on the part of the provider.

Clients are not monolithic entities. Although some clients may prefer the designation Latino, others may prefer the term Hispanic, while still others emphasize their ancestral origins as a means of self-identifying. As we discussed in Chapter 2, the client's racial or ethnic designation may be less salient than other identities, such as career, hobbies, and parenting status. The provider's effort to use designations that clients choose (e.g., in Hernando's case, it would be Latino) reflects culturally responsive behavior that communicates respect and an effort to honor the client's values. To add insult to injury, the provider also called Hernando by the wrong name (e.g., Fernando). Although forgetting the client's name may seem inconsequential, for some clients it signals that the provider doesn't value the client's sense of personhood.

The provider referred to the Latino community as a monolith, assuming that the entire Latino community opposed same-sex attraction. This presumption is shortsighted and disregards cultural nuances; moreover, it increases the prospects that clients may not feel psychologically safe within the counseling dyad. Although Hernando's provider apologized and possibly regards his counseling efforts as innocuous, insinuating that Hernando is an immigrant when he is not can be easily construed as microaggressive behavior. Owen et al. (2014) assessed the experiences of ethnic minority students in a college counseling center. More than 50% of respondents in their sample reported that their provider engaged in some type of microaggression during treatment. Seventy-six percent of the respondents who experienced microaggressions reported that their provider never discussed the microaggression in an effort to resolve the impasse. Regrettably, not discussing the microaggression had a decidedly negative impact on the therapeutic alliance. Several studies indicate that when providers make an effort to resolve cultural ruptures, clients have more favorable counseling outcomes (Eubanks et al., 2018; Yeo & Torres-Harding, 2021).

Although in this scenario the provider did apologize, his matter-of-fact response was poorly managed, as he did not take accountability for his behavior. He merely said he was sorry without exploring how the client was impacted by the comments, what feelings and prior encounters with microaggressions the provider's comments may have evoked, the extent to which the provider's comments may have reinforced potential feelings of marginalization, agreements about managing slights and indignities that may emerge in the future, and concerted efforts to rebuild trust. In the final chapter of this text, we will review strategies for recovering from ruptures (Chang et al., 2020). The inability or unwillingness to repair ruptures may reinforce feelings of marginalization in the client, damage trust, and contribute to premature termination.

Toward the end of the segment, the provider engaged in premature problem-solving. Although at this point in the relationship Hernando has revealed his ambivalence about coming out to his family, concern for how his family may be impacted, and the importance of his culture, the provider moved abruptly into a discussion about how the client may begin disclosing his sexual identity to his family members. Given the ambivalence the client has expressed, it's not clear that he is mentally or emotionally prepared at this time to engage in a coming-out discussion with his family. In the haste to help the client resolve his dilemma, the provider is rushing to explore solutions before having a more nuanced understanding of the client's experience and background. The provider could benefit from engaging in unhurried reflection in order to allow the client to process his concerns at a deeper emotional level.

Overview of First Three Broaching Categories

Whereas the first three categories along the *Continuum of Broaching Behavior* reflect less effective broaching styles in which the provider chooses not to broach or struggles to make facilitative responses, the final two categories along the continuum reflect more effective approaches to broaching clients' REC concerns (Day-Vines et al., 2018). Within the first three categories, providers' broaching efforts are poorly executed. For instance, an *avoidant* provider dodges the client's REC concerns and redirects the client's attention to more race/culture-neutral discussions, without attention to the manner in which the client's REC concerns are relevant to their presenting problems.

Isolating providers will at a minimum acknowledge the clients' REC concerns in order to get the broaching requirement out of the way, with little effort devoted to addressing the client's REC perspectives. As such, their broaching efforts are often misguided. Much like avoidant providers, isolating providers do not broach in a meaningful manner; they prefer to focus on more etic or generic topics. They engage minimally in their clients' REC concerns. If you scored highest on the *continuing/incongruent* category of the BABS, you likely experience some difficulty developing effective broaching statements, recognize the need for more training, and harbor concerns that your clients may experience you as ineffective.

Essentially, providers operating along the first three categories of the broaching continuum tend to stifle clients' cultural self-expression, which in turn hinders clients from talking openly and honestly about their culture-specific concerns. The lack of critical self-reflection, colorblind attitudes, and inattention to the structural elements that perpetuate and reinforce power dynamics both between the provider and client have the potential to undermine counseling progress.

The final two categories along the broaching continuum describe more advanced and effective broaching efforts that reflect highly stylized levels of cultural responsiveness. Essentially, *integrated/congruent* providers implement more individually oriented broaching interventions, and *infusing* providers engage in more systemic interventions that are oriented toward social change initiatives.

Integrated/Congruent Broaching Behaviors

Unlike providers operating at lower levels of the broaching continuum, *integrated/congruent* providers communicate to clients that REC discussions are permissible topics for discussion during treatment. Additionally, they exude relative ease, fluency, and comfort in both initiating and responding to clients' REC experiences (Day-Vines et al., 2018). As well, they encourage clients to make culture-specific interpretations of their concerns. Their deeper structural understanding about the way clients' REC factors impinge on their presenting concerns renders them more adept at broaching relative to their counterparts operating at lower levels of the broaching continuum.

Integrated/Congruent providers do not separate their clients' REC concerns from their presenting problems. In fact, they recognize that clients' REC experiences and presenting problems may be inextricably tethered to one another. Many clients, especially among those for whom REC is important, may appreciate the provider's effort to weave REC discussions into the counseling process (Lukowitsky et al., 2024). In fact, as stated in Chapter 2, omission of REC discussions from the counseling process contributes to client dissatisfaction with the counseling process, less favorable counseling outcomes, and reservations about returning for follow-up counseling sessions.

Integrated/Congruent providers listen empathically, validate and affirm clients' cultural concerns, identify their strengths, exhibit warmth and empathy, and create the psychological safety that permits clients to self-disclose, take risks, and demonstrate vulnerability without fear of reprisals or the withdrawal of emotional support. To build therapeutic trust, *integrated/congruent* providers honor the cultural meanings clients attach to their concerns. Instead of essentializing clients and reducing them to a single identity domain, integrated congruent providers recognize the full complement of clients' identity structures and the accompanying sources of oppression that may be associated with those identities. They create psychologically safe spaces for clients to discuss their REC concerns in order to reduce psychological distress and increase more effective problem-solving (Day-Vines et al., 2018).

To their credit, *integrated/congruent* providers move beyond surface-level reflections and help clients examine the source of their concerns by naming and labeling the intersectional domains, such as race, class, gender, and oppression, that contribute to clients' struggles. *Integrated/Congruent* providers address these concerns directly without tiptoeing around them, redirecting the client's attention to more generic or neutral topics, or minimizing clients' REC concerns. They believe clients' disclosures about the often-overwhelming impact of REC on their lives without second-guessing or blaming them, offering interpretations that divert the client's attention from salient REC concerns or engaging in premature problem-solving (Walker, 2024).

To their credit, *integrated/congruent* providers recognize the sociocultural, sociopolitical, and sociohistorical factors that clients confront. That is, they can make connections both between historical and contemporary encounters with varying forms of oppression and the resulting impact on everyday life and mental well-being. Additively, they can label feelings that are inextricably linked to clients' REC experiences in a very pointed and direct manner, thus integrating and synthesizing the technical, relational, and cultural dimensions of broaching (Williams, 2026). Taken together, these skills help providers facilitate productive conversations that contribute to deeper engagement with clients' REC concerns.

Technical broaching skills refer to the provider's ability to integrate foundational counseling skills with effective broaching behaviors, such as active listening, reflection of content, reflection of feeling, encouragers, open and closed questions, interpretations, metaphors, and silence (Williams, 2026). The melding of foundational skills with effective broaching behaviors helps clients feel heard and understood. Each of these verbal response modes has an intended purpose. For instance, reflection of content refers to the provider's restatement of the client's comments to check for accurate understanding of clients' REC concerns. The provider's effort to paraphrase clients' REC statements helps clients hear what they have said, how they sound, and what they mean (Hill, 2020).

The *integrated/congruent* provider's use of reflection of feelings to help clients identify specific emotions associated with their REC experience in ways that can lead to catharsis. This skill is especially important because studies show that clients largely perceive their providers as avoidant such that they dodge REC conversations for many of the reasons cited earlier in the text (Depauw, 2023). In their study, Williams (2026) examined the unfolding of broaching skill sets in a sample of counselor trainees matriculating in a multicultural counseling course and concluded that following a semester-long skill development process, students improved their ability to attend to clients' emic or culture-specific concerns in ways that helped them remain attuned with clients. Williams presented students with video-recorded vignettes. In turn, students generated broaching statements that were evaluated along the following behavioral markers such as (a) labeling clients' REC encounters directly, (b) addressing clients' encounters with varying forms of discrimination, (c) validating clients' experiences regarding REC, (d) conveying broaching statements clearly and concisely, and (e) broaching with confidence as opposed to hesitantly.

At the beginning of the semester, one trainee in the Williams (2026) study responded to a video vignette by generating the following broaching statement: "It sounds like you're upset about your brother's experience." This colorblind statement acknowledged the client's affective experience but ignored references to the client's racialized experience and stress. By the end of the semester, however, the same student generated a more pointed broaching statement that directly acknowledged the client's affective experience and the manner in which race shaped the client's personal struggles. The counselor trainee said the following: "It must be so painful to see your younger brother face exclusion because of his race, especially knowing you've been through similar experiences." The final statement captured both the emotional impact of the client's dilemma and its relatedness to racialized oppression. Effective broaching statements involving reflection of feelings incorporate both an acknowledgment of the client's emotional state as well as racialized components of the presenting concern. The provider's pragmatic integration and synthesis of foundational counseling skills with the deliberate and intentional discussions of REC create conditions that permit clients to talk freely and openly about the role of race in their lives.

Relational skills are associated with the provider's ability to establish a healthy therapeutic environment that exudes warmth, trust, and acceptance. Minimal encouragers are used to help the client continue talking and may involve a combination of verbal prompts such as "uh-huh" and "Say more…" that invite the client to talk in more detail about their concerns, as well as nonverbal encouragers that involve head nods, gestures, and facial expressions that imply the client should continue talking (Hill, 2020). In the context of broaching, providers use these skills to communicate that the client's REC concerns are permissible.

Much has been written about power imbalances within the counseling dyad and the detrimental impact they can have on the counseling relationship when not managed effectively (Chang et al., 2020). *Integrated/Congruent* providers recognize the importance of establishing more egalitarian connections with clients so as not to invoke power dynamics that reinscribe sociohistorical, sociocultural, and sociopolitical hierarchies within the counseling dyad. They recognize that imposing power dynamics may undermine a strong therapeutic alliance.

To their credit, *integrated/congruent* providers possess racial self-awareness such that they take inventory of their own attitudes and biases to ensure that they do not interfere with efforts to support their clients. *Integrated/Congruent* providers recognize their attitudes toward dominance, their social identity attitudes, levels of racial identity functioning, and the possible impact that their assumptions may have on their ability to work effectively with clients. Additionally, they can distinguish between normal and abnormal functioning without attributing client difficulties to pathology or presumed stereotypes.

Integrated/Congruent providers are less likely to make problematic comments that clients experience as offensive and interpret as microaggressive behavior. In the event the provider and client experience a cultural rupture or a therapeutic impasse, the provider is open to working toward recognizing and acknowledging ruptures, taking responsibility for their contribution to the rupture in a nondefensive manner, engaging in critical reflexivity, repairing the rupture in order to achieve reconciliation, and restoring therapeutic trust within the counseling dyad (Chang et al., 2020; Gaztambide, 2012).

Integrated/Congruent providers develop a working knowledge of clients' cultural backgrounds by listening attentively to clients. It is through the process of deep and authentic listening, engagement, and observation as clients disclose details of their REC dynamics and cultural value systems that providers learn about clients' core cultural worldviews. Providers also develop essential information about their clients by reading and remaining abreast of the conceptual and research literature, engaging various forms of media (e.g., movies, documentaries, podcasts, music, and listservs), participating in cultural events, connecting with community members, seeking out professional development activities, etc. Relatedly, a qualitative study of immigrant clients' perceptions of their providers' cultural responsiveness demonstrated that clients did not necessarily expect providers to have complete knowledge about their cultures but expected providers to exhibit empathy, demonstrate openness toward learning about their cultures, and discuss their cultural concerns in appropriate ways (Rogers-Sirin et al., 2015).

Providers who broach effectively practice multicultural orientation as a way of being. That is, they exhibit cultural humility, as evidenced by the fact that they have a sense of curiosity about clients' unique cultural contexts, engage clients comfortably in broaching discussions without getting flustered or distracted – unlike individuals who exhibit rhetorical incoherence described by Bonilla-Silva (2021), and talk directly about clients' specific and unique REC concerns. Providers who are committed to the principles of broaching possess a sense of critical consciousness that allows them to not only be aware of how issues of power and marginalization impact clients, but these providers also have the capacity to acknowledge, validate, and affirm their clients' reality.

The following transcript illustrates the interaction style of an *integrated/congruent* provider.

Provider: If our efforts together are successful, tell me what you would like to focus on specifically.

Client: Well, as a gay Latino male, I was hoping to talk about some of the challenges I'm having. I've known for a while that I'm gay, but I have struggled to come out to my family. I'm worried that they may not accept me completely. I listen to some of the comments and innuendos they make, and I'm concerned that my family will not accept me. My family is very important to me and in order to preserve peace in the family, I pretend to be someone I'm not and this is becoming way too exhausting for me. I'm tired of pretending that I plan to marry when I find the right woman or that my buddy is not my significant other. In my Latino family it's really unacceptable to be a gay man.

Provider: Wow! I imagine it must be incredibly challenging to want to talk to your family about your identity as a gay Latino man, but to worry about their possible responses. This is an enormous burden you're carrying.

Client: Exactly. I'm pretty sure many members of my family are homophobic, based on the things they say about the LGBTQIA+ community.

Provider: You're torn between coming out and remaining hidden because you don't want to risk rejection from family members. You've been playing charades and now it's becoming way too stressful for you.

Client: Absolutely. I feel stuck. Sometimes, I imagine coming out to my family and them acknowledging and embracing my gay identity and that feels pretty good; but other times, I envision the taunts, hostility, loss of respect, and rejection from certain family members. I'm concerned that my coming out may create divisions within the family and I don't want to contribute to any kind of family disruption.

Provider: You've given considerable thought to what coming out as a gay Latino man means for not only yourself, but also for your family members and how they may be impacted, and now you're in limbo.

Client: Yes, exactly. My mother and grandmother are very religious. My coming out would just crush them. They would probably be quite embarrassed and have concerns about how they would be treated by our local community and our church community. I'm 27 and I no longer live at home, but I live nearby. I believe my father would be far less accepting of me as a gay man. My siblings will be cool with me though.

Provider: You've talked about how your family members may react to your coming out as a gay man. I'm curious about how you see yourself as a gay Latino man and what your different identities mean to you.

Client: That's a good question. I'm somewhat ambivalent. Although I am completely unequivocal about being gay and I fully embrace my Latino identity. I'm a proud Latino man, but I think I've been conditioned with very traditional family values that emphasize heterosexual relationships. I was also raised Catholic which means I'm supposed to be straight. Even though I'm comfortable with my gayness, I'm constantly working to reconcile the conflict I experience about being both gay and Catholic.

Provider: Uh-huh (*Nods*).

Client: During my teenage years, I tried to combat my attraction to men by dating women, thinking that the desire would miraculously go away, but it didn't. In high school, students had the option of attending an alternative gay prom. I asked a girl to the straight prom, because at that time I was still ashamed of my sexuality. I prayed every night that God would make me straight. At times I even distanced myself from the Church, but not completely. Many of my gay friends have renounced Catholicism, but I was not prepared to do that, and it created some friction in my friendships with other gay people. Even though I don't agree with the Church's stance on same-sex attraction, my faith has not waivered. I'm a believer. Sometimes, I experience anger and resentment toward the church because there seems to be hypervigilance around same-sex attraction, but not on greed, adultery, substance abuse, or overeating. This kind of hypocrisy bothers me. I think it has even contributed to my bouts of depression and anxiety.

Provider: You have an incredibly strong sense of culture, family, religion, and personal identity that has sustained you, even as you have experienced considerable isolation. You're caught between multiple worlds. Your faith, family, religion, and personal identity are very important to you. You hold on to these values even though you feel rejected and judged. You have exhibited tremendous strength, courage, and resilience even as your experience a deep sense of woundedness. Talk to me more about the difficulty you sometimes experience reconciling your cultural, religious, and personal values.

Client: I'm not sure that I have reconciled these values. I'm torn and sometimes ambivalent and beat myself up even, because I haven't completely reconciled my cultural values with my religious values. In fact, I no longer attend mass. I find other ways to worship God and nurture my faith. At times, I still feel guilty that I'm not straight. I sometimes feel guilty because I'm not doing what the church or the family says I should do. But even as I struggle to honor these expectations, I feel convinced that my gay identity is an essential part of who I am. It's not something I can or I'm willing to abandon. I'm firm in that identity.

Provider: It's been necessary for you to compartmentalize your religious, gay, and Latino identities at times, so that you can coexist with each of your identities.

Client: That's true. I often emphasize my gay identity when I'm with my gay peers, my Latino identity when I'm with family, and my religious identity when I'm in religious settings or worshipping in my own way. I downplay different identities depending upon the setting I find myself in - to decrease my stress levels. I also find myself disagreeing and disregarding certain Church doctrine. Once I went to confession to get religious counsel on my sexuality. The priest said I was going to hell, and he did not grant me absolution. That left me feeling like he was denying my humanity. I refuse to let the priest dictate my sexuality or my humanity. I find that I have to constantly work to affirm my own religious identity.

Provider: I hear you saying that despite the boundaries that the Church imposes on the LGBTQIA+ community and the inner conflict you sometimes feel, you maintain an unwavering commitment to your faith as well as your gay male identity. Your refuse to be bound by cultural scripts.

Client: Exactly.

Each broaching transcript began identically; however, the provider's orientation toward broaching determined how they managed the counseling interaction. Providers at the lower end of the broaching continuum enlisted broaching strategies that did not facilitate the level of treatment engagement that would permit Hernando to explore the relationship between his presenting concerns and his REC. In marked contrast, the *integrated/congruent* provider assumed an effective broaching stance, by incorporating relevant technical, relational, and cultural elements in his broaching efforts. The provider used reflection of content to restate Hernando's disclosures in an effort to help him feel heard and understood. For instance, the provider paraphrased Hernando's comments and acknowledged that Hernando experienced a heightened level of distress and rejection from each of the systems that were important to him. Additionally, the provider noted that Hernando compartmentalized his religious, gay, and Latino identities in order to maintain peace among his family members. The provider's level of verbal tracking helped Hernando feel heard and understood.

The provider also used reflection of feeling to both mirror and clarify Hernando's stated and implied emotions. For instance, the provider noted that Hernando was worried that his family may respond negatively to the pronouncement of his sexual orientation as well as torn and ambivalent about the prospect of coming out. These reflective statements captured the emotions Hernando felt. Further they provided Hernando with nonjudgmental reassurance that helped him feel safe, and strengthened the therapeutic alliance. At several junctures during the exchange, Hernando responded by saying, "Exactly" and "Absolutely," as a result of feeling validated.

The provider's accurate listening and ability to convey empathy and understanding of Hernando's REC helped validate Hernando, reinforcing the premise that discussing REC perspectives is acceptable within counseling contexts. The provider used a metaphor as a figure of speech that provided a symbolic representation, noting that Hernando's closeted self is analogous to a game of charades. Specifically, the provider noted that Hernando engaged in charades by giving a misleading impression of himself to ward off speculation about his sexuality that has become increasingly more difficult to maintain. The provider's use of metaphor helped intensify meaning and allowed Hernando to explore the conflict he had about coming out. Additionally, the provider used Hernando's language. That is, Hernando described himself as a gay Latino male, and the provider used the same descriptor to refer to Hernando. Unlike the avoidant provider who imputed nationality and immigration status, the *integrated/congruent* provider did not make any such assumptions.

Each time the provider validated and affirmed Hernando's concerns, Hernando talked at a deeper emotional level, confiding about his ambivalence about coming out, anticipation of homonegativity from certain family members, the pride he maintains in his gay, Latino, and religious identities, etc. Hernando also described his early efforts to date women, the shame he internalized about being gay, and his hurtful interaction with his priest. This level of disclosure did not occur with the *avoidant*, *isolating*, or *continuing/incongruent* providers, as their nonfacilitative responses discouraged personal vulnerability and insight.

When Hernando described how he thought family members may react to his coming-out process, the provider acknowledged that Hernando had devoted considerable thought to possible reactions from family members. Although the family's reaction was helpful in orienting the provider's understanding of Hernando, the provider returned the focus to Hernando and probed deeper to explore how Hernando saw himself as a gay Latino male. This was a strategic decision on the part of the provider. Although he could have engaged Hernando in an extended dialogue about family members, the provider wanted to center Hernando's feelings, cultural beliefs, and value orientations, especially since Hernando was focusing more on how others see him versus how he regards himself. The provider foregrounded Hernando's intersectional identities by asking him to explore what it means to be gay, Latino, and male, recognizing that there is no singular way to be gay, Latino, or male. Additionally, he did not want to essentialize Hernando or reduce the discussion to only talking about Hernando's sexuality as opposed to the intersections of race, ethnicity, sexual orientation, and gender. As such, the provider encouraged Hernando to verbalize his inner concerns. The provider encouraged Hernando to express some of the cognitive and emotional dissonance associated with going against the values and viewpoints of the Church. Although Hernando described his ambivalence about coming out, he was firm in his gay Latino Catholic identity and was unwilling to abandon his core personal beliefs. Hernando was not going to be bound by cultural scripts that he experienced as rigid and confining.

The provider was adept at discussing clients' REC concerns. He exuded comfort and confidence that allowed Hernando to make culture-specific interpretations of his construals about himself and his family. Unlike the providers in the first three scenarios (e.g., *avoidant*, *isolating*, *continuing/incongruent*), the *integrated/congruent* provider did not shy away from Hernando's REC concerns. In fact, the provider leaned in and acknowledged the client's ambivalence about coming out to his family, validated and affirmed Hernando, and helped him explore his intersectional identities. The provider accepted Hernando's concerns and was open to exploring Hernando's multiple intersecting identities (race, gender, sexual orientation, religion) with an understanding that Hernando may experience multiple oppressions. In Hernando's case, the provider was able to help him examine oppressive cultural scripts. Unlike providers operating at lower categories of broaching behavior, the provider did not stifle Hernando's self-expression in ways that may limit the client's potential for healing.

The provider cultivated relational aspects of the therapeutic alliance by validating Hernando. For instance, he acknowledged how challenging it is for Hernando to withhold information about his sexuality from his family. The provider used strength-based language by praising Hernando's strong sense of culture, family, religion, and identity. In an effort to reinforce Hernando's unwavering commitment to his gay Latino identity, the provider noted that Hernando refused to be bound by cultural scripts, at which point Hernando smiled.

The provider also nurtured the therapeutic alliance by using the client's language. For instance, Hernando referred to himself as a gay Latino male. Similarly, the provider used Hernando's language and referred to Hernando as a gay Latino male. Unlike the *continuing/incongruent* provider who assumed Hernando was Mexican and immigrant, the *integrated/congruent* provider made no such assumptions. Although it may be helpful to know about the client's specific ethnic designation and documentation status, it is not necessary at this stage of the counseling session to interrupt the client's train of thought to pose questions in order to inquire about the client's background information, beyond what was available on the intake form. In light of the very contentious debate around documentation status and the volatile debate surrounding immigration enforcement, it may be wise to refrain from asking about the client's documentation status. It may be more appropriate to discuss the client's current sense of safety and security. In this moment, such a discussion is not relevant; there will likely be future opportunities to explore culture, immigration, and/or generational status when it becomes relevant to the client's goals for counseling. Further, in an earlier scenario we learned that Hernando is a US citizen.

As an aside, once I moved away from home and started working as a university professor, I would call my mother daily, so much so that when she called me, she would often say, "Norma, you didn't ask why I called." I would usually respond by saying that I did not need to ask why she called. If I listen long enough, I will learn exactly why she called. Similarly, with our clients we don't need to ask intrusive questions that diverge from their discussion points in order to satisfy our curiosity, because such questions derail the counseling process and center the provider's needs rather than the client's needs. Much of the client's personal information will come out in their own unique way without us redirecting the client's thought process. The unfolding of the client's experience does not always occur in a linear fashion.

Integrated/Congruent providers engage in open, honest, transparent conversations that permit clients to express themselves authentically, without fear of retribution or the withdrawal of emotional support. The acceptance clients experience from the provider precludes them from having to conceal important aspects of their REC experience and increases the possibility that the client will find the counseling experience cathartic and liberating.

Throughout the dialogue, the provider exuded comfort talking with Hernando and inquired about his culture without missteps. In subsequent counseling sessions, the provider may want to build on the client's earlier disclosures by considering other cultural opportunities to explore the client's personal values, past traumas, internalized homophobia, and the impact of sexuality on the experience of securing quality housing, employment, and health care in more depth.

If you completed the BABS measure and your highest score was on the *integrated/congruent* category, it is likely that you exhibit many of the characteristics described above. You likely feel comfortable engaging clients about the relatedness of their presenting concerns to issues of REC. With that said, it is reasonable to assume that your overall orientation may indicate that you are predisposed to engaging in meaningful conversations with clients. In fact, the *integrated/congruent* category is the ideal category for providers engaged in individual counseling sessions.

Burning Question

Norma, if I scored high on the *integrated/congruent* category of the BABS, does that mean I can work comfortably with all clients?

That's an excellent question. Although your BABS scores suggest that you may be comfortable broaching clients' REC concerns overall, there may be certain populations with whom you are more comfortable broaching. For instance, just because you are an American Indian provider doesn't mean you are comfortable working with all American Indians or indigenous persons. For instance, if you grew up in an urban community and have had minimal interactions with indigenous people who reside on reservations, you may be more comfortable with indigenous clients who share urban experiences compared to clients who grew up in more isolated enclaves. As stated at the outset of this book, culture is not static; it evolves constantly. Providers can never become too comfortable with their progress. Providers should maintain ongoing engagement in professional development opportunities to enhance the tools in their toolbox.

Infusing Broaching Behaviors

The major distinction between *integrated/congruent* and *infusing* providers is that *integrated/congruent* providers engage in broaching discussions within the counseling dyad and as part of the therapeutic process, whereas *infusing* providers engage in a broader repertoire of broaching behaviors that better reflect advocacy, social justice, and systemic change initiatives that reach a broad swath of clients both within and beyond the counseling dyad. *Infusing* providers effect change by advocating for clients by working to dismantle barriers to mental health and well-being.

Infusing providers possess some of the same attributes as *integrated/congruent* providers who are motivated to move beyond individually oriented counseling initiatives and effect change for larger swaths of people who need support. For instance, imagine that the providers within a counseling agency only speak English, yet the client population speaks languages other than English, making the delivery of counseling services rather difficult. An infusing provider who recognizes the challenges that her English language learners must surmount to access mental health services might consider lobbying for bilingual providers in a counseling agency. The provider recognizes that when language is a barrier to quality mental health care, clients in need of services may forego care. Similarly, a professor who prepares mental health practitioners in a university setting may lobby administrators for resources to hire a bilingual professor in order to improve the quality of training and preparation of students to work more effectively with clients for whom English is a second or even third language. The commitment to making mental health care more representative moves beyond lamenting about recognizable problems.

Infusing providers who endorse the hiring of bilingual therapists recognize the benefits that result when clients can move comfortably between their language of origin and English during treatment. The dearth of bilingual providers restricts mental health care for bilingual clients. Language switching can help clients explore their concerns in a more meaningful way (Seto & Forth, 2020). Numerous benefits accrue when clients have access to bilingual providers such as the ability to alternate between languages, provision of counseling services for individuals who might not otherwise have access to services. Similarly, a professor who recognizes that pre-service mental health providers who are bilingual may not have adequate instruction to facilitate counseling sessions. One professor lobbied for a section of practicum that enabled students to complete their clinical placements in settings with bilingual speakers. Clinical supervision addressed the specific and unique needs of multilingual clients.

Some providers disregard counseling activities for which they are not compensated. They contend that if they cannot secure billable hours, they are less invested in the work; however, mental health providers have an ethical obligation to support the best interest of clients, which at times will involve engaging in non-billable activities that can assist with the continuity of client care.

Dr. Cynthia Major Lewis is a Board-Certified Psychiatrist and the director of Adult Psychiatric Emergency Services at Johns Hopkins Hospital. As a psychiatrist, she recognized that many patients who were seriously mentally ill obtain mental health care through a kind of revolving-door access to treatment, wherein they may be committed to a psychiatric facility involuntarily, receive stabilization treatment, return to their routines, stop taking medication, and repeat this vicious cycle. Dr. Lewis's leadership and advocacy were instrumental in the passage of state legislation that now provides a continuum of care for seriously mentally ill patients through assisted outpatient treatment programs. This legislation is designed to reduce arrests, hospitalizations, homelessness, and costs to the state of Maryland. Using her professional credentials, clinical expertise, command of the scholarly literature, and commitment to not just having an awareness of challenges patients confront but also maintaining an abiding commitment to reducing the perpetual cycle of institutionalization, Dr. Lewis provided expert testimony to the state legislature. Her testimony contributed to the passage of a bill and corresponding funding that resulted in a statewide continuum of care for seriously mentally ill patients to receive comprehensive court-ordered outpatient treatment within their communities as opposed to in-patient facilities.

Burning Questions

Norma, what if I broach and my client isn't interested in discussing their REC concerns?

You may experience instances when you invite the client to discuss their REC concerns and they decline, believing that these issues are not germane to their presenting problem. Do not panic. Consider their response as diagnostic information. For instance, if you go to a restaurant and have a steak dinner and the server asks you if you want some type of steak sauce and you say, "No thank you," the server doesn't run to the kitchen and say to the other staff, "Oh my goodness, the patron doesn't want steak sauce." In all likelihood, the server would address you directly and say something reassuring like, "If you change your mind, please let me know, I'll be happy to get whatever steak sauce you prefer." Similarly, in a counseling session when a client indicates they do not have concerns around REC, we might tell the client something like,

> Topics related to race, ethnicity, and culture may not be a concern for you now, but at some point during our work together if issues of race, ethnicity, and culture do become relevant to you, I invite you to share any concerns around race, ethnicity and culture that are important to you.

Relatedly, the provider may inquire at a later point in treatment about how the client's presenting concerns are connected to experiences involving REC. My experience as a counselor educator suggests that clients do not always recognize these connections when REC issues are first introduced; however, over time they may come to recognize and choose to discuss these concerns more openly.

Burning Question

Norma, once we know what's troubling the client, can we move directly to problem-solving?

No, not at all. Often clients have spent so much time managing stress associated with oppression, being misunderstood, dealing with forms of trauma, etc., so it is important that we not rush through their problem situations and move abruptly to identifying counseling interventions. We must engage in unhurried reflection using foundational counseling skills such as reflection of content, reflection of feeling, and reflection of meaning to acknowledge what has transpired for the client. Only broaching once is like eating a single potato chip or French fry. It doesn't make sense.

Before moving to problem resolution, it's important to make sure you understand the client's concerns as fully as possible. In the case of Hernando, before moving summarily to whether or how he should come out to his family, the provider should create an affirming counseling space that helps Hernando engage in and explore his sexual identity, sexual health and wellness, relationships with partners, and sources of resilience, all while respecting the client's boundaries so as not to engender feelings of shame or embarrassment. In Hernando's case, it will be important to explore how REC factors impact his intersectional identity domains. In an effort to respond ethically, the provider should recognize their own limitations and seek supervision where appropriate, as well as determine when it may be appropriate to refer the client to someone who is more skillfully able to counsel the client.

Broaching Attitudes and Behavior Survey

Where do you fall on the broaching continuum? Please note that it is possible to have more than one high score along the continuum. For instance, you may have a high score on the integrated/congruent and infusing subscales, which suggests that you engage in effective broaching behaviors, and you also work toward eliminating barriers for clients by instituting social justice interventions.

It is important to recognize that your broaching skills may be context-dependent such that you exhibit greater depth of understanding and facility working with some populations versus other populations. For instance, you may work more comfortably with gay Gen-z clients as opposed to gay baby boomers. This may be in part because you have had more exposure or more opportunities to work with certain populations, you have more contextual knowledge about certain groups, or you are naturally drawn to certain groups.

I once had a 23-year-old student who was committed to working with the geriatric population. Out of curiosity, I asked her to share with me what drew her to geriatric clients, because she seemed to me to have a heightened sense of commitment, empathy, and compassion for the elderly. She responded that as a child she spent a significant amount of quality time with her grandparents who made her feel very special. Regardless of which population you have a natural affinity toward, it is important to develop an ease of manner working with multiple populations. You will continue to build on your broaching foundation as you develop more tools and dexterity working with a range of client populations.

Summary

The *Continuum of Broaching Behavior* is a heuristic device that describes providers' orientation toward facilitating REC discussions with clients. The continuum contains five categories that advance from less helpful to more helpful broaching styles. *Avoidant* providers ignore the contextual dimensions of REC. *Isolating* providers address clients' REC concerns minimally and with little follow-up; consequently, they soon return to more generic topics. *Continuing/Incongruent* providers broach mechanically and awkwardly. The first three categories along the broaching continuum (*avoidant*, *isolating*, and *continuing/incongruent*) tend to reflect less effective strategies for discussing clients' REC concerns. The final two categories along the broaching continuum represent preferred broaching styles. *Integrated/Congruent* providers engage in broaching efforts as part of the therapeutic process in order to help clients weigh the extent to which REC issues shape their presenting concerns. *Integrated/Congruent* broaching styles represent the preferred mode within the counseling dyad. *Infusing* providers engage in social justice interventions both within and outside the counseling dyad to eliminate barriers for clients. Infusing broaching styles represent the preferred broaching style when working outside the counseling setting on clients' behalf.

Discussion Questions

1 Review your BABS scores. What is your predominant broaching style?
2 With which client populations might you be more comfortable broaching? With which client populations might you be less comfortable broaching?

3 What factors contribute to your ease or difficulty broaching?
4 What attitudes, biases, and assumptions do you harbor that may interfere with your ability to work effectively with Hernando and other clients?
5 What cultural scripts have you developed that may undermine the counseling process? How will you both monitor and manage your biases as you work with Hernando?
6 What broaching strengths do you currently possess, and what factors have helped you hone your current skill set?
7 What goals do you have to enhance your broaching skill set? Hint: Finish reading this book. Consider revisiting chapters again and again.

References

Aydoğan, M., Middleton, T., & Britton, P. (2022). Barriers to broaching culture in counseling supervision: A Q methodology study. *Education and Science, 47*, 1–16. https://doi.org/10.15390/EB.2022.11302

Bonilla-Silva, E. (2021). *Racism without racists: Color-Blind racism and the persistence of racial inequality in America*. Rowman and Littlefield.

Brawner, R., Day-Vines, N.L., Gubara, S., Agorsor, C., Jackson, Z., & Ran, T., & Caldwell, N. (2025). Perceptions of racial, ethnic, and cultural ruptures in counseling: A qualitative case study of a client from a minoritized background. *Journal of Counseling and Development, 103*, 484–495. https://doi-org.proxy1.library.jhu.edu/10.1002/jcad.70004

Chang, D.F., Dunn, J.J., & Omidi, M. (2020). A critical-cultural-relational approach to rupture resolution: A case illustration with a cross-racial dyad. *Journal of Clinical Psychology, 77*(2), 369–383. https://doi.org/10.1002/jclp.23080

D'Andrea, M., & Daniels, J. (2001). RESPECTFUL counseling: An integrative model for counselors. In D. Pope-Davis & H. Coleman (Eds.), *The intersection of class, culture, and gender in counseling* (pp. 417–466). Sage. https://doi.org/10.4135/9781452231846.n17

Day-Vines, N.L., Booker Ammah, B., Steen, S., & Arnold, K.M. (2018). Getting comfortable with discomfort: Preparing counselor trainees to broach racial, ethnic, and cultural factors with clients during counseling. *International Journal for the Advancement of Counselling, 40*(2), 89–104. https://doi.org/10.1007/s10447-017-9308-9

Day-Vines, N.L., Bryan, J., & Griffin, D. (2013). The broaching attitudes and behavior survey (BABS): An exploratory assessment of its dimensionality. *Journal of Multicultural Counseling and Development, 41,* 210–223. https://doi.org/10.1002/j.2161-1912.2013.00037.x

Day-Vines, N.L., Cluxton-Keller, F., Agorsor, C., & Gubara, S. (2021). Strategies for broaching the subjects of race, ethnicity and culture. *Journal of Counseling and Development, 99*, 348–357. https://doi.org/10.1002/jcad.12380

Day-Vines, N.L., Cluxton-Keller, F., Agorsor, C., Gubara, S., & Otabil, N. (2020). The multidimensional model of broaching behavior. *Journal of Counseling and Development, 98,* 107–118. https://doi.org/10.1002/jcad.12304

Day-Vines, N.L., Wood, S., Grothaus, T., Craigen, L., Holman, A., Dotson-Blake, K., & Douglass, M. (2007). Broaching the subjects of race, ethnicity, and culture during the counseling process. *Journal of Counseling and Development, 85,* 401–409. https://doi.org/10.1002/jcad.12069

Day-Vines, N.L., Zhang, J., Cluxton-Keller, F., Hicks, D., Mwombele, B., Austin, M., Henderson, C., Henning, M., & Pecku, M. (2026). An Investigation of African origin clients' perceptions of their therapists' ability to broach racial, ethnic, and cultural concerns during the counseling process. *Unpublished Manuscript.*

Degruy, J. (2017). *Post traumatic slave syndrome: America's legacy of enduring injury and healing*. Joy Degruy Publications.

Depauw, H., & Van Hiel, A. (2024). Uncovering patterns in perceived therapist behaviour: A latent profile analysis of broaching experiences among ethnic minority group member clients. *Clinical Psychology and Psychotherapy, 31*, e3067. https://doi.org/10.1002/cpp.3067

Depauw, H., Van Hiel, A., De Clercq, B., Bracke, P., & Van de Putte, B. (2023). Addressing cultural topics during psychotherapy: Evidence-based do's and don'ts from an ethnic minority perspective. *Psychotherapy Research, 33*, 768–782. https://doi-org.proxy1.library.jhu.edu/10.1080/10503307.2022.2156307

Drinane, J.M., Owen, J., & Tao, K.W. (2018). Cultural concealment and therapy outcomes. *Journal of Counseling Psychology, 65*, 239–246. https://doi.org/10.1037/cou0000246

Dubois, W.E.B. (1903/1969). *The souls of Black folk.* New American Library.

Eubanks, C.F., Muran, J.C., & Safran, J.D. (2018). Alliance rupture repair: A meta-analysis. *Psychotherapy, 55*, 508–519. https://doi.org/10.1037/pst0000185

Foley, G.N., & Gentile, J.P. (2010). Nonverbal communication in psychotherapy. *Psychiatry, 7*, 38–44.

Gaztambide, D.J. (2012). Addressing cultural impasses with rupture resolution strategies: A proposal and recommendations. *Professional Psychology: Research and Practice, 43*(3), 183–189. https://doi.org/10.1037/a0026911

Hemmings, & Evans, A. (2018). Identifying and treating race-based trauma in counseling. *Journal of Multicultural Counseling and Development, 46*, 20–39. https://doi.org/10.1002/jmcd.12090

Hill, C.E. (2020). *Helping skills: Facilitating exploration, insight, and action.* American Psychological Association.

Jones, C.T., & Welfare, L.E. (2017). Broaching behaviors of licensed professional counselors: A qualitative inquiry. *Journal of Addictions & Offender Counseling, 38*(1), 48–64. https://doi-org.proxy1.library.jhu.edu/10.1002/jaoc.12028

Lukowitsky, M.R., Winseman, J.S., Feld, E, Kam, S.M., & Balkoski, V.I. (2024). Patients' perceptions of their therapist: Effects of race, culture, and cultural competency on the working alliance. *American Journal of Psychotherapy*. https://doi-org.proxy1.library.jhu.edu/10.1176/appi.psychotherapy.20230056

Menakem, R. (2017). *My grandmother's hands: Racialized trauma and the pathway to mending our hearts and bodies*. Central Recovery Press.

Mullan, J. (2023). *Decolonizing therapy: Oppression, historical trauma, and politicizing your practice*. W.W. Norton & Company.

Newton, C., & Steele, J.M. (2025). The broaching readiness framework: A path for psychologists to embrace cultural opportunities. *Counselling Psychology Quarterly, 38*, 1135–1152. https://doi-org.proxy1.library.jhu.edu/10.1080/09515070.2025.2458034

Owen, J., Tao, K.W., Imel, Z.E., Wampold, B.E., & Emil, R. (2014). Addressing racial and ethnic microaggressions in therapy. *Professional Psychology: Research and Practice, 45*, 283–290. https://doi.org/10.1037/a0037420

Rogers-Sirin, L., Melendez, F., Refano, C., & Zegarra, Y. (2015). Immigrant perceptions of therapists' cultural competence: A qualitative investigation. *Professional Psychology: Research and Practice*, *46*(4), 258–269. https://doi-org.proxy1.library.jhu.edu/10.1037/PRO0000033

Sadusky, A., Yared, H., Patrick, P., & Berger, E. (2024). A systematic review of client's perspectives on the cultural and racial awareness and responsiveness of mental health practitioners. *Culture and Psychology, 30*, 567–605. https://doi-org.proxy1.library.jhu.edu/10.1177/1354067X23115660

Seto, A., & Forth, N.L.A. (2020). What is known about bilingual counseling: A systematic review of the literature. *The Professional Counseling, 10*(3), 393–405. https://doi.org/10.15241/as.10.3.393

Walker, R. (2024). *No racial elephants in the room: An unapologetic approach to providing culturally affirming mental health care to Black and African American clients.* PESI.

White-Davis, T., Stein, E., & Karasz, A. (2016). The elephant in the room: Dialogues about race within cross-cultural supervisory relationships. *International Journal of Psychiatry in Medicine, 51*, 347–356. https://doi-org.proxy1.library.jhu.edu/10.1177/0091217416659271

Williams, J. (2026). Broaching race, ethnicity, and culture: Examining counselor trainees' growth through experiential training. *Journal of Multicultural Counseling and Development, 54*(2), 55–66. https://doi-org.proxy1.library.jhu.edu/10.1002/jmcd.70014

Yeo, E., & Torres-Harding, S.R. (2021). Rupture resolution strategies and the impact of rupture on the working alliance after racial microaggressions in therapy. *Psychotherapy, 58*, 460–471. https://doi.org/10.1037/pst0000372

Chapter 4

Multidimensional Model of Broaching Behavior

After developing the *Continuum of Broaching Behavior* with colleagues, I introduced the broaching model to students in my counseling techniques and social/cultural diversity courses. I also conducted presentations introducing the broaching framework to various mental health providers at conferences and professional development workshops. Much to my chagrin, I noticed that people inaccurately reduced the broaching framework to differences between the provider and client, much like the *isolating* provider in Chapter 3 who worked with Hernando. My students might say something similar like "How do you feel about working with me because I'm White and you are Black?"

Although consideration of sociodemographic differences between the provider and client warrants discussion within counseling contexts, provider–client differences alone are not the primary purpose for posing the question. As we will see later in this chapter, a superordinate purpose of inquiring about provider–client differences involves consideration of how the social locations of the provider (race, gender, class, age, sexuality, nationality, etc.) interact with the social locations of the client (race, gender, class, age, sexuality, nationality, etc.), in ways that impact the client's counseling experience. In other words, the social locations of the provider and client are not neutral. They are rooted in historical and contemporary inequities that may play out within the counseling dyad in ways that perpetuate power, oppression, faulty communication patterns, conscious and unconscious bias as well as trust, mistrust, and distrust. Discussions about provider and client social locations promote mutual understanding and opportunities for corrective action, especially when the client may have concerns about how the counseling process is unfolding.

In addition to the tendency for students to reduce clients' multicultural concerns to provider–client differences, I also observed students centering their broaching efforts exclusively on encounters with racism and discrimination. Although this tendency is not surprising, it curtails many other REC discussions that are relevant to clients' counseling concerns. In presentations, I usually acknowledge that I have been African American my entire life and that I have experienced enormous amounts of racism and discrimination; however,

DOI: 10.4324/9781003649311-4

I contend that I am a complex human being. As such, I am more than the sum total of the encounters I have endured with racism and discrimination. Similarly, providers cannot essentialize or reduce clients to a single identity domain (e.g., immigration status, disability, sexual orientation). Examining the totality of clients' REC concerns beyond their encounters with racism and discrimination helps mitigate mounting levels of psychological distress that contribute to depression, anxiety, trauma, internalized oppression, as well as poor health consequences (Carter & Pieterse, 2020). Providers must examine the complexity of the client's human experience, including but not limited to the manner in which racism and discrimination shape their sociocultural, sociohistorical, and sociopolitical realities.

In an effort to address clients' multifaceted concerns and provide further elaboration regarding the *Continuum of Broaching Behavior*, my colleagues and I developed the Multidimensional Model of Broaching Behavior (MMBB; Day-Vines & Holcomb-McCoy, 2013; Day-Vines et al., 2020). Whereas the *Continuum of Broaching Behavior* describes orientations that providers assume as they determine whether to broach clients' REC concerns (see Chapter 3), the MMBB examines multiple aspects of client identity, values, experience, emotion, as well as encounters with structural forces of oppression that undermine client well-being. Over the course of the next several chapters, we will review specific broaching dimensions in which providers can explore the contextual dimensions of REC. The MMBB provides a more elaborated opportunity for providers to address clients' REC concerns that include but are not limited to individual differences between the provider and client, the client's intersectional identities, level of connections to family and community, or encounters with racism and discrimination.

Conceptualizing MMBB Dimensions

The MMBB functions as a heuristic tool that identifies specific broaching contexts providers may use to guide discussions about the extent to which REC may be embedded within clients' presenting concerns (Day-Vines et al., 2021). By outlining broad topical areas for addressing clients' REC concerns, the MMBB offers recommendations that help providers explore the salience of REC within their clients' lives. Discussing a range of broaching concerns beyond provider–client differences or racism and discrimination can help facilitate client self-understanding, enhance the therapeutic alliance, reduce psychological distress, and promote more effective problem-solving. The MMBB dimensions are as follows: (a) intra-counseling or relational dynamics between the provider and client, (b) intra-individual or the client's intersectional identity domains, (c) intra-REC or the client's connection or disconnection with people from their own REC communities, and (d) inter-REC or the client's encounters with racism and discrimination. These domains add conceptual clarity that permit providers to consider the vast array of topical areas related to the client's REC concerns (Erby & White, 2020). The MMBB is not intended to unfold in a linear fashion, because the broaching dimensions are fluid, overlapping, and interacting and are not designed to be overly prescriptive. Providers may discuss the broaching dimensions in the order that seems most relevant in facilitating discussions about clients' REC concerns. Attention to the MMBB dimensions is contingent upon the client's needs. The remainder of this chapter focuses on intra-counseling broaching dimensions.

Intra-counseling Broaching Dimensions

The intra-counseling dimension of the MMBB refers to the discussion of interpersonal processes between the provider and client, as it pertains to REC. This is critically important because counseling relationships function as the foundation of the therapeutic process and rest heavily on therapeutic understanding, trust, respect, empathy, and psychological safety (Hill, 2020). Unaddressed relational dynamics between the provider and client can create an unhealthy power dynamic within the counseling dyad that may contribute to countertransference, ruptures, and, at the extreme, premature termination (Seligman, 2008). Incidentally, countertransference refers to situations in which the provider's unresolved concerns impact their reactions to the client. Those reactions include positive and negative responses such as overidentification with clients, as well as microaggressions directed toward the client, whether or not they are intentional (Sue et al., 2022).

Development of a strong therapeutic connection with clients involves not only cultivating the therapeutic alliance but also enlisting client perceptions about the viability of the helping relationship, especially as it pertains to REC. Components of the intra-counseling broaching dimensions involve provider efforts to (a) build a therapeutic alliance, (b) invite the client to explore the full range of their REC concerns, (c) elicit client feedback using cultural immediacy, (d) accept client feedback with a nondefensive posture, and (e) divest oneself of expert status in order to reduce the power imbalance. The feedback the client shares can help the provider adjust the counseling process to better meet the client's needs.

Building the Therapeutic Alliance

At the outset of counseling, providers have a small window of opportunity to create conditions for forging a strong therapeutic alliance, which includes establishing a relationship, creating realistic goals, and encouraging clients to talk freely and openly. The provider's broaching efforts operate as a necessary, albeit insufficient, criterion for establishing rapport and developing psychological safety within the counseling dyad. Before examining the contextual dimensions of REC with clients, the provider must engage in a preliminary set of counseling behaviors that convey empathy, respect, and openness. As we will discuss in much more detail in Chapter 8, providers exhibit invitational skills, or a sequence of actions, behaviors, and words to help clients develop a sense of comfort and ease within the counseling dyad (Schmidt, 2014). Invitational skills include the intentional and unintentional ways of encouraging or discouraging communication, as well as the choices that both the provider and client make in communicating effectively and accepting the messages being sent (Schmidt, 2014). These skills "invite" the client to converse freely with the provider and are demonstrated in both nonverbal and verbal interactions.

The provider's effort to build the therapeutic alliance begins long before the formal counseling process ever starts and includes a range of nonverbal and verbal communiqués (Brawner & Day-Vines, 2024). Whether deliberate or not, the provider conveys messages about how welcoming the counseling practice may be. For instance, the office location (e.g., near or far from public transportation), the provider's decision to operate in or out of network, the availability of sliding scale fees, as well as the display of representative artifacts (magazines, artwork, etc.) within the office environment, all convey metamessages about the provider's priorities and value orientations. Even when clients do not verbalize their reactions about the representativeness of the counseling setting, clients may have internal reactions. For instance, Than is a Burmese refugee who receives counseling services at a refugee resettlement site. Although she is grateful for the opportunity to address the trauma she experienced during her premigration, migration, and post-migration experience, she is baffled that few people on staff are bilingual or have a refugee background. This has impacted her ability to access essential services and information. Than wonders whether she will be assigned a provider who has the skillset, experience, and deep structural understanding of her needs. The volunteer interpreter who was assigned to attend Than's counseling session last week had a family emergency and canceled, which delayed Than's care. Few staff members are from minoritized backgrounds, nor does the artwork represent clients from refugee backgrounds. The artifacts serve as symbol systems that give Than the impression providers are not attuned to refugees' specific and unique cultural needs; however, she is beholden to her providers because they have the power to determine her mental health treatment and access to needed resources.

In addition to the visual cues that providers convey about their openness to diversity, clients gauge the interpersonal style, warmth, and welcoming nature of the provider, the practice, and the agency. As the reader will recall from previous chapters, clients from minoritized groups may be especially sensitive to cues about whether providers exude trust, mistrust, or distrust. Uncertainty about trust may activate clients' healthy paranoia antennae as an adaptive response given prior encounters with mistreatment and disrespect (Grier & Cobbs, 1968; Griffith et al., 2021). Under such circumstances, clients may rely less on what providers say and more on how providers make them feel. For instance, Adeola, a Nigerian American teacher, reveled in the fact that her provider invited her to explore multiple aspects of her cultural background as an integral part of the counseling process; however, Adeola noticed a disconnect in the provider's stated commitment to open conversations about REC yet recognized the reality that her provider was reluctant to engage in deeper, more meaningful conversations about her background. Adeola wanted to discuss her family's insistence that she pursue one of three careers that are valued in Nigerian households: engineering, medicine, or law. Adeola chose to become a teacher, which left her fulfilled and family members deeply disappointed. As Adeola lamented about her standing in the family, gender dynamics, and intergenerational tensions, the provider insisted that teaching was a noble and respected career choice. The provider's insistence about the value of teaching felt invalidating to Adeola because it did not give her the emotional space to explore the guilt, resentment, and ambivalence she internalized. Nor did it permit her to explore the role that gender and class played in shaping her family's stance on career choice. Clients need opportunities to explore the full depth and range of their emotional experience and its embeddedness in REC dynamics. In essence, the provider encouraged Adeola to self-disclose about her REC experience but subsequently minimized salient aspects of her experience. Namely, the provider seemed not to be aware of the premium many Nigerian families place on education, social mobility, family achievement, and the subsequent pressure that impacted Adeola. Inasmuch as Adeola felt silenced in her family about her own desires and aspirations, she felt similarly silenced by her provider's incapacity to discuss some of her deeper REC concerns. The provider's inattention to Adeola's needs undermined the establishment of a healthy therapeutic relationship.

Invite the Client to Explore the Full Range of Their REC Concerns

Broaching as a Pre-Counseling Activity

Much has been written about timing and broaching statements. For instance, I am constantly asked when exactly during the counseling process providers should broach with their clients. Essentially, providers want to know whether they should broach at the beginning, middle, or end of the counseling process. My colleagues and I have asserted vehemently that broaching is not a single or one-time event (Day-Vines et al., 2007). Other scholars concur that broaching should occur early in the counseling session and continue throughout the duration counseling process (Fuertes et al., 2002; Jones & Welfare, 2017). The provider's broaching behavior reflects an ongoing process that includes a set of dispositions and strategies that providers implement as they prepare clients for broaching discussions (Day-Vines et al., 2021). It is about orienting oneself to clients' needs. More recently, we have asserted that broaching is reflected in the way providers portray their practice even before they see their first client (Brawner & Day-Vines, 2024). There are numerous opportunities for providers to invite clients to explore their REC counseling concerns prior to the start of counseling without being dogmatic. For instance, providers can use advertisement portals like Psychology Today or Zocdoc, as well as websites that identify their areas of expertise, including experience working with specific populations (e.g., ethnic minority women, religious minorities, couples, trans people), languages, presenting problems (chronic health issues, employment concerns, grief), counseling modalities (EMDR, CBT), as well as attention to culture-based concerns (e.g., racialized stress, racial trauma, intersectionality). For clients who have an interest in exploring their REC concerns, knowing prior to the start of counseling that REC discussions can be integrated into the counseling process offers added assurances that counseling will be worthwhile and meaningful.

Providers may also share personal statements about their value orientations, belief systems, and counseling modalities. Such statements contextualize the counseling process and provide a basis for facilitating REC discussions once the counseling process unfolds. These professional statements signal to clients that providers recognize the significance of clients' REC concerns and perspectives. It also prompts clients that cultural experiences are relevant to the counseling process and prepares clients for the types of topics they can expect to discuss in session. By identifying their scope of practice, providers prepare clients for the types of topics that can emerge during treatment. Essentially, the series of questions normalize the discussion of REC during the counseling process by creating an opportunity to forge a trusting therapeutic alliance even before the counseling process begins.

Maria is a 21-year-old Guatemalan American. Her parents came to the United States as agricultural workers before she was born. In spite of their undocumented status, they built a family business and had three more children who are now between the ages of 10 and 16. Although Maria's parents lived with constant uncertainty about their precarious documentation status, they enjoy family life and the loving connection they have forged in their largely Latinx community. Yet, living in the shadows of deportation because of their mixed documented family status was exhausting. More recently, Maria's parents were apprehended during an immigration raid at their family business and remanded to an immigration detention facility. Fortunately, the family had planned for the possibility of deportation. They discussed what they should do with their underage children to maintain family cohesion. Maria's parents contemplated whether everyone should return to Guatemala as a family unit to a country and culture with which the children had no familiarity. They considered whether leaving the United States put their dreams in jeopardy of having all the children attend college and start on a trajectory of middle-class success and productivity. In the end, the family decided to leave the younger children in Maria's care because she was legally able to assume responsibility for the children and the business. This meant that Maria was suddenly parentified or thrust into an adult role as caretaker. Assuming responsibility for the family business meant that she would likely forego full-time college enrollment in order to care for her siblings. Maria was exhausted, overwhelmed, and grateful that her siblings would not have to move to Guatemala but simultaneously overwhelmed and somewhat resentful that she would now need to shoulder complete responsibility for the care of her siblings. Maria was annoyed that her parents did not include her in the family decision-making process.

Because she was a commuter student at a local university, Maria sought counseling services at the campus counseling center. When she registered for counseling services, she had the option of being assigned to a therapist or selecting a therapist. She chose to work with a therapist whose online bio indicated that she was a bilingual provider from Costa Rica. Although Maria and the prospective provider have different nationalities, she felt assured that the provider would have a strong enough understanding of her REC concerns to be helpful. Further, in moments of intense emotionality, Maria fluctuates between speaking English and Spanish, so having the option of a bilingual therapist felt even more comforting. The therapist's areas of expertise included immigrant trauma and feminist therapy, both expertise levels Maria felt she could benefit from therapeutically. In Maria's case, the broaching process began even before the start of therapy. Information about the provider reassured Maria that she could explore her REC concerns and made the prospect of therapy both necessary and enticing. Maria felt that a provider who had a deep structural understanding of immigrant concerns may be better poised to understand her current circumstances. Maria believed that with the right provider she might spend less time trying to be taken seriously.

As early as four years old, Bobby (née Roberta) felt trapped in a women's body. She never quite felt that who she was on the inside matched her assigned gender at birth. She enjoyed boys' activities more than the dainty activities that were expected of girls. She did not like dresses or the ribbons her mother put in her hair. Her peers picked on her because she seemed masculine while her friends observed in silence – seldom sticking up for her. Sometimes even the teachers joined in the antics. In middle school, she realized that she was uncomfortable with her developing body. Deep inside, Bobby felt a constant surge of masculine energy. This left Bobby confused. In high school, Bobby laid to rest his birth name. One teacher in particular insisted on using Bobby's dead name as a form of ridicule and to entertain other students. Over time, Bobby developed deep gender dysphoria. In the confines of his bedroom, he used social media sites to learn more about girls who wanted to become men. Bobby adopted new pronouns: he, him, his. This new declaration led Bobby to begin adopting a more masculine wardrobe, including men's blazers and button-down shirts confiscated from his father's closet. Bobby did not have many conversations with friends or family. Although family members tolerated Bobby's decision to transition, they did not necessarily support this decision. Imagine how liberated Bobby felt after discovering this provider's description on the *Psychology Today* website.

> As a Black, queer, trans person, I intimately understand how those with marginalized identities are often silenced and made to feel invisible. In my practice, I prioritize creating a space where your voice is centered and valued. I believe that true healing and growth come when we reconnect with ourselves and with others in meaningful ways, and I strive to create an environment where you can fully show up as yourself.
> Provider's name
> xxx.xxx.xxxx

This statement spoke volumes to Bobby and made him feel like he was reading parts of his own biography. At last, it seemed he found someone who really seemed to understand him. Bobby believed he would be able to come home psychologically and finally have someone who truly understood him and did not just feign support. He was tired of performative allyship with therapists who surreptitiously pathologized his existence. Clients should not have to play guessing games to determine whether the therapist is open to exploring their sociocultural and sociopolitical realities.

Prior to the start of counseling, many providers administer intake forms. These documents serve as an initial opportunity to gather a variety of data about the client. Providers may elicit information about clients' contact information, cultural backgrounds, values, religious orientation, sexual orientation, medical history, languages spoken, preferences for therapists (e.g., race, gender, language), etc. Additionally, providers may elicit information about clients' prior counseling experiences and whether counseling was helpful or unhelpful. They may also ask clients what topics they may be more or less comfortable discussing. This could give the provider an opportunity to follow up on responses made on the intake form. These questions prime the client by preparing them that REC discussions are permissible within the context of counseling; moreover, they alert clients that counseling discussions are broad and encompassing, and if interested, clients can delve into their REC concerns. Intake forms allow clients to describe their salient identities and communicate subtly that REC discussions are permissible. This topic is discussed in more detail in Chapter 8.

Inasmuch as providers communicate to clients prior to the start of counseling that REC discussions are welcome, providers must maintain that same commitment throughout the counseling process. It may be tempting to think that the right circumstances will arise that create a perfect broaching moment, but there is a certain amount of preliminary work that is necessary to create the conditions that contribute to the client's willingness to discuss their REC concerns. This includes the informed consent process, which occurs when the provider helps the client understand how the counseling process unfolds, practice or agency policies, state and federal laws, and the client's rights. This also includes discussions about the nature and purpose of therapy, the provider's qualifications and boundaries of competence, the voluntary nature of counseling unless clients are mandated, limits of confidentiality, management of emergency situations, etc. In addition to these standard topics, providers may use the informed consent discussion to address broachable topics clients can expect to explore in sessions. For instance, the provider may say something like:

> Sometimes clients wonder what types of personal concerns are appropriate for counseling. Ordinarily, clients may discuss things that are bothering them, such as concerns about friendship, family, and romantic relations, grief and loss, work related stressors, traumatic events, depression, anxiety, and so forth. Sometimes clients' cultural identities like race, ethnicity, gender, sexual orientation, religion and spirituality, language, immigration and other experiences are intertwined with their everyday challenges in ways that affect their sense of well-being. These topics are also important to discuss. I want you to know and understand that if you have a desire to discuss any particular cultural concerns you are welcome to do so. I am very open to discussing aspects of your cultural background and experience. There may be times when I inquire about how your cultural experiences are related to some of your counseling concerns. There will also be times when I will look to you to initiate those cultural conversations. My intention is to make counseling as meaningful as possible for you.

Boswell et al. (2025) provided a more concise statement inviting the client to address their REC concerns within the context of counseling:

> As part of our work together, I will be asking many questions to try to understand aspects of your identity related to race, culture, and gender. I may misunderstand despite my best efforts, and if you would be willing to let me know I have gotten it wrong, we can strengthen our working relationship. To help you the best that I can, it is important that you feel as comfortable as possible discussing all aspects of your identity.

Statements like these provide added assurance that clients can raise their REC concerns within the safety of the counseling dyad. As the counseling process unfolds, the provider will look for opportunities to broach the client's REC concerns. Recall from Chapter 2, where we discussed multicultural orientation, namely, the provider's cultural humility or sense of curiosity about the client and willingness to admit limitations; the cultural opportunities or efforts to identify broachable moments, as well as cultural comfort or the provider's ease of manner engaging clients in REC discussions. In the chapters that follow, we will discuss several other broaching domains (e.g., intra-individual, intra-REC, inter-REC) that permit providers to engage in more robust discussions about the extent to which REC shapes clients' counseling concerns.

Initiate and Respond to Broaching Discussions

Broaching refers to the provider's effort to initiate or respond to REC discussions. That is, there are instances in which the provider takes the lead by inviting the client to explore and examine the extent to which REC issues may be linked to their presenting concerns. At other times, the client may take the lead by sharing how REC concerns impact their lived experience. Because the provider wields the balance of power within the counseling dyad, it is incumbent upon the provider to address broaching concerns directly, deliberately, and with confidence, regardless of who initiates the discussion. As we discuss in much more detail in Chapter 9, whether initiating or responding to a broaching statement, the provider will use a range of foundational and advanced counseling skills such as reflection of content, reflection of feeling, reflection of meaning, and interpretation, to acknowledge, validate, and support the client as they address their REC concerns.

When providers invite clients to discuss their REC concerns, but then exhibit discomfort dialoguing about clients' concerns, redirect clients' attention away from their REC concerns prematurely, minimize or negate REC concerns, or only discuss clients' REC concerns following very public situations (e.g., immigration raids, state-sanctioned violence), clients may not feel comfortable engaging in REC conversations because the foundation of trust and security has not been brokered (Galán et al., 2022). Further, this emotional distancing may demonstrate a form of countertransference on the part of the provider (Seligman, 2008; Sue et al., 2022). Clients need opportunities to process their thoughts and feelings without sensing that REC discussions are an imposition for the provider (Brawner et al., 2025). In the section that follows, however, we explore strategies for gathering consistent feedback from clients about their counseling experience.

Elicit Qualitative Feedback from Clients Using Cultural Immediacy

The Dunning–Kruger effect indicates that, in general, people engage in self-assessment bias by exaggerating their competence levels (Dunning, 2011). Researchers have found similar patterns among mental health providers, noting that they tend to overestimate their general and cultural knowledge (Sadusky et al., 2024; Walfish et al., 2012). In order to reduce the likelihood of self-assessment bias, it is recommended that providers elicit continual feedback from clients.

The intra-counseling broaching dimension helps providers monitor the counseling relationship by inquiring about how clients experience REC dimensions of the therapeutic process. Providers may ask what is working or not working for the client and how provider–client REC similarities and differences shape and impact the counseling process, as well as what counseling behaviors would be more or less helpful during the counseling process. Eliciting feedback about clients' REC-related counseling experiences helps providers gain clinical insights that can be used to calibrate the counseling process and make adjustments that help maintain a healthy and viable counseling experience. At designated junctures during the counseling process, the provider may inquire about the client's counseling experience. In the counseling statement that follows, the provider inquires about how their differences may impact the counseling process:

> I know that this can sometimes be a difficult topic to discuss, but I was wondering how you feel about working with someone who is from a different racial/ethnic background? I ask because although it is certainly my goal to be as helpful to you as I possibly can, I also know that there may be times when I cannot fully appreciate your experiences. I want you to know that I am always open to talking about the topics whenever they are relevant.
>
> (Cardemil & Battle, 2003)

In this statement, the provider initiates a conversation about the differences between themselves and the client in a tentative manner. For instance, the provider states, "I was wondering." Use of the word wondering conveys the provider's sense of curiosity, not absolute certainty. The provider continued by inquiring about specific differences that may impact the counseling dyad. In this case, the differences center around race and ethnicity and reflect what Helms and Cook (1999) refer to as visible racial-ethnic group differences. As the label suggests, some differences are patently obvious because they are visible. Other provider–client differences may be less visible, as in the case of military status, sexual identity, social class status, etc. Another critical feature of this statement is the provider's use of cultural humility to acknowledge limitations in their counseling effectiveness. The provider does not assume an all-knowing stance. The provider's comments sound heartfelt.

In my teaching efforts, I share a video-recorded demonstration tape of myself counseling a Sudanese American woman. I say something to the effect that we are both African-origin women, and that as an African American, I identify as a descendant of enslaved African peoples, and that she identifies as Sudanese American. I continue by noting that although we share the same race and gender, we have different ethnic backgrounds and that there may be times when I don't fully understand elements of her cultural background. I also note that I intend to work to make sure we bridge our cultural understandings and misunderstandings. I acknowledge our shared and different identities because it is likely that the client knows beyond a shadow of a doubt that I do not understand the inner workings of Sudanese culture. My broaching statement acknowledges the obvious and exhibits a level of cultural humility. This broaching statement acknowledges that providers and clients who share the same racial designation are not monoliths.

In a related example, Selma is an experienced provider who identifies as an atheist. Her client is a devout Catholic who has centered religion as an important part of her core identity. At one juncture, the client inquired about Selma's religious background. Selma indicated that she identified as an atheist. Between sessions, Selma pondered whether her client felt she was a credible provider and the extent to which the client was benefiting from the counseling experience. Because religion was a core theme in the client's life and therapeutic goals, Selma broached by openly acknowledging their religious differences and inquired about how receiving services from an atheist provider impacted the client's counseling experience. The dialogue between Selma and her client unfolded as follows:

Selma: During our last session you inquired about my religious background and I shared that I am atheist. I am wondering how those differences in our religious background impact your counseling experience? I ask because I want you to experience the counseling process as a meaningful endeavor.

Client: Well, initially I had reservations when I asked you about your religious background, and you mentioned that you were a practicing atheist. I honestly wondered whether you would understand or appreciate how important my religion is to me.

Selma: You thought I might not take your Catholicism seriously.

Client: Yes, pretty much. I suspected that you might be judgmental and think my commitment to religion was meaningless. In actuality, I have appreciated the level of respect and thoughtfulness you have shown toward my religious beliefs. I realize that I have made some assumptions about you that were not accurate or fair. I was raised to believe that atheists do not have a moral compass, but I have been surprised and a little embarrassed that I judged you in that way.

Selma: Thank you for your honesty. Let me say that I too have come to appreciate how your faith is a core part of your identity and shapes how you see and understand the world. Your faith guides your beliefs and choices and is rooted in your compassion for humanity. I have observed that daily devotion and prayer ground you.

Client: Although I didn't expect to say this, I am moved by the gentleness of your spirit. This discussion is a reminder that I am working on my own efforts to improve my relationships with people who are close to me. Part of my difficulty has been that I have judged people in ways that push them away rather than connect us. You have helped me see that we don't have to share the same beliefs in order to accept one another.

Selma: During our work together, you have achieved some important insights about yourself, and you are using insights about our relationship to strengthen your relationships with people who are important to you.

Client: Yes, that's exactly right. I am definitely trying, and I thank you for acknowledging your observations and helping me through this process.

Selma: It's my pleasure. During our work together, I want to make sure that I am supporting your religious values and viewpoints in ways that you find helpful. I encourage you to bring up aspects of your religious identity as often as seems appropriate for you. I also want you to know that sometimes, there may be gaps in my knowledge and understanding. My goal is not to expect you to fill those gaps, but for me to deepen my own knowledge about your background so that I can be a better support to you. So far, we've discussed the fact that therapy is working for you, but circumstances could change, and you might feel that I have become less helpful to you. If you ever feel like I am saying or doing something that is unhelpful, I hope we can have a conversation about that too.

Client: Certainly. I appreciate your willingness to acknowledge mistakes that may arise during our sessions. I'm glad we're having this conversation.

During the course of their discussion, the client admitted that initially, she had reservations about Selma's atheist identity and feared that Selma would devalue her belief system. The client noted that to her surprise, Selma was deeply curious about the client's religious worldview and effort to find meaning and purpose in life. The client confided that Selma taught her how to be more human. This discussion created a powerful turning point in the counseling relationship. Basically, the question about their differences prompted a deeper discussion about how the client grew to better appreciate Selma and how Selma helped the client become less judgmental, which was at the root of some aspects of the client's presenting concerns. Their conversation also reflected a broader dynamic of status differentials, with the client holding a dominant religious identity within a Christian-majority society, and Selma representing a minoritized religious identity.

Cultural Immediacy

By engaging the client in a dialogue about their differing religious worldviews, Selma modeled cultural immediacy. Essentially, cultural immediacy refers to the provider's proactive and timely exploration of the relationship dynamics that are shaped by the social identities and power relations of both the provider and client (Day-Vines et al., 2021). Rather than ignore how their respective cultural values and viewpoints influence the therapeutic relationship, the provider explored the manner in which their social locations or shared and different identity dimensions affect the counseling process in real time. The use of cultural immediacy deepened their personal connection, strengthened the therapeutic alliance, promoted mutual respect, trust, authenticity, and positive client outcomes.

Based on guidelines prescribed by the Multicultural and Social Justice Counseling Competencies (MSJCC; Ratts et al., 2016), the counselor maintains a marginalized status given her religious positionality as an atheist in a Christian-dominated society, and the client maintains a dominant religious status. Incidentally, despite growing secularism in the United States, anti-atheist prejudice remains prevalent (Rill, 2022). Within the intra-counseling broaching domain, Selma and her client discuss their respective religious identities. Selma appears self-aware about her own respective values and viewpoints, without appearing to impose them on the client, which is an important premise of effective multicultural counseling. Selma is deeply invested in helping her client explore her religious concerns and addresses their similarities and differences by naming them explicitly, given the sociopolitical nature of religion within common parlance. Inasmuch as Selma enlisted the intra-counseling broaching dimensions appropriately and effectively, there are instances in which this dimension can be used inappropriately.

Problematic Uses of Cultural Immediacy

Broaching individual differences between the provider and client alone can be problematic when broaching statements are delivered without a particular intention or purpose. Much like any counseling skill, the provider must determine what skill to use, why the particular skill is necessary, and how it will support the client. As the reader will recall from Chapter 3, the isolating provider interrupted Hernando's train of thought as the client talked about some of the challenges he experienced as a gay Latino male, to ask how the client felt about their shared and different identity dimensions. This statement was poorly timed and came across as random, inappropriate, and lacking a specific purpose or value for the client by bringing up issues of race and ethnicity when it was unrelated to the current counseling discussion in that moment. Essentially, the provider's question seemed more about the provider than the client.

Focusing exclusively on individual differences ignores structural realities associated with clients' REC concerns. Recall from Chapter 2 where Sarah, a recently licensed 25-year-old White provider who worked with a 60-year-old Asian man who recently lost his federal government job. Sarah had concerns about the age differential and whether she was qualified to work with this particular client. If her broaching efforts focus exclusively on generational differences between herself and her client, without consideration of how those differences impact the counseling process, then Sarah's broaching efforts center her own self-absorbed concerns and apprehensions without consideration of the interpersonal dynamics between herself and the client. Further, an emphasis on individual differences between the provider and client may preclude Sarah from examining intersectional structural dynamics that may impact the client's presenting concerns (e.g., ageism, classism, racism). In other words, Sarah may perpetuate colorblindness by minimizing or ignoring larger structural forces that impinge on the client's life and well-being.

Collecting Empirical Feedback from Clients

In addition to inviting clients to verbalize their reactions to the counseling process, providers can administer surveys that permit clients to assess the provider's broaching effectiveness. For instance, Day-Vines et al. (2024) developed the Broaching Attitudes and Behavior Survey – Client version to elicit client reactions about their counseling experience and assess their perceptions about the client's belief that providers have addressed the contextual dimensions of REC in counseling. The measure invites clients to assess where the provider operates along the broaching continuum (e.g., *avoidant*, *continuing/incongruent*, *integrated congruent*, *infusing*), whether the provider exhibits qualities like cultural humility, demonstrates openness in discussing the client's REC concerns, and/or exhibits an ease of manner connecting with clients. The measure also assesses whether providers exhibit ineffective broaching behaviors such as ruptures and microaggressions. Client feedback can help providers calibrate their broaching efforts in order to increase the depth and strength of the counseling relationship, deepen the provider's understanding of the client, and enhance broaching effectiveness.

Similarly, Depauw and Van Hiel (2024) developed a measure to assess clients' perceptions of their providers' broaching behavior. Respondents evaluate providers along four dimensions: (a) proactive, or the client's perception that the provider makes a concerted effort to explore client concerns related to REC; (b) insensitive, or the client's perception that the provider broaches ineffectively and draws on biases and stereotypes; (c) open, or the provider's effort to hint or insinuate that it is acceptable for the client to discuss their REC concerns; (d) wait-and-see, wherein the provider expects the client to initiate REC conversations; and, avoidant, or the provider's inattention to the client's REC concerns.

Accept Client Feedback

Whether you obtain verbal indicators about the client's experience of your counseling efforts or quantitative feedback, it is important to consider seriously the information the client shares, whether or not you agree with the feedback. All client feedback will not be positive. Providers do not broach intra-counseling dimensions to seek validation or have clients stroke their egos, but to gain clarity about how the counseling process is working for the client, in the event the provider needs to adjust their counseling approach. Providers have an obligation to listen to client feedback, validate the client's concerns, and address the sentiments associated with the feedback. Client reactions are important, and providers can use continuous improvement to both gauge counseling effectiveness and integrate client feedback into provider behavior. That means specifically that providers must process the client's feedback in a nondefensive manner. In instances where the provider is unable to process feedback in the moment, it makes sense to take time outside of the counseling dyad to consider what the client has communicated. Clinical supervision may help as supervisors function as sounding boards to support providers in their efforts to better understand what the client is trying to communicate (Jones & Branco, 2020). Journaling about the experience may also be helpful. Where appropriate, providers should address less positive feedback shared by the client in an effort to restore the counseling relationship.

Many scholars discuss the importance of obtaining and implementing continual feedback from clients (Day-Vines et al., 2020; Mesa-Buitrago et al., 2025). For instance, when I first started teaching counseling skills to master's-level students, I would use demonstration tapes that I made with mock clients, usually family members and close friends. I recall a counseling tape I made with my husband in order to demonstrate counseling strategies and techniques. At the conclusion of the demonstration tape, I asked my husband for feedback. In particular, I used cultural immediacy to inquire about any general and cultural concerns he wanted to discuss that I may have omitted. Like respondents in the Dunning (2011) study, I assumed (erroneously, I might add) my counseling efforts were outstanding. Much to my surprise, my husband said that we did not discuss how religion influenced his worldview. He was accurate in that I had not raised the question about the importance of religion to his presenting concerns. Given that at that juncture we had been married for nearly 20 years, it should have been obvious to me that religion was a salient part of his identity structure. Although I was embarrassed, I did not become defensive. I acknowledged that I had not integrated his religious values into our discussion. There are likely a number of reasons for that oversight. First, I did not make the connection between his presenting concern and religion. Second, I may have been so hyperaware of his religious convictions that I assumed religion was understood. Vieten and Lukoff (2022) assert that providers may feel uncomfortable addressing religious and spiritual concerns for a variety of reasons, especially if their own religious and spiritual development is lacking, they have had minimal training in religion and spirituality, and they were trained in institutions where multicultural training devoted more attention to issues of race and ethnicity than religion. In any case, instead of becoming defensive and making excuses for my omission of religion and spirituality in our counseling session, I acknowledged my oversight and the salience of religion in his life. I noted that during our follow-up session we could address the role of religion in shaping his responses to life's stressors. A defensive response may have come across as me not taking responsibility for my oversight. A non-response may have been alienating. The provider's acknowledgment of the oversight of clients' REC concerns prevents the client from losing respect for the provider or from feeling that their concerns are being minimized. This openness can help strengthen the counseling relationship.

Reduce the Power Imbalance

As I have stated previously, the provider wields the balance of power in the counseling relationship. It is important to neutralize the power imbalance through a number of strategies. Inviting the client to share feedback, especially about the REC dimensions of the counseling process, is one strategy for neutralizing the power imbalance because it amplifies the client's voice and gives them a more active role in the counseling process. The client has the opportunity to offer an honest appraisal of their counseling experience, which gives added assurance that their concerns will be taken seriously. This stance may differ from how clients have experienced previous counseling relationships where they remain in a subordinate position without an opportunity to discuss their REC concerns. Inviting clients to share their perspectives helps legitimize clients' perspectives and provides client autonomy that gives clients a say in their lives and lived experiences.

Self-Disclosure

Self-disclosure serves as another strategy for neutralizing the power imbalance between the provider and client. It involves the provider sharing information about their own experience in order to facilitate client self-understanding and to make the client feel less alone. By the time the client enters counseling, they have likely lost enormous amounts of objectivity, such that they may feel demoralized, voiceless, and like their problems will not end. Some clients may find it helpful when providers self-disclose their own encounters with life's challenges. Frequently, clients see providers as paragons of excellence who are immune to the vagaries of life. By engaging in self-disclosure, we acknowledge our own humanity, fallibility, and shortcomings, as well as resilience. Because the client discloses so much of themselves in the counseling process, it is important for us to share our concerns. I like to use the metaphor that within the counseling dyad, the client is sitting across from us butt naked and fully exposed, while we counsel, fully garbed in fur coats, hats, and gloves. Self-disclosure allows a modicum of reciprocity between the provider and client.

Trina is an Asian American doctoral student in a mental health discipline. She has experienced a number of challenges with her advisor. As her challenges have mounted, she sought counseling services from a clinical psychologist in the campus counseling center. As she shared her woes about her doctoral process, she disclosed her interest in a research agenda examining the experiences of sex-trafficked women from immigrant backgrounds. Trina's doctoral advisor has encouraged her to consider a more neutral topic because she lacks expertise in Trina's specific area of interest. Trina senses that her professor's objections to her dissertation topic are now laced with indifference and hostility. She feels dejected and not sure she can continue working with this particular professor. Trina felt that her advisor wanted her to select a more neutral topic without considering issues of race and representation, yet Trina felt convinced that this topic was part of her calling. In an effort to validate her concerns, Trina's provider surmised that they shared a number of parallels given her own doctoral journey. Trina's provider disclosed that during her doctoral program, she too felt mounting tension between herself and her advisor and was not sure she would be able to complete her doctorate under her advisor's supervision. As a result, the provider sought out a new advisor who recognized that her study would serve as a important contribution to the scholarly literature. Trina felt relieved and less alone with her provider's disclosures. Soon after that acknowledgment, the provider returned the focus to the client, careful not to impose her own values and viewpoints on Trina. The provider's intent was to provide reassurance to Trina. This discussion helped Trina feel closer to her therapist, reduced the power imbalance by fostering greater communication and trust, and modeled strategies for managing problem situations but leaving the final decision to the client.

Burning Question

Norma, am I obligated to broach my identities with clients?

It is important to remember that the provider is bound by confidentiality. This same requirement is not mandated of the client. In determining whether or what you are going to broach with clients, it is important to only share those identity domains that you are comfortable with and that you would not mind have repeated by the client. It's also important to share experiences that are relevant to the counseling process. Before a self-disclosure, you should ask yourself whether sharing this experience supports the client. It is important that providers not focus on their own encounters in ways that detract from the client's concerns or make the client feel that they must now provide emotional support for the provider. Consider your intentions for disclosing whatever identity domains you choose to share with the client. After a self-disclosure you want to return the focus back to the client. Culturally based self-disclosures model that discussions about REC are permissible within the safety of the counseling dyad.

Burning Question

Norma, when should I address intra-counseling dimensions with clients?

Although there is no consensus about timepoints in the counseling process when broaching is most beneficial. Fuertes et al. (2002) noted that experienced White psychologists in their study emphasized the importance of broaching early and consistently. Choi et al. (2015) noted that

> There is a growing consensus among experts in multicultural training that, especially when there are obvious cultural differences between a client and provider, it is the responsibility of the counselor to take the lead early – perhaps in the first session – to make a cultural broaching statement that introduces a discussion of how culture, race, and ethnicity might influence the ongoing work.
>
> (p.25)

More recently, Bayne and Branco (2018) interviewed African American therapists about their broaching behavior with clients. Some respondents reported broaching toward the beginning of the therapeutic relationship, others reported that they postponed broaching events until they became better acquainted with clients and could gauge the benefits of broaching, and still others reported uncertainty about initiating racialized discussions that prevented them from broaching at all. Be that as it may, a number of studies link the provider's broaching behavior to greater depth of client self-disclosure, symptom reduction, increased likelihood of returning for follow-up sessions, and provider credibility Day-Vines et al., 2024; (Fuertes et al., 2002; Hicks, 2026; Knox et al., 2003; Zhang & Burkard, 2008). With specific regard to intra-counseling broaching domains, think about your intentions for broaching. Be sure not to broach intra-counseling dimensions in the middle of the client's REC discussion, because it becomes more about you than about the client's experience. Sometimes, it is helpful to address this question at the beginning of a session when you have had a number of prior sessions where REC has been discussed and before getting into the content of the current session. At other times, it may be helpful to broach intra-counseling dimensions at the conclusion of the session so that it does not interfere with other content the client has discussed. Certainly, future research will help clarify this question.

Summary

The MMBB is a conceptual model for considering specific broaching contexts or foci that providers can use as they facilitate broaching discussions with clients. The model contains four dimensions: (a) *Intra-Counseling dynamics* or negotiation of interpersonal processes governing the provider–client relationship; (b) *Intra-Individual concerns* or the manner in which power, oppression, and privilege pervade several intersectional identity dimensions; (c) *Intra-REC* or sources of stress and/or support that arise between clients and their family or community members; and (d) *Inter-REC* or encounters with racism and discrimination. This chapter focused specifically on intra-counseling broaching dimensions and addressed the provider's effort to explore relational dynamics with the client by (a) building the therapeutic relationship so that the client feels safe and willing to discussing REC concerns; (b) communicating to clients that broaching discussions are permissible; (c) using cultural immediacy to elicit feedback from the client about cultural aspects of the counseling experience; (d) accepting client feedback nondefensively; and (e) reducing the power imbalance. Without deliberate efforts on the part of the provider, clients may assume that broaching discussions are not permissible.

Discussion Questions

1 Identify distinctions between immediacy and cultural immediacy.
2 Discuss factors that make it important for providers to facilitate broaching concerns between them.
3 Identify two to three of your social locations and discuss how they may impact your ability to broach and work effectively with clients who have different social locations.
4 Identify two to three of your social locations and discuss how they may impact your ability to broach and work effectively with clients who have shared social locations.

References

Bayne, H., & Branco, S. (2018). A phenomenological inquiry into counselor of color broaching experiences. *Journal of Counseling and Development, 96*, 75–85. https://doi-org.proxy1.library.jhu.edu/10.1002/jcad.12179

Boswell, N., Barghini, R., Bhatt-Mackin, S., Murray, A., Topor, D., Nakamura, A., Pellegrino, L., & Ruble, A.E. (2025). Repairing cultural ruptures in psychotherapy: Strategies to enhance the therapeutic alliance. *American Journal of Psychotherapy, 78*, 119–123.

Brawner, R., & Day-Vines, N.L. (2024). Invitational skills as a precursor to counselors' efforts to broach racial, ethnic, and cultural factors with clients. In K. Butler and A.S. Butler (Eds.), *Intersectionality: Becoming a culturally competent counselor* (pp.83–120). Cognella.

Brawner, R., Day-Vines, N.L., Gubara, S., Agorsor, C., Jackson, Z., Ran, T., & Caldwell, N. (2025). Perceptions of racial, ethnic, and cultural ruptures in counseling: A qualitative case study of a client from a minoritized background. *Journal of Counseling and Development, 103*, 484–495. https://doi-org.proxy1.library.jhu.edu/10.1002/jcad.70004

Cardemil, E., & Battle, C. (2003). Guess who's coming to therapy? Getting comfortable with conversations about race and ethnicity in therapy. *Professional Psychology: Research and Practice, 34*, 278–286.

Carter, R.T., & Pieterse, A.L. (2020). *Measuring the effects of racism: Guidelines for the assessment and treatment of race-based traumatic stress injury*. Columbia University.

Choi, G., Mallinckrodt, B., & Richardson, J.D. (2015). Effect of international student counselors' broaching statements about cultural and language differences on participants' perceptions of counselors. *Journal of Multicultural Counseling and Development, 43*, 25–37. https://doi-org.proxy1.library.jhu.edu/10.1002/j.2161-1912.2015.00062.x

Day-Vines, N.L., Cluxton-Keller, F., Agorsor, C., & Gubara, S. (2021). Strategies for broaching the subjects of race, ethnicity and culture. *Journal of Counseling and Development, 99*, 348–357. https://doi.org/10.1002/jcad.12380

Day-Vines, N.L., Cluxton-Keller, F., Agorsor, C., Gubara, S., & Otabil, N. (2020). The multidimensional model of broaching behavior. *Journal of Counseling and Development, 98,* 107–118. https://doi.org/10.1002/jcad.12304

Day-Vines, N.L., & Holcomb-McCoy, C. (2013). Broaching the subjects of race, ethnicity, and culture as a tool for addressing diversity in Counselor Education classes. In J. West, D. Bubenzer, J. Cox, & J. McGlothlin (Eds.), *Teaching in Counselor Education: Engaging students in meaningful learning* (pp. 151–166). Association for Counselor Education and Supervision.

Day-Vines, N.L., Wood, S., Grothaus, T., Craigen, L.,Holman, A., Dotson-Blake, K., & Douglass, M. (2007). Broaching the subjects of race, ethnicity, and culture during the counseling process. *Journal of Counseling and Development, 85,* 401–409. https://doi.org/10.1002/jcad.12069

Day-Vines, N.L., Zhang, J., Cluxton-Keller, F., Hicks, D., Jones, C.T., Spann, T., Daga, D., & Agorsor, C. (2024). An investigation of the construct validation of the broaching attitudes and behavior scale – clients. *Journal of Multicultural Counseling and Development*. https://doi.org/10.1002/jmcd.12300

Depauw, H., & Van Hiel, A. (2024). Uncovering patterns in perceived therapist behaviour: A xlatent profile analysis of broaching experiences among ethnic minority group member clients. *Clinical Psychology and Psychotherapy, 31*, e3067. https://doi.org/10.1002/cpp.3067

Dunning, D. (2011). The Dunning–Kruger effect: On being ignorant of one's own ignorance. *Advances in Experimental Social Psychology, 44*, 247–296. https://doi.org/10.1016/B978-0-12-385522-0.00005-6

Erby, A.N., & White, M.E. (2020). Broaching partially-shared identities: Critically interrogating power and intragroup dynamics in counseling practice with trans people of Color. *International Journal of Transgender Health, 23*(1–2), 122–132. https://doi-org.proxy1.library.jhu.edu/10.1080/26895269.2020.1838389

Fuertes, J.N., Mueller, L.N., Chauhan, R.V., Walker, J.A., & Ladany, N. (2002). An investigation of European American therapists' approach to counseling African American clients. *The Counseling Psychologist, 30*(5), 763–788. https://doi.org/10.1177/0011000002305007

Galán, C.A., Tung, I., Tabachnick, A.R., Sequeira, S.L., Novacek, D.M., Kahhale, I., Jamal-Orozco, N., Gonzalez, J.C., Bowdring, M.A., Boness, C.L., & Bekele, B.M. (2022). Combating the conspiracy of silence: Clinician recommendations for talking about racism-related events with youth of color. *Journal of the American Academy of Child and Adolescent Psychiatry, 61*(5), 586–590. https://doi.org/10.1016/j.jaac.2022.01.001

Grier, W.H., & Cobbs, P.M. (1968). *Black rage*. Basic Books.

Griffith, D.M., Bergner, E.M., Fair, A.S., & Wilkins, C.H. (2021). Using mistrust, distrust, and low trust precisely in medical care and medical research advances health equity. *American Journal of Preventive Medicine, 60*, 442–445. https://doi.org/10.1016/j.amepre.2020.08.019

Helms, J.E., & Cook, D.A. (1999). *Using race and culture in counseling and psychotherapy: Theory and process*. Allyn & Bacon.

Hicks, D. (2026). *Counselors' broaching skills influence on the mental health outcomes of chronically ill racial and ethnic minoritized clients: A serial moderated mediation model* [Unpublished doctoral dissertation]. The Ohio State University.

Hill, C.E. (2020). *Helping skills: Facilitating exploration, insight, and action*. American Psychological Association.

Jones, C.T., & Branco, S.F. (2020). The interconnectedness between cultural humility and broaching in clinical supervision: Working from the multicultural orientation framework. *The Clinical Supervisor, 39*(2), 198–209. https://doi-org.proxy1.library.jhu.edu/10.1080/07325223.2020.1830327

Jones, C.T., & Welfare, L.E. (2017). Broaching behaviors of licensed professional counselors: A qualitative inquiry. *Journal of Addictions & Offender Counseling, 38*(1), 48–64. https://doi-org.proxy1.library.jhu.edu/10.1002/jaoc.12028

Knox, S., Burkard, A.W., Suzuki, L.A., & Ponterotto, J.G. (2003). African American and European American therapists' experiences of addressing race and cross-racial psychotherapy dyads. *Journal of Counseling Psychology, 50*, 466–481.

Mesa-Buitrago, D., Cardemil, E.V., & Heberle, A.E. (2025). A critical-cultural-relational exploration of Latinx emerging adults' experiences of rupture. *Journal of Counseling Psychology*. https://doi.org/10.1037/cou0000842

Ratts, M.J., Singh, A.A., Nassar-McMillan, S., Butler, S.K., & McCullough, J.R. (2016). Multicultural and social justice counseling competencies: Guidelines for the counseling profession. *Journal of Multicultural Counseling and Development, 44*, 28–48. https://doi.org/10.1002/jmcd.12035

Rill, S.M. (September, 2022). Oppression against atheists. *The Elm: Voices and opinions*. https://elm.umaryland.edu/voices-and-opinions/2022/Oppression-Against-Atheists.php

Sadusky, A., Yared, H., Patrick, P., & Berger, E. (2024). A systematic review of client's perspectives on the cultural and racial awareness and responsiveness of mental health practitioners. *Culture and Psychology, 30*, 567–605. https://doi-org.proxy1.library.jhu.edu/10.1177/1354067X231115660

Schmidt, C.D. (2014). Integrating continuous client feedback into counselor education. *Journal of Counselor Preparation and Supervision, 6*(2). https://doi.org/10.7729/62.1094

Seligman, L. (2008). *Conceptual skills for mental health professionals*. Pearson.

Sue, D.W., Sue, D., Neville, H.A., & Smith, L. (2022). *Counseling the culturally diverse: Theory and practice* (9th ed.). Wiley.

Vieten, C., & Lukoff, D. (2022). Spiritual and religious competencies in psychology. *American Psychologist, 77*, 26–38. https://doi.org/10.1037/amp0000821

Walfish, S., McAlister, B., O'Donnell, P., & Lambert, M.J. (2012). An investigation of self-assessment bias in mental health providers. *Psychological Reports, 110*, 639–644. https://doi-org.proxy1.library.jhu.edu/10.2466/02.07.17.PR0.110.2.639-644

Zhang, N., & Burkard, A. (2008). Client and counselor discussions of racial and ethnic differences in counselling: An exploratory investigation. *Journal of Multicultural Counselling and Development, 36*, 77–87. https://doi.org/10.1002/j.2161-1912.2008.tb00072.x

Chapter 5

Intra-Individual Broaching Dimensions

The intra-individual broaching dimension refers to the provider's effort to explore the confluence of identity dimensions that are embedded within the client's presenting concerns. At the same time, the provider acknowledges how issues of power, oppression, and privilege shape identity dimensions in ways that may exacerbate psychological distress. All too often, providers zero in on a single identity domain of the client, such as their race or sexual orientation or immigration status, without exploring the client's experience more holistically. Attending to only a single domain or axis of the client's experience falsely implies that individuals within a particular demographic group experience the world identically. Such an approach minimizes the magnitude of the client's concerns (Day-Vines et al., 2020). When only recognizing marginalization the client encounters on the basis of, say, their disability status, the provider essentializes the client, as if the client's only challenge involves experiences related to disability, without attention to other forms of subordination and privilege that exacerbate disability concerns. Broaching the client's intra-individual dimensions permits the client to consider the extent to which issues of individual and systemic oppression are embedded in the client's presenting concerns.

To illustrate, Katrina – a Caribbean immigrant, who is a professional, gay, Black, female with a physical disability – navigates multiple interlocking sources of power, oppression, and privilege that exacerbate the discrimination she encounters above and beyond her disability. She uses a wheelchair on account of her degenerative bone disease and needs several accommodations including an accessible workspace, ergonomic seating so that she can transfer from her wheelchair to her seat, and wider pathways for restroom access. After six months of employment, Katrina contacted human resources, once again, to inquire about when she could expect the accommodations she needs in order to complete her work. The human resources officer brushed Katrina off as if she were being difficult. No matter how demure or assertive her demeanor, human resources personnel perceive Katrina's efforts to secure accommodations through negative tropes and stereotypes, such as the angry Black woman depiction and perpetual foreigner.

DOI: 10.4324/9781003649311-5

Because she speaks accented English as opposed to a standardized variety of English, Katrina experiences raciolinguistic oppression. Raciolinguistics is the practice of discriminating against an individual or group of individuals based on both their language and race (Rosa, 2019). Katrina's co-workers make subtle innuendos about her race, immigration status, and accented discourse style. During treatment, Katrina may withhold concerns about her sexual orientation until she can determine whether or not her provider is homophobic. Although Katrina is well-educated and her social class status should serve as a source of privilege, she constantly combats derogatory assumptions and resentment regarding her accomplishments. All too often co-workers treat her as an affirmative action baby. The cumulative impact of being multiply marginalized necessitates that providers consider the full complement of Katrina's multiple oppressions and not focus on a single domain of her experience if they intend to foster psychological safety, validation, personal empowerment, and healing.

Broaching clients' intra-individual dimensions or intersectional sources of oppression addresses how issues of race, class, gender, disability, nativism, and sexual orientation converge to create complex layers of marginalization that impact clients' lived realities (Collins, 2023). Such an orientation shifts the focus from addressing a single identity dimension at a time (e.g., disability or race) and considers the confluence of oppressive forces (e.g., race, class, gender, disability, and sexual orientation) that create obstacles for the client. To be clear, the specific identity domain is not the obstacle; however, the social hierarchies and the frequent maltreatment that result from having a particular identity domain create problematic experiences for the client. The fact that clients confront multiple sources of oppression suggests that oppressive forces may mirror each other in ways that compound harm and vulnerability. In other words, the oppression Katrina experiences on account of her disability is likely similar to the oppression she confronts on the basis of her race, gender, and sexual orientation. The combined effects of the individual oppressions serve as a debilitating weight that takes its toll on her well-being. Providers who facilitate conversations that recognize the cumulative effect of multiple oppressions on the clients' well-being are better poised to deliver culturally responsive care. Conversely, providers who have difficulty addressing clients' complex stressors may inhibit important conversations that preclude clients from gaining a greater sense of control over their lives.

As we discussed in Chapter 2, cultural concealment refers to instances in which clients choose not to share important aspects of their cultural identity with their provider. Presumably, this decision results from the fear of being judged or out of concern that the provider may withdraw emotional support. In any case, research indicates that cultural concealment is associated with less favorable treatment outcomes (Drinane et al., 2018). Based on these findings, clients like Katrina may refrain from discussing connections between her disability and the related challenges associated with her race, social class, gender, and sexual orientation due to concerns the provider may respond as dismissively as the human resources officer responded and construe her concerns as unwarranted or a figment of Katrina's imagination. A growing body of scholarship has documented the extent to which clients' disability experiences occur concurrently with other sources of marginalization.

Mireles (2022) examined the experiences of ethnic minority college students with disabilities and concluded that Asian students were treated more favorably when requesting disability services, compared to other students of color. In particular, Asian students were seen as more deserving of accommodations and less likely to be regarded as trying to take advantage of the system. Mireles speculated that Asian students may benefit from model minority myths, while students from other minoritized groups may be viewed from more deficit framings.

In the case of Katrina, there may be multiple explanations contributing to the delay in securing accommodations, including the fact that materials may be on back order. Given what we have learned about Katrina's current on-the-job experience, it is more than reasonable to consider also that the delay in meeting her requests for accommodations involves some level of conscious or unconscious bias. Within recent years, anti-immigrant bias has intensified precipitously in the United States, as has anti-Blackness. Anti-Blackness refers to society's inability to recognize the humanity of African Americans and reflects contempt that targets African Americans in an effort to valorize Whiteness (Ross, 2020). The dismantling of federal and corporate DEI programs, federal layoffs, budget cuts, structural inequality, etc. serves as examples. Between February and July, Black women lost 319,000 jobs, while White and Hispanic women saw an increase in 142,000 and 176,000 jobs, respectively, during the same time period (Green, 2025). Similar layoffs are also cycling through corporate America. Experts suggest that these actions may serve as a model for other employers (Green). Against this backdrop, Katrina's private college education may be seen through the prism of affirmative action, and if she exudes confidence, she may be deemed arrogant.

Additively, Bell and Hunter (2025) recommend that providers consider the racialized ableism that clients confront, such as stereotypes about both their disability and status as Black women who may be perceived as less deserving of accommodations, or less capable of high-performance levels given her disability. According to noted sociologist Bonilla-Silva (2021), the inability to acknowledge how race contributes to Katrina's dilemma represents a semantic tactic referred to as colorblind racial attitudes. Previous research indicates that providers who avoid or disregard the discussion of clients' REC concerns were more likely to endorse items indicating that race is unnecessary in the counseling arena, on a measure assessing providers' openness to discussing clients' REC concerns (Day-Vines et al., 2013). Similarly, clients who completed a measure about their providers' broaching efforts and who also perceived their providers as avoidant reported that their providers missed opportunities to discuss their REC concerns and engaged in ruptures and microaggressions

(Day-Vines et al., 2024). An emerging body of research suggests that clients who reported one salient identity were more likely to report that their provider demonstrated cultural humility and that they experienced improvement in therapy (Anders & Kivlighan, 2023).

The successful provider will need to broach the complex interplay between issues of race, class, gender, national origin, linguistics, sexual orientation, and ableism and the combined impact that each of these identity domains pose to Katrina's sense of well-being. The provider must also be mindful not to privilege one identity domain over another and should instead focus on those identity dimensions and sources of oppression that are most salient to the client (Bell & Hunter, 2025). In other words, the provider cannot emphasize the client's encounters with ableism while simultaneously minimizing or dismissing how issues of race, gender, class, immigration status, and sexual orientation impinge on her encounters with ableism.

As we discussed in Chapter 3, providers are sometimes more comfortable discussing some topics versus others. For instance, a provider may feel more comfortable discussing sexual orientation versus race, or gender versus disability status. Focusing on topics that place the provider at ease centers the provider's needs more so than the client's needs. Emphasis on counseling topics that the provider feels more comfortable addressing prevents the client from focusing on their most salient counseling concerns. Moreover, centering the provider's needs to the exclusion of the client's needs erodes trust, reinforces the provider–client power imbalance, perpetuates systemic oppression by silencing the client, signals that such topics are not relevant for counseling, and negatively impacts treatment effectiveness. Disability-affirming care implies that providers must integrate and synthesize each of the client's salient identity domains into the treatment process, in ways that acknowledge multiple sources of strength and marginalization. Regrettably, a paucity of scholarship considers disability and its connection to other systems of oppression (Bell & Hunter, 2025; Shin et al., 2017). The intra-individual broaching dimensions draw heavily on the groundbreaking work of Kimberle Crenshaw (1989) in an effort to examine the client's encounters with individual and systemic oppression.

Background Information about Intersectionality

Kimberle Crenshaw (1989) coined the term intersectionality in response to a legal case involving five Black women who filed a discrimination lawsuit against General Motors. The court dismissed the lawsuit, noting that the plaintiffs did not defend their case sufficiently given that General Motors had actually hired both Blacks and women. Crenshaw insisted that when addressing racial discrimination, the company centered the interests of Black men. Similarly, when addressing gender discrimination, the company centered the interests of White women. The focus on Black men and White women clearly excluded

Black women. Crenshaw argued that focusing on single-axis concerns such as gender or race left other sources of marginalization unexamined, which resulted in a biased legal decision. In the case of General Motors, the bias targeted Black women, primarily because Black women experienced both race and gender discrimination.

Essentially, intersectionality is more than the sum total of people's identities and more accurately encompasses multiple oppressions. Frequently, providers focus on client traits or descriptive characteristics (e.g., race, gender, class, religion) without considering the dynamic interaction between these identities and the way power structures contribute to clients' experiences with inequality and marginalization. Simply noting that Katrina is a gay, Black, female with a disability reveals her social identity without attending to how she confronts homophobia, racism, and ableism as a routine part of her life. Intersectionality theory insists that providers take into consideration oppressive systems that render clients' lives unnecessarily difficult. Since Crenshaw's groundbreaking theorizing, intersectionality has been applied to a number of disciplines, including counseling, psychology, social work, and psychiatry (Shin et al., 2017). In the context of counseling, providers cannot ignore the multifaceted needs of clients. They must do their best to examine the plurality of clients' concerns and experiences with oppression; otherwise, clients' mental health needs may remain unmet.

Broaching the client's intra-individual dimensions, then, positions providers to address clients' intersectional concerns and experiences, or the manner in which issues of power, oppression, and privilege pervade clients' sociopolitical, sociocultural, and sociohistorical realities. Notably, the client's identity status is comprised of multiple overlapping identities that include sources of power and privilege that contribute to the client's worldview and encounters with oppression (Crenshaw, 1989; Ratts et al., 2016).

Intersectionality as Lived Reality

Frequently, providers oversimplify the notion of intersectionality and mistakenly assume that intersectionality refers to multiple identity domains. Intersectionality does in fact involve multiple identity domains; however, this interpretation is only partially correct. A more fulsome definition of intersectionality acknowledges how issues of power, oppression, and privilege shape the client's presenting concerns. For instance, when I am teaching, I disclose my own intersectional realities by revealing several of my intersecting identities involving sources of both privilege and marginalization. I note that if you ask me what it's like to be a professor, that's one answer that involves a generic description of the roles and responsibilities academics perform in a university setting. Emphasizing identity from a role function perspective implies a modicum of privilege; however, if you contextualize the question by asking me what it's like to be an African American professor, that's a second answer that has a decidedly different answer. Although the response captures the essence of academic life, it also reflects how issues of race and representation shape my experiential reality within the academy. To illustrate, early in my career, students would ask if they could call me by my first name because I was young. They were often put off when I established boundaries and said no because it felt disrespectful, contemptuous, and condescending, especially since they routinely referred to older White male professors by their professional titles. Often, I would provide a detailed explanation about honorifics within African American culture, as well as the historical context in which Black women, no matter how old or accomplished, were not accorded the respect of a title. In fact, using Black women's first names functioned as a means of putting Black women in their place – an effort to reify social hierarchies and status differentials (Collins, 2022; Cooper, 2018; hooks, 1981). In fact, even having to provide a rationale for a boundary operates as a source of oppression. In any case, if you ask me what it's like to be an African American female professor, that's a third answer that reflects gendered and racialized ways African American females are expected to remain impervious to racist, sexist attacks by not expressing strong truths and opinions that may upset White counterparts, for fear of being seen as arrogant, difficult, aggressive, or woke. Being resolute and standing tall in my African American pride and commitment to social justice (for all groups, not just my own) is often interpreted as threatening and has been costly. If you ask me what it's like to be an African American female professor that is married and actively parenting, that's a fourth answer. As a new mother more than 20 years ago, I worried that if I talked too much about the birth of my daughter and the abundant joy she brought my husband and me, I might not be taken seriously as an academic. Being perceived as more concerned with parenthood than academia might in turn jeopardize prospects for tenure.

If you asked me what it's like to be an African American female professor who is actively parenting, wife-turned-widow, that's a fifth answer that taps into the gravity of managing my own grief while simultaneously navigating the pervasive sense of loss and abandonment experienced by a teenager who was fiercely devoted to her loving father. All this in addition to sustaining a career. In a counseling setting, each context would require cultural attunement to various sources of power, privilege, marginalization, and resilience. A provider's inability to engage with any of these intersections with an abiding sense of social consciousness, cultural curiosity, or compassion would render the counseling session superficial at best, and harmful at worst. Inattention to my specific worldview would minimize the complexity of my experience as well as the cumulative impact of systemic forces of oppression that shape my well-being and identity development – ultimately eroding my experience of psychological safety within the counseling dyad. The next section of this chapter provides contextual information about intersectionality theory.

Counseling Considerations Regarding Intersectionality

Shin et al. (2017) conducted a content analysis of 40 articles in leading counseling psychology journals that addressed intersectionality with clients. They classified intersectionality scholarship along three dimensions: (a) weak, (b) strong, and (c) transformational. Weak intersectional scholarship merely incorporated various demographic categories without considering larger systemic issues associated with inequality. A provider engaged in weak intersectional approaches makes no mention of power or oppression encountered by the client and does not consider the combined effects of multiple sources of oppression. Nearly two thirds of articles in the study were classified as weak.

Strong intersectionality considers the client's multiple social identities as co-constitutive systems of power and privilege that can undermine psychological well-being. Shockingly, only eight of the 40 articles were characterized as strong. Transformative intersectionality examines clients' exposure to multiple oppressions and their connection to structural inequality and involves the provider's commitment to social justice action in order to dismantle systems of oppression. Only four articles contained content that endorsed transformative intersectionality.

Xiong et al.'s (2022) research incorporates transformational intersectionality. They recognized the specific challenges encountered by international students related to acculturative stress, language, lack of social support, immigration challenges, safety concerns, as well as encounters with racism and discrimination. To combat the obstacles students encountered, they implemented a successful mindfulness support group to reduce stress, anxiety, and depression. At a minimum, providers should be committed to exhibiting strong intersectionality with their clients, with aspirations of achieving transformational intersectionality.

In Chapter 8, readers will be introduced to a heuristic device that facilitates the identification of intersectional identity domains that providers can explore with clients – RESPECTFUL model (D'Andrea & Daniels, 2001). This framework contains ten specific multicultural areas of consideration that help providers determine specific identity domains that may be relevant for the client. This holistic framework helps providers assess sources of support and identify oppressive forces that influence clients' lived realities and can be used as a point of departure for engaging in broaching discussions. Providers can consider the following identity domains: religious and spiritual, economic/class background, sexual/gender, psychological maturity, ethnic-racial, chronological development, threats to one's well-being, family background history, unique physical characteristics, location of residence, and language differences. These domains help providers understand the client's worldview. The section that follows provides a dialogue between Katrina and her provider.

Counseling Dialogue

Provider: Thank you for sharing these challenges with me. Based on our discussion last week, you have been balancing a lot of personal stressors, and I want to acknowledge the weight you are carrying.

Katrina: Yes, it's been very difficult.

Provider: Hmm-mm (*uses a head nod and silence to allow the client to continue talking*).

Katrina: I don't even know where to start. It just seems so overwhelming. I'm wrangling with human resources to get the accommodations I need in order to do my job effectively. My wheelchair is too wide for me to access my office. This is clearly a violation of the Americans with Disabilities Act, but each time I reach out to human resources, they say they have put in a work order, and I should just use the conference room for now. The conference room can work as long as no other meetings are scheduled for that room. But using the conference room, is an imposition because if it is in use, I have nowhere to really work. Also, I requested these accommodations almost six months ago. My requests are not unreasonable, but they act like I'm a nuisance. I'm only asking for resources I'm entitled to by law.

Provider: Although getting accommodations has been a struggle, it seems that the lack of validation, dignity, and respect you experience concerning your disability is also hurtful.

Katrina: Absolutely. I see their quiet exasperation when I come into the office. They make some patronizing comments about how hard they are trying to meet my needs, and it just seems disingenuous. Really, it seems like gaslighting to me.

Provider: Hmm-mm (*uses silence again to allow the client to continue talking*).

Katrina: They exchange furtive glances with each other and give excuses about why things have not been taken care of yet. They definitely are not prioritizing my needs.

Provider: What emotions come up for you when you observe your co-workers' behavior?

Katrina: (*shaking her head*) Just sheer exhaustion from constantly having to defend myself and not being able to trust that I will get what I'm supposed to get. Righteous indignation. Feelings of invisibility. Frustration with my manager who observes exactly what is happening to me but is more concerned about not alienating the higher-ups or the clerks in HR than addressing a real injustice.

Provider: As I listen to you, I hear the sense of pain and abandonment you have experienced. I realize there's more to this issue than just accommodations. This is also about invisibility and lack of belonging. It seems you navigate the workplace as someone with multiple marginalized identities – as a highly accomplished Black woman from the Caribbean who speaks accented English, is gay, and has a physical disability. If you're comfortable sharing your experience, I think it would be helpful to hear your thoughts about how these dynamics contribute to some of the challenges you experience at work.

Katrina: Well, that's a great point. Thank you for asking. Sometimes I feel like a unicorn because I am so different from everyone else. This company is definitely not accustomed to dealing with people like me. In fact, I have not even disclosed my sexuality because I feel my co-workers are not ready for that. I believe that although I have cordial relations with the people on my job, I sense that sometimes the employees that report to me have difficulty taking directives from a Black woman, especially someone from the Caribbean. They will often ask me to repeat what I'm saying, as if they don't understand my accent. They second guess my requests and will sometimes say things like, "Are you sure?" I find that behavior utterly disrespectful. I contribute enormously to the success of this company. My metrics are stellar, and I know for a fact that I make less than several of my colleagues even though I have more education and experience than many of them. Some days I feel like I am going to break even though I put up a tough veneer.

Provider: At every turn you face push back. It must be exhausting to constantly have to prove yourself. You are experiencing multiple forms of oppression. As a Black woman working in a managerial position some of your employees question your authority. They treat you in a condescending manner which seems to be related to your differences. You're also underpaid and not getting the support you expected from human resources. Whether intentional or not, you find these multiple forms of bias are taking their toll on you. You are approaching a breaking point.

Katrina: Absolutely. That's why I thought it was important to start counseling now. I don't know how much more I can take.

Provider: Perhaps, part of the difficulty may be that your work environment does not feel psychologically safe, yet despite the obstacles you face, you continue to show up as a leader.

Katrina: Thank you for acknowledging that. I get very little recognition for my efforts.

Provider: You are quite welcome. In our next session, how do you feel about continuing this discussion about racialized stress and the multiple oppressions that you experience?

Case Analysis

Integration of Broaching Strategies and Counseling Techniques

In order to center the client's specific and unique REC contexts, the provider integrated broaching strategies with important counseling techniques. The provider both elicited information about the basis of Katrina's concerns and accepted her narrative as legitimate, without requiring her to justify her perceptions. This helped Katrina feel heard and understood without having to respond from a defensive stance. As a consequence, Katrina poured out her difficulties at a deeper emotional level. In particular, the provider acknowledged Katrina's difficulty securing accommodations, the dismissive demeaner of human resources personnel, the ostracism she experiences from her co-workers and direct reports, her sense of pain and humiliation, especially having her decisions questioned by direct reports, and the fact that she is highly qualified yet underpaid.

Throughout the session, the provider integrated broaching techniques with foundational counseling strategies. As the excerpt continues, the provider validated Katrina's concerns using interpretation. Essentially, interpretation involves the provider's effort to move beyond the client's stated concerns and address certain unstated and underlying concerns. For instance, although Katrina initially described her effort to secure accommodations, she also indicated that the company has violated her disability rights. She senses that human resources personnel may be annoyed because she is persistent about her needs. The provider has listened perceptively to Katrina and recognizes that accommodations may be the safest, most concrete concern for her to address, even as there seem to be underlying concerns that warrant consideration. In the absence of some type of update or explanatory rationale from human resources about the lack of resources, the provider reframes the lack of accommodations as a possible form of disrespect and personal invalidation. The provider's tenor was direct and explicit and moved beyond Katrina's access to disability services. The provider's comment pinpointed the consequences of not having adequate materials to perform her job, such as an increasing sense of self-doubt, an erosion of confidence, and at the extreme, Katrina's compromised sense of mental wellness, and the increased likelihood of conditions like depression and anxiety. It seems the provider recognized that like many women of color, Katrina vacillates between hypervisibility or being under constant surveillance by co-workers who question her competence, and hyper-invisibility, such that her essential needs remain ignored. Katrina signaled her agreement with the provider's assessment by saying, "Absolutely." As a result of feeling heard and understood, Katrina provided an explicit example of the disrespect she experiences by referencing what she sensed as inauthentic efforts to help her secure needed resources. Katrina specifically described feelings of manipulation by noting that she considered human resource responses to her request as a form of gaslighting.

Burning Question

Norma, what if I make an interpretation about the client's experience that is inaccurate?

Frequently when a provider offers an inaccurate interpretation, the client may point out how the provider's interpretation differs from the client's interpretation. That clarification provides added understanding for both the provider and client. For this reason, it is helpful to offer tentative interpretations that permit the client to adjust the interpretation. Following an interpretation, check in with your client to gauge whether the client agrees with the interpretation. In instances where the client may see the issue differently, invite the client to provide alternative interpretations. Listen for opportunities to restate your understanding of the revised interpretation. In instances when you want to explore the client's concern at a deeper level, but may not have identified a relevant interpretation, it may be helpful to use an open question for interpretation. This technique permits the client to offer her own assessment about what may be going on.

As the session continued, the provider used silence to encourage Katrina to keep talking in order to process her thoughts more thoroughly. The silence permitted Katrina to continue her train of thought without interruption. Notably, the provider did not give advice, which can be especially tempting for novice providers who sometimes experience difficulty resisting the impulse to offer suggestions. Providers who lack a sense of comfort or an ease of manner with clients, especially minoritized clients, may be inclined to talk excessively by giving advice or engaging in unnecessary chatter to camouflage their limited efficacy levels. The provider's attention to her own behavior and the impact it may have on clients is especially warranted because unsolicited advice may be inconsistent with Katrina's needs, core values, or self-understandings, not to mention principles of culturally responsive counseling. Essentially, the provider's recommendations may not work for reasons known principally to the client. It is important for providers to understand the magnitude of the client's presenting problems by engaging in unhurried reflection and by leading with a sense of curiosity.

During the dialogue, the provider did not bombard Katrina with questions. In fact, questions were appropriately spaced, and the provider used them sparingly. She asked an open question for feelings and a question about possible directions for follow-up counseling sessions. Sometimes, novice providers ask questions as the default counseling technique. Such questions derail the client's train of thought; however, listening for understanding allows the provider to organize their understanding of the client's central concerns without interruptions. The provider should not commandeer the conversation, by posing questions the client will eventually answer in their own time and at their own pace. In fact, much of the information we acquire as providers is revealed to us in a nonlinear manner. It is through the process of deep listening that we work to understand the client, reflect what we heard the client say, and check for understanding.

During the session, the provider used an open question for feeling to elicit information about Katrina's perception of her co-workers' behavior. Katrina described feelings of anger, marginalization, exhaustion, and resentment, especially given that her boss has observed many of these troubling dynamics but remains conspicuously silent for fear of turning off other employees in the organization. Afterward, the provider reflected those feelings back to Katrina and then broached the client's REC concerns by asking her to describe her social location as a gay, Black female from the Caribbean who speaks accented English and has a disability. Before answering the question, Katrina acknowledged how appreciative she was that the provider was open to exploring her intersectional identities, which helped her feel validated. Katrina continued by noting the sense of alienation she experiences and discussed the ostracism and second-guessing she encounters on a routine basis at work. She described working incredibly hard but making less money than her peers. She also confided that she feels like she's at her breaking point.

Recognizing that several of Katrina's dilemmas may be related to issues of power, oppression, and privilege, the provider broached the client's intersectional identities by inviting her to describe her social locations. In particular, she said,

> You navigate the workplace as someone with multiple marginalized identities – as a highly accomplished Black woman from the Caribbean who speaks accented English, is gay, and has a physical disability. If you're comfortable sharing your experience, I would like to hear your thoughts about how these dynamics contribute to some of the challenges you experience.

The provider perceptively acknowledges that Katrina's concerns are deeper than just not receiving accommodations and may be related to her unique identity status. The provider used an intersectional approach to invite Katrina to talk about how her multiple identities impact her experience. Importantly, the provider communicated that Katrina should only share information that she feels comfortable divulging. This gives Katrina a sense of autonomy and choice in determining what she will share. The provider's request is not coercive and consequently leaves Katrina with a sense of personal agency, reduces the power imbalance, and facilitates trust. Additionally, the provider has normalized REC discussions as integral to the counseling process and the client's sense of psychological safety. The provider's effort to invite REC discussions is especially warranted given that as a society, we are in the throes of a highly contentious political climate in which many of the gains of the civil rights movement have been dialed back considerably. On a routine basis, the country witnesses deep partisan division and backlash against immigrants, DEI, sexual minorities, ethnic minorities, environmental and climate groups, etc. Each setback perpetuates debilitating forms of vicarious trauma for clients who are members of targeted groups and who navigate their own personal concerns in conjunction with societal realities.

Several years ago, in the immediate aftermath of the George Floyd murder, I was conducting a program evaluation for a private independent school that was concerned about growing campus tensions and missteps that had very flagrant racial overtones. One of the focus group sessions I conducted included a group of African American parents who reported that the day after Floyd's murder, African American students returned to class, and no one bothered to check in with them and inquire about how they may have experienced George Floyd's death. The video loop, which showed an unarmed African American civilian, pleading for his life as he lay prostrate with his hands cuffed tightly behind his back on a Minneapolis street corner, left many of the African American students emotionally jarred. Former police officer Derek Chauvin disregarded Floyd's pleas for air, while nonchalantly positioning his knee on Floyd's lifeless neck for more than nine minutes. The visual of Floyd's murder looped in constant rotation on television as well as multiple social media platforms. Parents were disturbed and dismayed that teachers did not think to inquire about how the young men may have been impacted. Teachers conducted business as usual in ways that left the young men reeling emotionally. Inattention to their pain was insensitive. Each replay of the murder seared an unforgettable memory in their mind's eye.

Much has been written about vicarious trauma, which results from not necessarily experiencing an emotionally jarring situation but witnessing events or hearing about events that are on constant loop in the media, prompting individuals to perseverate over the fact that it could have been them. Culturally responsive counseling necessitates that providers, at the very least, acknowledge what is going on for clients. This is particularly important for clients from nonwestern cultures where the psychosocial unit of measurement is the community and not necessarily the individual client. In other words, the needs of the collective take precedence over the needs of the individual, and feeling deeply for group members takes on personal significance. In future sessions, the provider may consider inquiring about any connections between what is going on in society and how it impacts Katrina's personal and professional life.

During the session, the provider used the positive asset search to acknowledge Katrina's strengths as a leader who persists despite the vast number of work-related struggles she encounters. This statement acknowledged how Katrina was able to manage despite working under difficult, if not toxic, circumstances. The provider engaged in realistic optimism by acknowledging the client's resilience in a hostile work environment without minimizing or avoiding the magnitude of racialized stress Katrina experiences. Ostensibly, the provider remained attuned to the client's affective state and maintained a hopeful outlook. One caveat, however. The positive asset search can sometimes function as a double-edged sword. Inasmuch as persistence operates as a necessary client strength, persisting in a toxic work environment could be detrimental to Katrina's health and well-being and demonstrate a form of false optimism. Providers who feel compelled to put a positive spin on Katrina's difficulties despite the structural oppression she faces, yet ignore the immediate structural challenges she confronts, may not prepare Katrina to strategize and move forward. False optimism does not position Katrina to face her challenges and may in fact promote harm. When identifying client strengths, it is imperative that providers refrain from reinforcing problematic coping styles and attributes that can exacerbate problem situations, which may leave the client ill-equipped to take action.

Future Directions with Katrina

Much has been written about strong Black woman phenomenon, which refers to the notion that in the face of enormous individual and structural oppression, many Black women exude unrelenting strength and resilience, suppress strong emotions, and resist being vulnerable or dependent in order to succeed. Such a stance may be detrimental to client well-being (Graham et al., 2022; Jones & Shorter-Gooden, 2025; Villarosa, 2022). In this vein, persevering in a toxic work environment may take its toll on Katrina's mental and physical health and place her at risk of burnout. For instance, internalizing discriminatory treatment without identifying support systems and advocacy efforts may lead to self-doubt and internalized oppression, such as Katrina's belief that she has contributed to her own problems. Cumulative exposure to racialized stress and other forms of marginalization contribute to weathering.

Arline Geronimus (2024) coined the term weathering to describe the health consequences of prolonged exposure to racialized stress. The term weathering is a double entendre that aptly captures the dictionary definition of weathering both as a means of withstanding colossal forms of oppression, and weathering as a form of physical deterioration. In humans, severe health consequences result from chronic exposure to stress, systemic racism, and marginalization. Unrelenting forms of racialized stress damage the nervous system and put the body in a perpetual state of flight-or-flight. Flight-or-flight modes were intended to occur infrequently; however, for some individuals like Katrina, the flight-or-flight response may activate at regular intervals. Exposure to chronic stress, as well as social and economic inequities, accelerates biological aging such that individuals become physiologically old at a young age, as evidenced by chronic diseases such as hypertension, diabetes, cancer, and weakened immune systems. African Americans and other minoritized group members are especially susceptible to weathering (Villarosa, 2022). The consequence of which is premature death. Future sessions with Katrina should consider the impact of weathering on her social, psychological, and physiological health.

The provider's broaching efforts should be intentional and deliberate, focused on the specific and unique cultural needs of the client. Notice that during the dialogue, the provider did not launch directly into a broaching statement. Instead, the provider sequenced her broaching efforts by gathering information about Katrina's specific situation, listening attentively, validating her experience, reflecting content and feeling, organizing her thoughts, and hypothesizing that the client's presenting concerns may be shaped by intersectional encounters with power, oppression, and privilege, before inviting Katrina to describe how her intersectional identities influenced the struggles she was currently experiencing. This approach toward exploring clients' REC concerns is consistent with *integrated/congruent* providers operating along the *Continuum of Broaching Behavior*, whose orientation toward broaching involves consideration of the client's specific and unique REC circumstances. On the other hand, *avoidant* providers, or those individuals who believe that discussing the contextual dimensions of REC have little relevance to the client's presenting concerns, would likely focus their attention on the difficulty Katrina has experienced securing accommodations. Avoidant providers may dissuade Katrina from identifying the relationship between her intersectional sources of power, oppression, and oppression and inquire about other interpretations of her presenting concerns.

Clinical psychologist Rheeda Walker (2024), author of *No Racial Elephants in the Therapy Room: An Unapologetic Approach to Providing Culturally Affirming Mental Health Care to Black and African American Clients*, contends that redirecting the client away from discussions about individual and systemic mistreatment dismisses the client's legitimate reality. Similarly, David Archer (2021), author of *Anti-Racist Psychotherapy, Confronting Racism and Healing Racial Trauma*, contends that dismissing clients' encounters with racism and discrimination functions as a form of gaslighting and contributes to racial and psychological violence. Archer also asserted that violence does not have to be physical to result in harmful consequences. Be that as it may, there may be clients for whom REC discussions are not relevant to their counseling needs and preferences, as we described in an earlier chapter. In that case, we would not force clients to address REC concerns if they do not see them as germane to their presenting concerns.

During the session, Katrina disclosed that she has not yet divulged her sexual orientation because the workplace does not seem psychologically safe enough for such a disclosure. Even though her sexual orientation may not surface as a work-related concern, it warrants discussion in the context of counseling more generally. In subsequent counseling sessions, the provider may also want to explore how Katrina navigates her sexual orientation outside work, whether she has found a support system within the gay community, and the impact of her race, gender, disability, and sexual orientation within the gay community. The provider may also want to explore Katrina's mechanisms of support within both the Caribbean and/or African American communities. For instance, does she feel a sense of belonging within Caribbean and/or African American communities, or does she feel a similar sense of exclusion from her own cultural groups that she experiences in her workplace, such that she is permitted to express her racial and ethnic identity but not her sexual orientation? The provider may also want to explore other sources of support such as religious and spiritual connections, especially since traditionally the Black church has been less receptive to sexual minorities. Determining whether Katrina meets her religious and spiritual needs through organized religion, connecting to the natural world, meditation and mindfulness, connecting with others, and the extent to which these practices sustain her seems important. The provider may also want to explore Katrina's sense of self-acceptance and pride in her identity as a gay, Black, Caribbean woman with a disability.

Understanding Katrina at a deep structural level is relevant to broaching clients' REC concerns. This includes understanding the client's individual and collective experience with oppression. Frequently, there is a tendency to regard African origin people as monolithic entities without attention to their similar and distinctive experiences. Although African, Caribbean, and descendants of enslaved people have shared experiences around oppression, colonialism, and African ancestry, they also have very distinctive racial-ethnic experiences (Collins, 2023). Many Caribbean Blacks are misconstrued as African American, although they identify strongly with their ethnic background or country of origin. Understanding the client's specific historical context is important (Mullan, 2023). Katrina's providers need foundational knowledge of how historical and cultural trauma, combined with her contemporary experiences, affect her well-being.

When I teach, I find that sometimes students believe that historical information about the client is optional. That puzzles me. When patients visit a doctor, the medical staff routinely gather information about the patient's medical history in order to better understand the patient's risk for disease and ascertain what medical issues clients and their families have dealt with previously. Understanding the patient's health history better positions the doctor to comprehend root causes of medical issues and deliver more effective treatment.

Similarly, when people take their car in for maintenance, the mechanic will often document the car's past history of services, repairs, and accidents that are stored in a central repository that helps future buyers determine whether they want to invest in the car. Similarly, providers must understand the client's history in order to better understand how past events shape the client's presenting concerns. This includes understanding cultural values, vocabularies of distress, and biopsychosocial background. The provider closes the session by inquiring about continuing subsequent sessions with a discussion of Katrina's intersectional concerns. In this way, the provider is extending the discussion without engaging in premature problem-solving.

In light of the foregoing discussion, there is more than enough fodder for the provider to facilitate meaningful dialogue with the client. Effective counseling requires a nuanced understanding of multiple identities and sources of oppression that the client navigates. Providers must have foundational information about culture-specific concerns that clients confront and be willing to understand, recognize, and explore the client's experience, sociopolitical realities, and vocabularies of distress. For instance, the provider may explore a dynamic referred to as "strong Black woman phenomena," which results in clients feeling that they have to possess enormous strength and they cannot demonstrate any vulnerability for fear of being seen as weak (Graham et al., 2022). The provider may want to explore the extent to which the client feels pressure to maintain these unreasonably high expectations. The provider may also want to explore the physical and emotional consequences of maintaining a "tough veneer," as Katrina put it. That may also involve helping Katrina navigate the controlling images that accompany the strong Black woman trope.

In the current political climate, where democracy is teetering on the brink of collapse, the provider may want to explore how the client is faring in the current political climate, especially since many individuals from marginalized groups seem to be under attack. In light of the fact that more than 300,000 Black women lost their jobs since January 2025, Katrina may want to explore job security, the racial climate, etc. Additionally, the provider may want to examine the systems of support that help sustain Katrina. For some Black women, family, friendship, and religious connections may provide emotional sustenance.

Summary

The intra-individual broaching dimension refers to the provider's consideration of the client's intersectional identity domains. Far too often, there is a tendency to focus on clients' singular identity dimensions, such as race or gender. Intersectionality emphasizes the interconnected systems and power systems that impact clients' lives (Crenshaw, 1989). That is, clients seldom have single-axis concerns. Providers working with multiply marginalized individuals must consider the unique combinations that clients experience. The RESPECTFUL model outlines ten specific identity dimensions that providers can use to better understand their clients and facilitate more meaningful broaching discussions (D'Andrea & Daniels, 2001). Effective broaching behaviors include the integration of foundational counseling skills with broaching efforts to name and explore interconnectedness between multiple sources of oppression.

Discussion Questions

1 What intersectional identity topics might you want to broach with Katrina?
2 What are your salient intersectional identities, and how might they interface with Katrina's intersectional identities?
3 Generate a broaching dialogue that you might facilitate in a follow-up session with Katrina.
4 How prepared do you feel to broach Katrina's intersectinal identity domains?

References

Anders, C., & Kivlighan, D.M. (2023). Salience: An intersectional approach to understanding cultural processes and outcomes in psychotherapy. *Journal of Counseling Psychology, 70*, 477–485. https://doi.org/10.1037/cou0000688

Archer, D. (2021). Anti-racist psychotherapy: Confronting systemic racism and healing racial trauma. Each One Teach One Publications.

Bell, T.R., & Hunter, T. (2025). Black, disabled, and Gay: A pragmatic approach to counseling clients at multiple intersections. *Journal of Multicultural Counseling and Development, 53*, 161–168. https://doi-org.proxy1.library.jhu.edu/10.1002/jmcd.12322

Bonilla-Silva, E. (2021). *Racism without racists: Color-blind racism and the persistence of racial inequality in America* (6th ed.). Rowman & Littlefield.

Collins, L.H. (2023). *Overlooked: Counselor insights for the unspoken issues in Black American life*. Rowman and Littlefield.

Collins, P.H. (2022). *Black feminist thought: Knowledge, consciousness, and the politics of empowerment* (30th anniversary ed.). Routledge.

Cooper, B. (2018). *Eloquent rage: A Black feminist discovers her superpower*. St. Martin's Press.

Crenshaw, K. (1989). Demarginalizing the intersection of race and sex: A Black feminist critique of antidiscrimination doctrine, feminist theory and antiracist politics. *University of Chicago Legal Forum, 1989*, 139–167.

D'Andrea, M., & Daniels, J. (2001). RESPECTFUL counseling: An integrative model for counselors. In D. Pope-Davis & H. Coleman (Eds.), *The intersection of class, culture, and gender in counseling* (pp. 417–466). Sage. https://doi.org/10.4135/9781452231846.n17

Day-Vines, N.L., Bryan, J., & Griffin, D. (2013). The Broaching Attitudes and Behavior Survey (BABS): An exploratory assessment of its dimensionality. *Journal of Multicultural Counseling and Development, 41,* 210–223. https://doi.org/10.1002/j.2161-1912.2013.00037.x

Day-Vines, N.L., Cluxton-Keller, F., Agorsor, C., Gubara, S., & Otabil, N. (2020). The multidimensional model of broaching behavior. *Journal of Counseling and Development, 98,* 107–118. https://doi.org/10.1002/jcad.12304

Day-Vines, N.L., Zhang, J., Cluxton-Keller, F., Hicks, D., Jones, C.T., Spann, T., Daga, D., & Agorsor, C. (2024). An investigation of the construct validation of the broaching attitudes and behavior scale – clients. *Journal of Multicultural Counseling and Development*. https://doi-org.proxy1.library.jhu.edu/10.1002/jmcd.12300

Drinane, J.M., Owen, J., & Tao, K.W. (2018). Cultural concealment and therapy outcomes. *Journal of Counseling Psychology, 65*, 239–246. https://doi.org/10.1037/cou0000246

Geronimus, A.T. (2024). *Weathering: The extraordinary stress of ordinary life in an unjust society*. Little, Brown Spark.

Graham, J., Welfare, L.E., Day-Vines, N.L., & Ghoston, M. (2022). Stress, coping, and the strong Black woman: An empirical analysis. *Journal of Multicultural Counseling and Development, 50*, 162–170. https://doi-org.proxy1.library.jhu.edu/10.1002/jmcd.12235

Green, E.L. (August 31, 2025). In Trump's federal workforce cuts, Black women are among the hardest hit. *New York Times*. https://www.nytimes.com/2025/08/31/us/politics/trump-federal-work-force-black-women.html#

hooks, b. (1981). *Ain't I a woman: Black women and feminism*. South End.

Jones, C., & Shorter-Gooden, K. (2025). *Shifting: The double lives of Black women in America*. Harper Perennial.

Mireles, D. (2022). Theorizing racist ableism in higher education. *Teachers College Record, 124*, 17–50. https://doi-org.proxy1.library.jhu.edu/10.1177/01614681221111428

Mullan, J. (2023). *Decolonizing therapy: Oppression, historical trauma, and politicizing your practice*. W.W. Norton & Company.

Ratts, M.J., Singh, A.A., Nassar-McMillan, S., Butler, S.K., & McCullough, J.R. (2016). Multicultural and social justice counseling competencies: Guidelines for the counseling profession. *Journal of Multicultural Counseling and Development, 44*, 28–48. https://doi.org/10.1002/jmcd.12035

Rosa, J. (2019). *Looking like a language, sounding like a race: Raciolinguistic ideologies and the learning of Latinidad*. Oxford University.

Ross, K.M. (June 4, 2020). Call it what it is: Anti-Blackness. *The New York Times*. https://www.nytimes.com/2020/06/04/opinion/george-floyd-anti-blackness.html#

Shin, R.Q., Welch, J.C., Kaya, A.E., Yeung, J.G., Obana, C., Sharma, R., Vernay, C.N., & Yee, S. (2017). The intersectionality framework and identity intersections in the Journal of Counseling Psychology and The Counseling Psychologist: A content analysis. *Journal of Counseling Psychology, 64*, 458–474.

Villarosa, L. (2022). *Under the skin: The hidden toll of racism on American lives and on the health of our nation.* Doubleday.

Walker, R. (2024). *No racial elephants in the room: An unapologetic approach to providing culturally affirming mental health care to Black and African American clients.* PESI.

Xiong, Y, Prasath, P.R., Zhang, Q, & Jeon, L. (2022). A mindfulness-based well-being group for international students in higher education: A pilot study. *Journal of Counseling and Development, 100*, 374–385.

Chapter 6

Intra-Racial, -Ethnic, and -Cultural Broaching Dimensions

When I first started teaching entry-level counseling techniques courses, I would have students engage in peer-counseling dyads with their classmates to help build their counseling skill sets. Students would partner with someone in the class and serve as the provider delivering counseling services to their peer client. Afterward, they exchanged roles, and the provider would become the client. Typically, students conducted three videotaped peer counseling sessions that would enable them to serve in both the capacity of provider and client. During the first two counseling sessions, students would practice active listening skills based on the client's presenting concerns. Typically, the first two sessions focused on more generic counseling concerns. During the third counseling session, students would broach an REC concern with their peer client.

I recall one instance in which a student shared information about her involvement in a long-distance dating relationship as a counseling concern. During the first two sessions, she talked in detail about the difficulty she experienced trying to stay connected with her partner since they seldom had opportunities to see each other because they lived on different continents, and the different time zones hindered daily communication. The core counseling concern involved the client's effort to preserve a healthy long-distance relationship.

During the third session, however, I instructed students to broach the contextual dimensions of REC with their client. Consequently, the peer provider invited Zara to explore the connection between her presenting concerns and relevant REC variables. Zara and her boyfriend were both South Asian nationals, but she was studying abroad in the United States while he worked in their homeland. The peer provider's effort to initiate a conversation about how REC shaped Zara's presenting concerns shifted the discussion about cultivating a long-distance relationship from a generic frame of reference to reconciling cultural challenges. In particular, Zara disclosed that her boyfriend felt adamant about marriage and starting a family. Her nuclear and extended family shared similar sentiments. To the contrary, Zara felt that although the relationship was meaningful, she was not prepared for marriage at this point in her life. She was

DOI: 10.4324/9781003649311-6

ambivalent and experienced tremendous tension between her desire to explore her career interests and experience life as a young adult woman with few encumbrances, relative to the pressure to marry and start a family.

This case illustrates how Zara talked openly in the first two sessions about her involvement in a long-distance relationship and the related logistical challenges that impacted her relationship (e.g., communication, distance, time zones). Zara omitted some of the cultural variables concerning her relationship and her internal dilemma about meeting family expectations. It was not until the peer provider broached or explicitly inquired about culture during the third counseling session that Zara was more forthcoming about the connection between her presenting concern and her REC values. Without the intentional broaching efforts of the provider, Zara may not have disclosed her inner thoughts involving culture at all or until much later in the counseling process. During the third session, the focus of attention shifted from the challenges of sustaining a long-distance relationship to underlying cultural tensions.

To reiterate, broaching refers to the provider's effort to either *initiate* or *respond* to REC concerns that emerge during the counseling session (Day-Vines et al., 2018). When providers initiate broaching discussions, they inquire about how REC influences a client's presenting concerns. Providers often initiate broaching discussions and invite the client to discuss REC values that may inform how the client interprets life experiences. This is especially important when those values differ from mainstream American culture. Providers who implement intra-REC broaching dimensions recognize the importance of having a more holistic discussion about the totality of the client's experience.

Culturally responsive providers are also attuned to the reality that in Western culture, decisions about marriage and family life may reside ostensibly between the dating couple, whereas in many but certainly not all non-Western cultures, family involvement may exert stronger influence on marital decisions. The provider's understanding of cultural nuances is an important variable in the delivery of culturally responsive care. Be that as it may, the provider will need to explore the specific needs, values, and interests of the client because tremendous variability exists from client to client, even when they are members of the same cultural group. In any case, decisions to initiate discussions about the client's REC concerns may arise from something the client stated or implied that warrants further elaboration. The provider's inquiry about REC may also result from understanding differences between Western and non-Western cultural values. By exhibiting curiosity about the client's REC concerns, the provider facilitates client self-understanding and permits the client to discuss concerns beyond surface-level conversations. In Zara's case, the peer provider's understanding that distinctions between Western and non-Western cultures prompted subsequent discussion.

In instances where the client's REC concerns are germane to the presenting problem, the client would likely seize an opportunity to discuss their REC concerns in more detail. Conversely, if REC concerns were not relevant to the client's presenting concern, the client may forego an opportunity to discuss REC concerns in that moment. This may result because the client may not have conscious awareness about the embeddedness of REC within their presenting problems and perceive that insufficient trust levels exist, or developmentally, REC concerns may assume less salience.

In Chapter 3, we used a restaurant analogy and noted that if a waiter asked the customer if they would like steak sauce to boost the flavor of their steak and the customer said, "No thank you," the waiter would not panic and feel they had made a dreadful mistake. Instead, the waiter would use that information as diagnostic information and recognize that steak sauce was not important to the customer in that moment. The waiter would be amenable to the possibility that at some later point the customer may want steak sauce and revisit that original request if and when it became more relevant. Similarly in a counseling context, the provider may introduce a broaching statement. If the client is not ready in that moment to explore REC concerns, the provider may revisit the matter at a later time, assuming REC concerns become more relevant. In instances where the client initiates conversations about REC, the provider would explore the client's REC concerns by acknowledging and validating the concerns the client has raised. There are primary distinctions between initiating and responding to a broaching statement. Chapters 8 and 9 provide more detailed information about strategies for broaching clients' REC concerns and the distinctions between initiating and responding broaching behaviors.

Providers who broach *Intra-REC* concerns address those culture-specific issues that may arise between the client and people with whom they share a common REC designation (Day-Vines et al., 2020). That is, clients may have personal beliefs, value orientations, and behaviors that are at odds with values and viewpoints sanctioned by the cultural group. Contrariwise, clients may derive enormous support and sustenance from their families and communities. Sometimes, clients experience family, peers, and community members as both a source of support and strain. For instance, Tiffany is a middle-class African American high school student who lives with her parents in a suburban community outside a major metropolitan city. Her parents grew up in impoverished communities but were able to transition into the middle class through hard work and education. They have been able to shield Tiffany from many of the hardships they endured. Their effort to protect her by moving to an affluent suburb limited her contact with other African American children. Consequently She looks forward to gatherings with extended family members during holidays and family reunions. She gets to visit with her cousins who keep her abreast of African American culture, style, and music; however, their efforts to keep her up to date are always accompanied by a fair amount of teasing. They accuse her of acting White, suggesting that she is not Black enough because she speaks a standardized variety of English in lieu of African American Vernacular English, plays violin, and is a member of the fencing team. Tiffany believes that her cousins may be expressing pride about her accomplishments and some envy. Although she laughs in a good, humored way, it makes her feel distant and disconnected from her family members, especially at a time when she is navigating important aspects of her own racial identity. She has been meeting with her school counselor to discuss college selections. Tiffany wants to consider a historically Black college or university, but worries about having a strong enough cultural fit with her African American counterparts because she perceives that she is not "Black enough." Tiffany's school counselor recognized the intra-REC identity concerns with which she was grappling, such as her limited sense of belonging with other African American students, self-acceptance, and her evolving racial identity. The school counselor helped Tiffany recognize that there is no absolute way to be Black. Healthy identity functioning indicates that youngsters can exhibit a strong ethnic identity and maintain an orientation toward success without assuming that these identities are mutually exclusive (Day-Vines et al., 2003; Tatum, 2017).

Far too frequently, there is a tendency to assume that just because people share the same REC designation, they may be identical, without consideration for nuanced ways of expressing cultural values and viewpoints. These differences may cause intra-group tensions, as in the case of Tiffany. These tensions and conflicts may occur across a number of domains, such as nationality, immigration, linguistic diversity, documentation status, acculturation levels, socioeconomic status, religion and spirituality, sexual orientation, and, with regard to the case illustration that follows, colorism. Colorism refers to intra-racial stratification based on skin tone within communities of color that result in preferences for people who have lighter versus darker complexions as a determinant of one's beauty, dignity, and worth (Joshi et al., 2017; Monroe & Hall, 2018).

Case Illustration

Sahil is a biracial South Asian and White 25-year-old. His mother is White, and his father is South Asian. He grew up in a loving nuclear household, although extended maternal family members made no pretense about their resentment toward Sahil's father because he was not White. Similarly, his father's family resented Sahil's mother because she was not Indian. This led to fierce disagreements that strained their marital relationship. By the time Sahil was six, his parents' marital relationship had become unbearable. The dissolution of their marriage was imminent, and soon after, they divorced. Sahil's mother retained custody of him, although he spent summers with his father. His mother soon began dating, and within a year she was remarried to a White man and pregnant with her second child. Sahil was thrilled to learn he was going to be Chad's big brother. He could hardly wait to teach him soccer and basketball and how to read.

Following the birth of his baby brother, Sahil struggled to understand why his blended biracial family received puzzled looks when they were together or why people assumed that he and his little brother were not related. Children would ask insensitive questions about why his skin did not match the skin color of the rest of the family. Sahil has olive-colored skin and dark hair, and his brother has blond hair and blue eyes. Sometimes, adults even told Sahil that his brother was not his brother. His mother tried to help him understand the physical differences by addressing parentage from a genetic stance. After Chad's birth, Sahil felt an even greater sense of rejection by his mother's family, who ignored him, talked in derogatory ways about people of color, and heaped enormous amounts of praise on Chad. Sahil tried to dismiss the differential treatment, but he found it demoralizing. He felt tormented by the disconnect he experienced from his family. In early adulthood the emotional weight took a toll on him, especially as he watched what looked like the meteoric rise of his young brother. Sahil experiences frequent bouts of anger, sadness, and isolation.

Provider: Sahil, family dynamics seem to have taken an emotional toll on you. From what I hear you saying, you feel marginalized in your own family. You have limited contact with your father and your brother seems to commandeer most of the family's attention. I get the impression that these issues have been an enduring part of your childhood and have continued into young adulthood, but now they are beginning to weigh on you in ways that are becoming increasingly more painful.

Sahil: I would agree. I love my little brother dearly, but he's 18 now and in college on a full soccer scholarship. I take partial credit for that because I'm the one that gave him his first soccer ball when he was three. I taught him a lot. When he was a kid, I would babysit for him sometimes, and we spent a lot of time playing soccer. I'm not sure how much he understands about blended families, particularly multiracial blended families. He seems oblivious to many of the racial dynamics I experience. He's the all-American kid – blond hair, blue eyes, good looks, athletic build, smart, cocky. He gets unlimited attention at home and at school. My stepdad dotes on him. I know he's not my father, but I seem like an intrusion on the family. I've always felt like I was unwanted by him – disposable. That he wished it were just the three of them. My mother tries to be a little more objective, but she's caught in the middle.

Provider: You continue to love your brother despite the hurt.

Sahil: Yes, I support him. I try to. It's not his fault. I do sense that we may be growing apart. I attended his first college soccer match. Afterwards I went on the field to congratulate him. He introduced me to his teammates as Sahil, not as his brother. That made me wonder whether he was trying to distance himself from me. You know, like not wanting his teammates to know that he has an Indian half-brother. Like maybe he's ashamed of me because of my race. We don't look very much like brothers even though we have the same mother.

Provider: In that moment on the field, you felt rejected by your brother because he seemed to view you as a member of a minority group, more so than your brother.

Sahil: Definitely. In that moment and many other moments (*fighting back tears*). He's the only family member I have ever really felt connected to. The possibility that our brotherhood may vanish is devastating.

Provider: That loss is unimaginable to you. You have experienced ostracism on the basis of your skin color and race. Are you familiar with the term colorism?

Sahil: Yes, I am. I know that in many communities of color lighter skin tones are more valued than darker skin tones. I have experienced that from both sides of my family. My father's side of the family shows some favoritism towards me because I'm lighter than my cousins who are monoracial and darker skinned. I look exotic, but I also get pushback because I don't understand Hindi. To them I'm not really Indian. On my mother's side of the family, my brother receives favoritism because he is all White.

Provider: Sahil, it sounds like you have been carrying this burden for a long time.

Sahil: Yes, I have. Pretty much most of my life. I try to minimize or ignore it. I can't understand why people put so much weight on skin color. I tried talking to my mother about it, but she said people are people and I put too much stock into color and race. She doesn't realize that I've lived with this most of my life – with people constantly questioning whether I belong to the family – making insensitive comments because I look different from everyone else. One time, I went to pick up my brother from aftercare at his elementary school. I was authorized to pick him up, but the attendant basically interrogated me, contacted the principal, and asked for additional identification, before she released him into my custody. I was convinced it was because we don't look like brothers.

Provider: You tried to discuss the hurt you experience with your mother and how your appearance influences the prejudice you experience as a South Asian American in a White family, but she dismissed your feelings. I imagine her response made you question your own reality.

Sahil: Definitely. In my head I go back and forth feeling this is a big deal, but then again – maybe it's not. Maybe I'm distorting this issue. I do think my mother's dealing with her own sense of guilt and probably ambivalence and doesn't know what to say or do. I know she loves me dearly. I'm her first child, but it seems that because she lives in an all-white bubble, she has been forced to choose sides. When she remarried, I don't think she thought about what it would mean to have a blended biracial family, especially with a bigot. Blended families are hard enough, but a blended biracial family? Go figure.

Provider: Your mother's inability to acknowledge your experience as a person of color has left you feeling invalidated and very alone. Would it be okay if we discussed how colorism has impacted you and your family, especially since you say you have grown up in a household feeling that you were neither Indian enough nor White enough?

Sahil: Sure. That's a loaded question. It's been really tough. I think I have suppressed a lot of these feelings until now – thinking that if I just ignore them, they will go away. I've numbed myself by connecting with my brother, studying, and trying to minimize what may actually be happening to our relationship. I feel a sense of personal confusion because I sometimes don't know who I really am.

As the counseling session opened, the provider summarized Sahil's intra-REC concerns and acknowledged the cumulative effect of years of emotional estrangement and disconnection from his family. Throughout the dialogue, the provider integrated and synthesized broaching statements with foundational counseling skills. For instance, the provider used reflection of feelings when Sahil disclosed his deep devotion and affection for his brother and the simultaneous lack of belonging he internalizes from family members. The provider responded by saying, "You continue to love your brother despite the hurt." As a result of feeling heard and understood, Sahil elaborated at a deeper emotional level, citing an illustrative example about the sense of woundedness he has experienced. He surmised that his brother introduced him to his soccer teammates as Sahil and not his brother because he is Indian and has a different phenotype. Rather than challenge Sahil's comment as a cognitive distortion, the provider acknowledged and accepted Sahil's feelings of rejection. Questioning Sahil's belief about why Chad did not introduce Sahil as his brother might have eroded any trust that had been built. In any case, the provider noted that "in that moment" Sahil felt a sense of rejection. Sahil clarified by noting that there have been many other moments, which suggests that this experience is ongoing and oppressive.

As the session continued, the provider asked Sahil if he knew about colorism. The provider did not lecture and advise Sahil about colorism, as if he may have been oblivious to the term and assume he needed education around the construct. Instead, she exhibited cultural humility and a sense of curiosity, allowing Sahil to elaborate on his understanding of colorism. As a consequence, Sahil disclosed the colorist treatment he receives from each side of the family. Sahil described the preferential treatment he experiences on the paternal side of his family because he is lighter than his South Asian cousins and the ostracism he experiences on the maternal side of his family because his skin is dark. He also disclosed a disturbing incident in which he attempted to pick his brother up from aftercare as a child, and the attendant almost did not release Chad from aftercare because she assumed they were not related. Toward the end of the dialogue, Sahil shared that he continues to feel unsupported by his mother who takes a neutral stance on the dilemma of race and color. In talking with Sahil, the provider gains a deep awareness about the cumulative stress that results from him feeling like an outsider in his own family. Sahil feels wounded that he does not have more support from his mother but attempts to rationalize her behavior. It seems that Sahil has endured so much pain that he has become immune to many of his own feelings.

In Chapter 4, we described each of the components of the MMBB and noted that they unfold in a nonlinear fashion and that the model should not be overly prescriptive. To that end, the provider addressed not only intra-counseling dimensions, such as colorism, but also addressed intra-individual dimensions concerning Sahil's identity and inter-REC concerns regarding the experience of discrimination given that he described his stepfather as bigoted.

In subsequent counseling sessions, it may be tempting to problem-solve by exploring how Sahil would like to manage his family dynamics; however, it is important to completely flesh out Sahil's concerns in more detail using unhurried reflection. There are opportunities for much further elaboration about Sahil's situation. For instance, what made Sahil decide to pursue counseling at this moment as opposed to any prior time, or not at all? What impact have colorist attitudes had on him personally? The provider could explore what it means to be the only person of color in his family and to be subjected to colorism as well as prejudicial attitudes from his stepfather and complicity from his mother. Sahil lives in two racially divergent worlds but seems not to belong fully to either of them. This may be important to discuss. Sahil has described the sense of disconnect he experiences within his blended biracial family. Sahil seems to adore his younger brother. What has prevented him from holding a grudge against Chad? Has Sahil ever expressed his sense of hurt and woundedness to Chad? If not, what has prevented him from having an earnest conversation with Chad?

During the session, Sahil indicated that his mother is White, and his father is South Asian. He did not disclose how he identifies racially and ethnically and the salience his identities have for him. Does his identity evoke a sense of pride, shame, security, insecurity, etc.? How have family dynamics shaped his identity, sense of self, belonging, and core values? Given that Sahil feels a sense of ostracism within his family, how does that shape his identity and his self-esteem? What messages has Sahil internalized about his multiracial identity? Collins (2022) recommends that providers explore identity development with biracial clients using models that enumerate transformations in growth, maturation, and understanding that shift as individuals move through the developmental trajectory.

The U.S. Census Bureau has updated the way people classify themselves racially to include people identifying as multiracial and having two or more races, opportunities to write in their racial designation, and efforts to combine race and ethnicity. Since the 2010 US census, the multiracial population has grown by 276% from 9 million people to 33.8 million people in 2020 (Jones et al., 2021).

There are a number of multiracial identity development frameworks (e.g., James H. Jacobs, Maria Root). Rockquemore and Brunsma (2002) identified four specific variations in racial self-understanding among biracial individuals. Individuals may endorse a (a) singular identity in which a biracial individual identifies exclusively with a single race, (b) border identity, where individuals see themselves as some combination of both races, (c) protean identity, where the racial identity one assumes is contingent upon the specific social context, and (d) transcendent identity, where people align with their humanness as opposed to a specific racial category. As part of their theory, Rockquemore and Brunsma studied a push-pull factor that influences whether biracial individuals are pushed or pulled in particular directions that validate or unvalidate their identity. Individuals with validated identities experience acceptance by others. Contrariwise, individuals with unvalidated identities do not experience acceptance by society and are pushed toward a monoracial identity rather than the ability to embrace a biracial or multiracial identity. Based on Rockquemore and Brunsma's theory, Sahil appears to have an unvalidated identity because neither his paternal nor maternal family members regard him as similar to themselves; however, further exploration in counseling about his racial identity seems important.

Sahil stated that he experiences very little social support from his family. If in fact this is the case, where and how does he derive social support from other sources? Before problem-solving, the provider needs to fully understand the nature and scope of Sahil's REC concerns.

Similarly, after the provider has processed Sahil's concerns more fully, it may be helpful to pivot and examine how Sahil may begin his healing process. Future efforts with Sahil may include having him examine and process feelings of loss and grief that have rendered him all alone with little emotional support. After more thoroughly comprehending the problem and encouraging catharsis, Sahil may begin to consider his healing journey. Group counseling interventions with other biracial and multiracial individuals may help Sahil resolve some of the difficulties he has internalized within his family system. More specifically, group counseling may help him feel less alone, develop a healthy appreciation of his biracial identity, and develop support systems with others who have a shared experience around their racial identity development. For Sahil, problem-solving approaches might include grieving fully, increasing self-acceptance, boundary setting, and addressing relational dynamics with family members.

Burning Question

Norma, how will I know when the client and I have exhausted the discussion about biracial identity?

That's a good question. Sometimes the client will signal their readiness to move on to new clinical territory because they have had ample time to process their emotions about what it means to be biracial and how these experiences have impacted their sense of well-being. Often clients signal their readiness to move from focusing on the weight of their stressors to the meaning and significance of those experiences, which suggests they have greater self-understanding. Additionally, providers may inquire about whether the client would like to move on to other topics or continue exploring their biracial identity.

Summary

The intra-REC broaching category refers to within-group sources of support and stress that impact the relationship between clients and those with whom they share a common REC designation. Sometimes, individuals presume that group members have shared, nearly identical values and viewpoints. In fact, there is tremendous variability within groups. That variability may occur with regard to race, ethnicity, religion, socioeconomic status, nationality, immigration status, linguistic diversity, etc., in ways that warrant counseling consideration.

Discussion Questions

1 What are some indicators that broaching Sahil's concerns about colorism warrants counseling consideration?
2 What category of Rockquemore and Brunsma's (2002) biracial identity model best represents Sahil's level of racial identity functioning?
3 How would you evaluate your level of cultural comfort broaching Sahil's concerns around colorism?
4 Identify areas that you might explore in more depth if Sahil were your client.
5 If Tiffany were your client, what intra-REC counseling concerns might you explore with her?
6 What barriers may make it difficult for you to broach Zara, Sahil, and Tiffany's REC concerns?
7 What strengths and skills do you possess that would facilitate your ability to broach Zara, Sahil, and Tiffany's REC concerns?
8 What intra-group pressures contribute to Zara, Sahil, and Tiffany's REC concerns?

References

Collins, L.H. (2022). Beyond either/or: Serving biracial, multiracial, and multiethnic clients in counseling. *Counseling Today*.

Day-Vines, N.L., Booker Ammah, B., Steen, S., & Arnold, K.M. (2018). Getting comfortable with discomfort: Preparing counselor trainees to broach racial, ethnic, and cultural factors with clients during counseling. *International Journal for the Advancement of Counselling, 40*(2), 89–104. https://doi.org/10.1007/s10447-017-9308-9

Day-Vines, N.L., Cluxton-Keller, F., Agorsor, C., Gubara, S., & Otabil, N. (2020). The multidimensional model of broaching behavior. *Journal of Counseling and Development, 98,* 107–118. https://doi.org/10.1002/jcad.12304

Day-Vines, N.L., Patton, J., & Baytops, J. (2003). African American adolescents: The impact of race and middle-class status on the counseling process. *Professional School Counseling, 7,* 40–51.

Jones, N., Marks, R., Ramirez, R., & Rios-Varga, M. (August 12, 2021). 2020 Census illuminates racial and ethnic composition of the country. *United States Census Bureau.* https://www.census.gov/library/stories/2021/08/improved-race-ethnicity-measures-reveal-united-states-population-much-more-multiracial.html#:~:text=to%20self%2D identify.-,Black%20or%20African%20American%20Population,in%20combination%20 population%20grew%2088.7%25

Joshi, S.N., Balaji, M., & Deshpande, P. (2017). De-hue-manizing them: Color and acculturation among second generation South Asians. In C.R. Monroe, (Ed.), *Race and colorism in education* (pp. 132–146). Routledge.

Monroe, C.R., & Hall, R.E. (2018). Colorism and US immigration: Considerations for researchers. *American Behavioral Scientist, 62*(14), 2037–2054. https://doi.org/10.1177/0002764218810753

Rockquemore, K.A., & Brunsma, D.L. (2002). Socially embedded identities: Theories, typologies, and processes of racial identity among Black/White biracials. *The Sociological Quarterly, 43,* 335–356. https://doi-org.proxy1.library.jhu.edu/10.1111/j.1533-8525.2002.tb00052.x

Tatum, B.D. (2017). *Why are all the Black Kids sitting together in the cafeteria? And other conversations about race.* Basic Books.

Chapter 7

Inter-Racial, -Ethnic, and -Cultural Broaching Dimensions

Providers who address inter-racial, -ethnic, and -cultural (inter-REC) concerns during the counseling process explore clients' encounters with racism and discrimination. In Chapter 1, we used Jones's (2000) framework to identify three specific forms of racism: (a) institutional racism, which is embedded in policies, laws, resources, and opportunities; (b) personally mediated racism, which is conceptualized as individual acts of meanness directed toward a minoritized target; and (c) internalized racism or the tendency of racially minoritized targets to believe stereotypes that are perpetrated about them. Similarly, Scheurich and Young (1997) developed a multilevel model of racism and asserted that racism at higher operational levels (e.g., civilizational) reinforces and perpetuates racism at lower operational levels, such that people from dominant groups may feel emboldened and compelled to enact individual acts of meanness toward minoritized group members (e.g., microaggressions).

We learned by reviewing Kimberle Crenshaw's (1989) intersectionality theory in Chapter 5 that inequality cannot be reduced to a single identity dimension (e.g., race, gender, sexual orientation, immigration status). There are usually multiple, complex, and competing identity structures that impact a client's experience with racism, discrimination, powerlessness, and stigma. Moreover, a client can experience both oppressed and privileged identities that providers may fail to consider when addressing identity singularly (Ratts et al., 2016). Incidentally, oppression operates as an umbrella term that captures multiple forms of domination and control, including but not limited to racism, sexism, classism, homophobia, religious intolerance, and ableism. These varying forms of domination represent an abuse of power that grants resources and opportunities to some individuals while withdrawing them from other individuals in ways that create harm (David & Derthick, 2017). Privilege, on the other hand, reflects unearned power available to some individuals on the basis of their membership in dominant groups (McIntosh, 1989). Whether maltreatment is structurally or individually mediated, clients' encounters with oppressive systems often overlap in ways that compound

DOI: 10.4324/9781003649311-7

psychological distress, and can lead to depression, anxiety, and hypervigilance (Archer, 2021; Carter et al., 2017; Chan & Westcott, 2025; Cogburn et al., 2024; Steele, 2025).

In each of the case illustrations we have explored in this text, clients have experienced intersectionality such that they confront both oppressed and privileged identities. As you will recall from Chapter 3, Hernando, the gay Latino male client who sought counseling services to explore ambivalence about coming out to family members, experienced oppression on the basis of his sexual orientation, race, and ethnicity, but privilege on the basis of his male sex. In Chapter 4, Selma, a White female provider, worked with a White female client who experienced oppression on the basis of her gender but privilege on the basis of her race and religious identity. In Chapter 5, Katrina, the gay Caribbean female immigrant with a disability, experienced oppression on the basis of her accent, sexual orientation, disability status, race, ethnicity, and gender but experienced privilege on the basis of her education and income. In Chapter 6, Sahil, a biracial South Asian and White man, experienced oppression on the basis of his biracial status and phenotype, but privilege on the basis of his male sex.

The vignettes described above demonstrate that clients cannot be reduced to a single identity dimension because they are likely to experience multiple, complex, and overlapping forms of oppression based on their identity statuses in ways that impact their sociocultural, sociopolitical, and sociohistorical experience. Culturally responsive broaching behavior necessitates that providers explore the multidimensionality of clients' experiences (Day-Vines et al., 2020). In the case illustration that follows, we observe how racism and discrimination unfold within the healthcare system and rattle a terminally ill pancreatic cancer patient's sense of trust and security within medical systems, but first we review a specific form of oppression related to healthcare disparities.

Much has been written about healthcare disparities and their impact on people from marginalized communities (Cogburn et al., 2024). According to the American Society of Clinical Oncology (Patel et al., 2020), healthcare disparities reflect the fact that minoritized group members experience preventable differences in cancer outcomes at all stages of disease, including but not limited to incidence (e.g., new cases), prevalence (e.g., all existing cases), stage at diagnosis, morbidity (e.g., cancer-related health complications), and mortality (e.g., death). Numerous factors contribute to healthcare disparities such as patients' health literacy rates, access to health insurance, quality health care, transportation, and environmental factors such as clean water or air and nutritious food (National Cancer Institute [NCI], 2025). Much like their financially constrained peers, ethnic minority individuals with higher incomes who have quality insurance are also susceptible to healthcare disparities resulting from institutional racism, distrust of medical systems, and unconscious bias from healthcare providers (NCI). For many African Americans, irrespective of their social class positionality, the long history of medical abuses that include both mental and physical health disparities has contributed to medical distrust and people's reluctance to seek care (Hylton, 2024; Jones, 2022; Summers, 2019; Thomas & Sillen, 1991; Washington, 2008).

Case Illustration

Byron is a 55-year-old African American man who was diagnosed three years ago with pancreatic cancer, a rare and very aggressive cancer of the digestive tract. This disease is considered a silent killer because doctors usually do not diagnose patients until advanced stages, once the cancer has already begun to ravage the body (Noel & Fiscella, 2019). Notably, African Americans are more predisposed to pancreatic cancer than any other racial or ethnic group (Rosenzweig, 2025). Initially, doctors removed the tumor from Byron's pancreas, but more recently, the cancer has metastasized. Although doctors can no longer offer any curative treatment, Byron's oncologist provided him with a referral for palliative care services, which include individual and group counseling, access to medication that helps him manage pain levels, and a patient navigator who assists him traverse a very complex healthcare system. Byron reports that the care and support he receives from his family, church, and co-workers make him feel less alone and permit him to better manage such a debilitating disease.

In previous counseling sessions, Byron has expressed concerns regarding his fear and trepidation about living with significant pain as the cancer begins to consume other parts of his body. He continues to grieve the reality that his cancer is not curable and address feelings related to anticipatory grief. Incidentally, anticipatory grief refers to the mourning process that occurs for individuals before an expected loss. Byron has experienced the full range of emotions such as inner turmoil, sadness, and worry. Early on in his diagnosis, he isolated himself from friends and family and spent considerable time perseverating about how family members might live without him and feeling devastated because he would not experience longevity. The overwhelming emotions resulted in mental exhaustion and irritability. Within the last six months, Byron has experienced each of the stages of the grief cycle, including denial, anger, bargaining, depression, and he is now approaching acceptance, even as he vacillates between each of these emotional states. This type of mental preparation occurs as individuals anticipate the end of life and their departure from earth.

Byron has discussed with his provider concerns about when he might die and anxiety about the afterlife. In turn, Byron and his provider have identified goals that would help him live with a sense of purpose and acknowledge aspects of life he appreciates. For instance, he has been asked to co-facilitate a Black men's cancer support group in a neighboring town because of his strong leadership skills. Additionally, he recognizes that he has the loving support of his family and community, and since his diagnosis, he has received quality medical attention. Byron feels a sense of reassurance because years ago, he and his wife made financial provisions for his family to function in the event either of them had an untimely death. Watching his children graduate from college and receiving family support and assistance from church members gives him a great sense of relief.

In an early counseling session, Byron confided that his faith helps him reconcile the grief and anxiety he experiences. Byron quotes scriptures and listens to gospel music because he says they provide him with a sense of comfort, reassurance, strength, peace, and hope. As time passes, he has begun to accept the inevitability of death and is working toward facing loss of life with dignity, as well as mental and spiritual clarity. Despite the emotional strides he has made, Byron vacillates from time to time between feeling hopeful and experiencing confusion about how and why he was diagnosed with cancer.

In today's session, Byron talked about the progression of his disease. He shared with his provider that he has been combing through the healthcare literature to better understand his diagnosis, how it developed, why it is so prevalent in African American men, and how it goes undetected until the disease has progressed into a deadly cancer. Byron realizes that he cannot alter the course of his disease, but he is interested in processing root causes with his provider. He realizes that pancreatic cancer is a disease of the digestive tract but never connected his history of digestive problems to cancer. Throughout the course of his adult life, Byron has visited his primary care physician regularly and was prescribed several over-the-counter and prescription medications. Ironically, weeks before his cancer diagnosis, his primary care physician gave him a clean bill of health. Byron imagines what might have resulted had the doctor ordered more invasive tests or referred him to a specialist who might have been able to detect the cancer at an earlier stage.

Case Illustration

Provider: In our last session, we discussed how you vacillate between accepting your cancer diagnosis and being filled with deep sadness and inner turmoil. You also shared that your family, friends, church, and men's support group have provided you with a sense of security. The men's pancreatic cancer support group helps you feel less alone, and you are now finding your emotional and spiritual rhythm. You are finalizing your affairs, so you've made a tremendous amount of progress. You also talked about gratitude for being able to see your children grow up, and you expressed pride in knowing that you've made financial provisions for your family. In our last session, things seemed to be looking up.

Byron: Well, in the last two weeks, I have regressed again. You know I meet with my Black men's support group weekly. Last week one of the fellas was talking about the disproportionate rate of pancreatic cancer in the African American community. After that discussion, I started researching information on this topic and I found out that not only is pancreatic cancer more deadly than other cancers, but Black men in particular are more predisposed to the disease and that the symptoms go undetected until late stages when little can be done. I knew most of that information, but what I didn't know is that early symptoms of the disease go undetected and unaddressed by many medical professionals.

Provider: It must be pretty unsettling to hear that African American men are disproportionately impacted by pancreatic cancer and early warning signs often go unheeded by doctors.

Byron: Exactly. I know that pancreatic cancer is a disease of the digestive tract. But I learned that many people who eventually develop pancreatic cancer have had digestive difficulties that they did not associate with the disease. For instance, I've always had digestive problems, and I have always shared this information with my doctor. I now realize I've been treating symptoms, and I actually had cancer growing inside me all this time. I went to the doctor consistently for annual check-ups because I am not one to skip appointments. I informed my doctor about the indigestion, heartburn, nausea, and back pain that I have lived with for years. The doctor seemed to minimize those symptoms as related to dietary practices and lifestyle habits. That really pisses me off. At the very least, if the doctor had been more aggressive about connecting my symptoms to other ailments, he might have ordered tests or referred me to a specialist. It's possible that sooner testing would have allowed my cancer to be detected at an earlier stage. You know what? I was prescribed antacids instead.

Provider: Basically, you were proactive. You met with your doctor regularly, shared your symptoms, but your doctor ignored those symptoms. This happened through no fault of your own, but learning this information is upsetting.

Byron: Absolutely! I've had the same doctor for more than ten years. It seems that he would have recognized that my chronic digestive difficulties were more than coincidental, even as I changed my diet. It's not like I don't have good insurance.

Provider: You sense the doctor dropped the ball.

Byron: No doubt – he really dropped the ball (*takes a deep breath*). Based on what I've read and what has been discussed in my Black male support group, I am grateful that my cancer was diagnosed early, that I was able to have a surgery that extends my life even though it may not cure the disease. Because I have quality insurance I have received more aggressive care. I also live near a hospital that does this surgery regularly. Being middle class means that I have insurance, and I have received recommended treatment regimens once I was diagnosed. That's a real blessing.

Provider: You feel relieved that being gainfully employed, middle class, and having quality insurance has increased your prospects for receiving life extending care, but it's still hard to accept the fact that more could have been done sooner. This news is pretty devastating.

Byron: Definitely. Based on everything I've read, if I had no insurance or public insurance, the chances of having surgery to remove the tumor on my pancreas would probably not have happened, especially as a Black man. In fact, a few of the men in my group did not survive more than six months after their diagnosis. I'm on year three.

Provider: It sounds like issues of race and class have affected the type of care you received. Being middle class and gainfully employed provided you with care you might not have had if you were poor and uninsured. And being African American contributed to the doctors perhaps taking your symptoms less seriously. So, while you were advantaged around social class, you still experienced healthcare disparities on the basis of your race. I imagine that there's a part of you that feels betrayed.

Byron: You damn right. I had symptoms that should have been attended to years ago given my regular complaints about chronic indigestion, heartburn, nausea, and back pain. I believe the doctor should have done more. You know, just before I was referred for palliative care, I asked my oncologist for a referral to a new primary care doctor. I asked him about his doctor since I did not feel my primary care physician did enough. He told me that he only uses specialists. I did not think anything of that comment in the moment, but as I reflect now, I think my oncologist was insinuating that a specialist has so much more in-depth expertise than a primary care physician. Damn (*shakes his head*).

Provider: In retrospect, you felt ignored by your primary care physician and wonder if a specialist may have recognized your symptoms earlier.

Byron: I go back and forth. There's nothing I can do about that now. I have experienced so many blessings in spite of this disease. This is the third year since my diagnosis and I'm still here. Like I said before, my faith has sustained me. I don't know where I would be without my faith. There are times however (*hesitates*).

Provider: Yes, go on.

Byron: I'm a faithful man but sometimes my faith wavers. Are you familiar with the passage in the Bible where a man's son is experiencing convulsions, and he asks Jesus to help him? Jesus tells the man that everything is possible if he just believes. The boy's father told Jesus that he did believe, but he asked Jesus to help his unbelief. That's where I am with this disease some days.

Provider: I'm not familiar with that scripture but it sounds like your experience is similar to that father who experienced faith and doubt at the same time. You vacillate between these two distinct emotional states – having enormous faith even as you question God.

Byron: That's true. I do go back and forth. Basically, I'm prepared to die, and I know that given my condition I will not get cured. I've made peace with that. There's a part of me that just doesn't want to die in this moment.

Provider: You have accepted the inevitability of your condition, even while you have a strong desire to live.

The provider opens the counseling session by summarizing the contents of the previous session with an acknowledgment of Byron's emotional state and tendency to vacillate between hope and despair, a theme that continues throughout the case illustration. The provider also uses the positive asset search to mention aspects of Byron's life that are going well. For instance, Byron seems to derive a sense of comfort from the African American men's support group, watching his children reach adulthood, and finalizing his affairs. Throughout the session, the provider's comments balance acceptance and longing without expecting Byron to assume an overly happy stance, or what scholars label toxic positivity. Toxic positivity refers to the expectation that clients exude a positive mindset despite the experience of emotional pain. Toxic positivity creates an unhealthy counseling dynamic and negates the client's experiential reality by invalidating justifiably negative emotions. Minimizing pain can lead to suppression of authentic emotions (Cross, 2022). Emphasis on happy emotions can protect the provider from grappling with personal discomfort and the gravity of the client's condition. Such a posture demonstrates an actual lack of empathy. Without an opportunity for emotional release, clients may feel ashamed and marginalized in ways that exacerbate suffering and psychological distress. Further, clients may engage in cultural concealment by withholding pertinent information about their REC concerns (Drinane, 2018). The provider's acceptance of strong emotions permitted Byron to talk openly and earnestly about his consternation surrounding his impending death.

Broaching refers to the provider's effort to initiate or respond to REC concerns that emerge during the counseling process (Day-Vines et al., 2018). Ordinarily, providers introduce broaching conversations, but there are many instances in which clients introduce broaching discussions. Studies demonstrate that in counseling dyads with White providers and Black clients, clients tend to initiate broaching discussions (Jones & Welfare, 2017; Paul, 2024). Moreover, findings indicate that addressing racial experiences results in deeper self-disclosures from the client. In any case, regardless of who begins the broaching process, it is incumbent upon the provider to acknowledge or respond to the client's REC concerns. In this instance, Byron notes the disproportionate rate of pancreatic cancer among African American men. Rather than assuming a colorblind racial stance and using a generic paraphrase indicating that Byron learned more information about his disease, the provider remained fully engaged and receptive to the client's sociopolitical concerns. This stance allowed the provider to attend carefully to Byron's shocking revelation about the presence of a fairly common set of symptoms prior to his cancer diagnosis. More specifically, the provider used a paraphrase and paid selective attention to Byron's concerns about healthcare disparities and the disproportionate impact on African American men. The provider's statement validated Byron's consternation about the symbiotic relationship between race and healthcare disparities. As a result of feeling heard and understood, Byron responded, "Exactly," and continued talking at a deeper emotional level about feelings of injustice. Had the provider sidestepped or minimized Byron's statement about healthcare disparities, Byron may have withheld his follow-up response. Instead, Byron continued talking and described the cancer-related symptoms he experienced throughout the course of his life. He also expressed his deep regret that his primary care physician did not associate his symptoms with digestive disorders that may have led to an earlier diagnosis or a referral. Byron recognizes that an earlier diagnosis may not have reversed the course of the disease, although it may have extended his life.

The provider's warmth and compassion created a marked degree of psychological safety which allowed Byron to explore his emotions fully and completely without having to self-monitor. Fortunately, the provider remained attuned to Byron's expression of emotional vulnerability which in turn permitted Byron to express grievances with the healthcare system. The provider did not just focus on Byron's cancer diagnosis but integrated an intersectional approach that opened a discussion about how power, oppression, and privilege interact. Notably, the provider demonstrated willingness to discuss the lack of aggressive diagnostic efforts on the part of Byron's primary care physician by demonstrating what Metzl and Hanson (2014) refer to as structural awareness, wherein providers name and label structural sources of oppression. In this instance, the provider articulated the complex interplay between Byron's medical condition and the systems that have failed him. The provider noted that Byron's cancer diagnosis occurred through no fault of his own and validated Byron's concern that the physician seems to have dropped the ball. The provider's acknowledgment of how the system contributed to Byron's health decline, through delayed diagnosis and failure to receive treatment from a specialist, is corroborated by literature demonstrating the tendency for medical practitioners to minimize Black patients' physical symptoms (Blackstock, 2024; Sabin, 2020). Regardless of how these breakdowns occur, the provider's acknowledgment served as an important affirmation that Byron seemed to appreciate.

The provider also acknowledged Byron's intersectional tensions, by labeling race as a source of oppression that jeopardized his health and class as a protective mechanism that provided him access to quality health care. Just as the provider engaged Byron's concerns about race and class directly, the provider also demonstrated cultural comfort or an ease of manner discussing Byron's concerns about religion and spirituality. When Byron inquired about the provider's familiarity with biblical scripture, the provider exhibited cultural humility by indicating lack of familiarity with the passage. As the reader will recall, cultural humility refers to the provider's sense of curiosity about the client, willingness to admit mistakes, and admission about the limits of their knowledge (Hook et al., 2017). The provider expressed curiosity about Byron's meaning and interpretation of the passage. This willing admission on the part of the provider likely enhanced credibility with Byron. Several studies demonstrate a link between cultural humility and a stronger therapeutic alliance as well as more favorable counseling outcomes (DeBlaere et al., 2023; Hicks, 2026; Hook et al., 2013). Conversely, missing opportunities to discuss clients' counseling concerns is associated with more negative counseling outcomes (Owen et al., 2016).

An emerging body of research literature suggests that providers may struggle to exhibit cultural humility as the client's number of salient identities increases (Anders & Kivlighan, 2023). This was not the case for the provider who not only addressed the intersectional identity domains but also helped Byron explore the tensions between race and class, faith and doubt, gratitude and injustice, as well as acceptance and longing. Throughout the session, the provider created a holding environment and maintained an emotional presence with Byron, as opposed to distancing from Byron's feelings. In this way, the provider served as a container and held various feelings that Byron expressed throughout the session, thus allowing Byron to achieve emotional depth. The importance of the provider's role in supporting Byron cannot be understated, especially given that family and community members may be taxed emotionally and with his physical care in ways that make it difficult to engage with some of the existential issues that preoccupy Byron. Further, Byron's support system may also experience their own anticipatory grief that precludes them from providing in-depth of emotional support, beyond instrumental care.

The provider consistently integrated and synthesized foundational counseling skills with broaching skills. To illustrate, the provider used the basic listening sequence, reflection of content, reflection of feeling, reflection of meaning to explore Byron's inner concerns. The provider identified feeling words that accurately matched the intensity of Byron's affective state and helped him process his emotions more completely. For instance, the provider noted Byron's feelings of sadness, betrayal, devastation, of being ignored, and being unsettled, as well as his sense of spiritual doubt concerning his illness. Similarly, the provider acknowledged Byron's competing feelings of gratitude, pride, support, and faithfulness. The use of feeling words helped validate and normalize Byron's subjective experience.

Sometimes, my students will say to their clients that they understand exactly how they feel, when in reality, providers do not know exactly how their clients feel. The presumption of knowing invalidates clients' feelings and demonstrates a kind of false empathy that may interfere with the client's ability to engage in further self-exploration. Once a provider communicates a feeling statement, the client needs an opportunity to acknowledge, disagree or clarify the felt-level experience. The provider's identification of specific feeling words serves as a point of departure that helps the client elaborate about their feelings in more depth. In this case illustration, each time the provider labeled a specific feeling, Byron talked in more depth about his inner experience. The use of emotion within the counseling dyad has been linked to positive counseling outcomes (Peluso & Freund, 2018).

Future Counseling Directions

During follow-up sessions, the provider may explore how Byron navigates the paradox between his spiritual belief system and his personal doubt. The provider may explore Byron's specific source of skepticism that intensifies his sense of spiritual doubt. This may involve pinpointing the extent to which Byron's relationship with God has shifted over time and identifying varying emotions that have resulted from his illness. The provider would need to accept and normalize feelings that may be related to unanswered prayers, frustration with God's timing, feelings of abandonment, as well as reconciliation with God. Efforts to explore how Byron resolves these competing orientations seem appropriate. For instance, how does Byron prevent unbelief from undermining his actual belief? These questions may lead to greater depth of exploration and personal understanding.

The provider may also explore components of the Multidimensional Model of Broaching Behavior. For instance, a discussion of intra-counseling dimensions may result in the provider encouraging Byron to talk in more depth about his REC concerns. As such, the provider may use cultural immediacy to invite Byron to consider their shared and different identity dimensions and how their similarities and differences shape Byron's counseling experience. Further, the provider may explore whether Byron has some unmet counseling needs that warrant consideration.

Given that the intra-individual broaching dimension focuses on the client's intersectional identities, the provider may explore other identities. So far, they have explored how issues of race, class, and religion have contributed to Byron's experience as a cancer patient. Byron may also benefit from discussing his diagnosis at the intersection of race and gender. For instance, how do beliefs about Black masculinity, strength, and courage shape Byron's perceptions of himself as a Black man with cancer?

Intra-REC broaching dimensions may warrant exploration of how Byron navigates issues of family and community meaning-making within an African American cultural context. This may involve a discussion of whether and how health beliefs within the African American community contribute to Byron's understanding of his cancer diagnosis. For instance, what cultural patterns does Byron maintain about the causes of his disease, and how do religion and spirituality impact Byron's health beliefs and attitudes? Future discussions about inter-REC broaching dimensions may address recourse Byron may take to create a legacy that seems most congruent with not only his values but also the capacity he has. For instance, the invitation to co-facilitate a Black men's group seems like an important contribution to other survivors who are engaged in a journey similar to Byron's. Byron may explore what legacy he wants to leave his family and community, whether through written correspondence, videography, storytelling, or advocacy. However, whatever Byron plans to do in the time he has remaining should be his choice.

Burning Question

Norma, I've never worked with terminally ill patients before. Should I refer out?

It is normal for you to have some fear and trepidation about issues of death and dying, especially if you have not had to face the loss of a loved one previously. Remember that as a provider, the focus is on the client who needs your support, strength, and compassion. If you have a lot of misgivings about death, you may want to explore your own attitudes about death anxiety and what makes you uncomfortable. As you know, death is an inevitable part of the life cycle; moreover, it is not contagious.

As a provider, you will do many of the same things with your terminally ill client that you would do with any other client in terms of validating and affirming their thoughts and feelings, being present, building a sense of psychological safety, and working to understand the client's internal frame of reference. When working with minoritized clients, it would be appropriate to inquire about the cultural meanings they attach to life and explore any intersectional dimensions of death that may be related to race, gender, class, religion, etc. If you are completely immobilized by the prospect of discussing death with your client, you may seek consultation or secure your own counseling to better understand your personal attitudes about death and dying.

Summary

The inter-REC broaching dimensions address the client's encounters with racism and discrimination, which are not limited to overt and covert acts of individual meanness. Instead, racism and discrimination are inextricably bound to structural forms of racism that invoke harm at higher operational levels and are simultaneously reinforced and perpetuated at the individual levels. Racism and discrimination manifest across myriad institutions, including healthcare systems that predispose individuals from minoritized groups to preventable disease outcomes that have the potential to reduce health outcomes and life expectancy, relative to individuals from more dominant groups. Providers will, of necessity, address clients' concerns around racism and discrimination.

Discussion Questions

1. How comfortable do you feel exploring a client's concerns about death and dying from a cultural standpoint?
2. What steps might you take as a provider to avoid toxic positivity with clients?
3. How would you support Byron if you did not believe he was impacted by healthcare disparities?
4. What is the advantage of addressing intersectional identity domains versus focusing on a single identity domain?
5. How might you explore a client's spiritual angst without advice giving?

References

Anders, C., & Kivlighan, D.M. (2023). Salience: An intersectional approach to understanding cultural processes and outcomes in psychotherapy. *Journal of Counseling Psychology, 70*, 477–485. https://doi.org/10.1037/cou0000688

Archer, D. (2021). *Anti-racist psychotherapy: Confronting systemic racism and healing racial trauma.* Each One Teach One Publications.

Blackstock. (2024). *Legacy: A Black physician reckons with racism in medicine.* Viking.

Carter, R.T., Johnson, V.E., Roberson, K., Mazzula, S.L., Kirkinis, K., & Sant-Barket, S. (2017). Race-based traumatic stress, racial identity statuses, and psychological functioning: An exploratory investigation. *Professional Psychology, Research and Practice, 48*, 30–37. https://doi.org/10.1037/pro0000116

Chan, C.D., & Westcott, J.B. (2025). Structural vulnerability framework: An application to professional counselors. *Journal of Counseling and Development, 103,* 257–266. https://doi-org.proxy1.library.jhu.edu/10.1002/jcad.12558

Cogburn, C.D., Roberts, S.K., Ransome, Y., Addy, N., Hansen, H., & Jordan, A. (2024). The impact of racism on Black American mental health. *The Lancet, 11*(1), 56–64. https://doi.org/10.1016/S2215-0366(23)00361-9

Crenshaw, K. (1989). Demarginalizing the intersection of race and sex: A Black feminist critique of antidiscrimination doctrine, feminist theory and antiracist politics. *University of Chicago Legal Forum, 1989*(1), 139–167.

Cross, K.L. (2022). Platitudes and toxic positivity. *Journal of Palliative Medicine, 25,* 1168–1169. https://doi-org.proxy1.library.jhu.edu/10.1089/jpm.2022.0295

David, E.J.R., & Derthick, A.O. (2017). *The psychology of oppression.* Springer.

Day-Vines, N.L., Cluxton-Keller, F., Agorsor, C., Gubara, S., & Otabil, N. (2020). The multidimensional model of broaching behavior. *Journal of Counseling and Development, 98,* 107–118. https://doi.org/10.1002/jcad.12304

Day-Vines, N.L. Booker Ammah, B., Steen, S., & Arnold, K.M. (2018). Getting comfortable with discomfort: Preparing counselor trainees to broach racial, ethnic, and cultural factors with clients during counseling. *International Journal for the Advancement of Counselling, 40*, 89–104. https://doi.org/10.1007/s10447-017-9308-9

DeBlaere, C., Zelaya, D.G., Dean, J.B., Chadwick, C.N., Davis, D.E, Hook, J.N., & Owen, J. (2023). Multiple microaggressions and therapy outcomes: The indirect effects of cultural humility and working alliance with Black, indigenous, women of color clients. *Professional Psychology: Research and Practice, 54*, 115–124. https://doi-org.proxy1.library.jhu.edu/10.1037/pro0000497

Drinane, J.M., Owen, J., & Tao, K.W. (2018). Cultural concealment and therapy outcomes. *Journal of Counseling Psychology, 65*, 239–246. https://doi.org/10.1037/cou0000246

Hicks, D. (2026). Counselors' broaching skills influence on the mental health outcomes of chronically ill racial and ethnic minorities clients:A. Serial moderated mediation model (Unpublished doctoral dissertation). The Ohio State University.

Hook, J.N., Davis, D., Owen, J., & DeBlaere, C. (2017). *Cultural humility: Engaging diverse identities in therapy.* American Psychological Association. https://doi.org/10.1037/0000037-000

Hook, J.N., Davis, D.E., Owen, J., Worthington, E.L., Jr., & Utsey, S.O. (2013). Cultural humility: Measuring openness to culturally diverse clients. *Journal of Counseling Psychology, 60*(3), 353–366. https://doi.org/10.1037/a0032595

Hylton, A. (2024). *Madness: Race and insanity in a Jim Crow asylum*. Legacy.

Jones, C. (2022). *The organ thieves: The shocking story of the first heart transplant in the segregated south*. Gallery/Jeter.

Jones, C.P. (2000). Levels of racism: A theoretic framework and a gardener's tale. *American Journal of Public Health. 90*, 1212–1215.

Jones, C.T., & Welfare, L.E. (2017). Broaching behaviors of licensed professional counselors: A qualitative inquiry. *Journal of Addictions & Offender Counseling, 38*(1), 48–64. https://doi-org.proxy1.library.jhu.edu/10.1002/jaoc.12028

McIntosh, P. (1989, July/August). White privilege: Unpacking the invisible knapsack. *Peace and Freedom*, 10–12.

Metzl, J.M., & Hansen, H. (2014). Structural competency: Theorizing a new medical engagement with stigma and inequality. *Social Science and Medicine, 103*, 126–113. https://doi.org/10.1016/j.socscimed.2013.06.032

National Cancer Institute. (2025, January 31). *Cancer disparities*. National Institutes of Health. https://www.cancer.gov/about-cancer/understanding/disparities

Noel, M., & Fiscella, K. (2019). Disparities in pancreatic cancer treatment and outcomes. *Health Equity, 3.1*, 532–540.

Owen, J., Tao, K.W., Drinane, J.M., Hook, J., Davis, D.E., & Kune, N.F. (2016). Client perceptions of therapists' multicultural orientation: Cultural (missed) opportunities and cultural humility. *Professional Psychology: Research and Practice, 47*(1), 30–37. https://doi-org.proxy1.library.jhu.edu/10.1037/pro0000046

Patel, M.I., Lopez, A.M., Blackstock, W., Reeder-Hayes, K., Moushey, E.A., Phillips, J., & Tap, A. (2020). Cancer disparities and health equity: A policy statement from the American Society of Clinical Oncology. *Journal of Clinical Oncology, 38*, 3439–3448.

Paul, L., Chang, D.F., & Bitney, C. (2024). Psychotherapy in Black and White: An examination of how race is discussed in a sample of Black American clients and White American counselors. *Training and Education in Professional Psychology, 18*, 230–238. https://doi-org.proxy1.library.jhu.edu/10.1037/tep0000446

Peluso, P.R., & Freund, R.R. (2018). Therapist and client emotional expression and psychotherapy outcomes: A meta-analysis. *Psychotherapy, 55*(4), 461–472. https://doi.org/10.1037/pst0000165

Ratts, M.J., Singh, A.A., Nassar-McMillan, S., Butler, S.K., & McCullough, J.R. (2016). Multicultural and social justice counseling competencies: Guidelines for the counseling profession. *Journal of Multicultural Counseling and Development, 44*, 28–48. https://doi-org.proxy1.library.jhu.edu/10.1002/jmcd.12035

Rosenzweig, A. (2025, June 16). *Black Americans at increased risk for pancreatic cancer*. Pancreatic Cancer Action Network. https://pancan.org/news/black-americans-at-increased-risk-for-pancreatic-cancer/

Sabin, J.A. (June 6, 2020). How we fail Black patients in pain. *American Association of Medical Colleges*. https://www.aamc.org/news/how-we-fail-black-patients-pain

Scheurich, J., & Young, M. (1997). Coloring epistemologies: Are our research epistemologies racially biased? *Educational Researcher, 26*, 4–16.

Steele, J.M. (2025). *Racism and African American mental health: Using cognitive behavior therapy to empower healing*. Routledge.

Summers, M. (2019). *Madness in the city of magnificent intentions: A history of race and mental illness in the nation's capital*. Oxford University.

Thomas, A., & Sillen, S. (1991). *Racism and psychiatry*. Carol Publishing Group.

Washington, H. (2008). *Medical apartheid: The dark history of medical experimentation on Black Americans from colonial times to the present*. Vintage.

Chapter 8

Strategies for Broaching the Subjects of Race, Ethnicity, and Culture

Years ago, I co-presented a conference workshop with a colleague on the Broaching framework. The workshop was a condensed version of material contained in this textbook. At the conclusion of our presentation, participants approached us to ask additional questions about how they might apply the framework. One man whom we'll call Fred sought my attention and proudly announced that he applied the skills we described during the workshop but glibly informed me they did not work. My colleague overheard him and took a step in our direction, smiled graciously, and said, "Perhaps you didn't apply the skills appropriately." This exchange reinforced my contention that broaching clients' REC concerns is a process, not an event. That is, before engaging in a broaching discussion, the provider must perform a series of preliminary steps that we describe in this chapter.

Broaching requires intention, thought, analysis, timing, and planning. Broaching is not a statement that a provider merely blurts out without paying selective attention to the client's REC concerns – considering the intended purpose of the broaching statement, determining how a broaching statement, question, or probe may propel a client forward to think in more depth about their inner experience, the relational dynamics between the provider and client that may help or hinder the delivery of a broaching statement, and the actual framing of the broaching discussion. The provider's broaching behavior is contingent upon a strong counseling relationship and requires that the provider remain congruent such that their outward presentation of self matches their inner experiences, and that the provider has navigated their own biases, so they do not interfere with the creation of a safe therapeutic relationship. The provider's level of cultural humility, ease of manner, willingness to explore the client's REC concerns are integral to the broaching process. More importantly, the client must perceive the provider as genuine, honest, trustworthy, and engaged, because the client's perceived sense of psychological safety gives rise to the disclosure of personal thoughts and feelings about the embeddedness of REC within the client's presenting concerns (Fuertes et al., 2002).

Throughout this book, I have reiterated that the provider wields the balance of power within the counseling dyad. As such, the provider assumes responsibility

DOI: 10.4324/9781003649311-8

for cultivating a healthy therapeutic environment that allows the client to reflect, grow, heal, and discuss the embeddedness of their REC experiences within their presenting concerns. Effective broaching behavior includes building the therapeutic alliance with the client in order to cultivate trust and set the stage for the eventual broaching process. In earlier chapters, we discussed components of the continuum of broaching framework and the multidimensional model of broaching behavior. This chapter introduces the Strategies Model of the Broaching Framework and encompasses four interrelated components: (a) joining, (b) assessment, (c) preparation, and (d) delivery. Together these components provided a coherent approach to facilitate a positive broaching experience with clients. Because joining and assessment emphasize relational and clinical foundation upon which the broaching framework rests, they are the primary focus of this chapter. The subsequent chapter addresses the preparation and delivery components of the broaching framework and demonstrates how providers can translate this foundation into intentional and meaningful broaching dialogue.

Step 1: Joining

Invitational Skills

During high school, I ran track and cross-country. I was invigorated by distance running and continued as an avid runner until only a few years ago, when my body imposed physical limitations that made walking far more feasible. In any case, I recall that each run started with a warm-up, a series of stretching exercises that progressively loosened and prepared my limbs and joints for the process my body was about to undertake. At one point, I began training for a marathon; however, I did not always stretch before my runs – after all, I was young, felt invincible, and did not think stretching was as important as experts advised. I by-passed that recommendation and three to four weeks before the actual marathon, I was sidelined with painful shin splints that made even walking difficult. In a very similar vein, by-passing the relational aspects of the counseling process may be injurious to the counseling relationship and, by extension, the broaching process. As with any counseling approach, engaging in a meaningful counseling relationship requires certain obligatory steps, such as joining with the client.

Joining refers to the provider's effort to connect with the client by establishing rapport, demonstrating empathy, and exuding respect. During the joining process, providers who intend to broach their clients' REC concerns must establish therapeutic conditions that will facilitate their subsequent broaching efforts. These behaviors communicate the provider's genuine acceptance and appreciation of the client, acknowledgment of the legitimacy of the client's concerns, and the creation of a psychologically safe therapeutic connection that allows the provider to enter the client's perceptual world. This step is critically important because many clients have internalized the notion that REC discussions are taboo and consequently off limits for counseling.

A study of more than 10,000 counseling sessions with nearly 2,000 clients concluded that clients reported having cultural conversations less than 50% of the time, and REC discussions usually occurred with ethnic minority providers, although the rate of discussion varied by provider (Kuo et al., 2024). These findings suggest that although providers may be attuned to ethnic minority clients' need for discussing their REC concerns, joining serves as a prerequisite for building a therapeutic alliance. The establishment of a healthy therapeutic relationship permits the client to be vulnerable and share more intimate details of their REC concerns. Providers have a small window of opportunity in which to create conditions for developing a therapeutic alliance with the client. We know this given the incidence of microaggressions within counseling dyads, the impact on the working alliance, and the high rate of premature termination among minoritized clients in particular (Owen, 2014). Taken together, the skills designed to establish rapport set the stage for the provider's broaching efforts at the appropriate time. That is, before the provider broaches with the client, there should be a secure connection between the provider and client based in part on the provider's use of invitational skills. That connection is developed through a series of verbal and nonverbal behaviors that communicate respect for and acceptance of the client.

Nonverbal Invitational Skills

Invitational skills refer to a sequence of actions, behaviors, and words that help clients develop a sense of comfort and safety within the counseling dyad (Schmidt, 2004). Invitational skills include nonverbal and verbal behaviors, as well as gestures that convey acceptance of the client. Nonverbal invitational skills include policies and practices such as whether a provider is out-of-network and does not accept Medicaid or private insurance from clients. Similarly, when counseling costs are prohibitive, in the absence of sliding scale options, providers may inadvertently convey the message that their services are designated for more materially privileged clients. Whether intentional or not, such policies may discourage prospective clients from seeking counseling services (Brawner & Day-Vines, 2024).

To illustrate, Karen is a poor White woman who lives in a rural part of her state with very few options for providers. She recently gave birth to her third child who was born 12 weeks prematurely with significant medical challenges. The pressure of managing a household with a toddler, a first grader, and a newborn seems daunting to Karen. Additionally, the precarity of her husband's employment situation has left her feeling overwhelmed, such that her mental resources are diminishing. Karen's neighbor told her about an online counseling service that would work perfectly given her time constraints. Karen contacted the provider, only to find that the agency did not accept insurance. Dejected, Karen decided that counseling is only for clients who are wealthy, so she abandoned the idea of counseling altogether, concluding that the prohibitive cost may signal that the provider does not have the capacity to attend to her specific concerns around gender, social class, and geography. As a consequence, Karen questioned whether she might feel misunderstood by and disconnected from her provider. Would her provider understand her struggle to obtain affordable childcare, judge her need to choose between medicine and groceries, pathologize her family's tenuous financial predicament, behave in a condescending manner given their social class differences, ridicule her rural roots, invalidate her self-disclosures, or invoke elitist class-based antagonisms? Although it is the provider's prerogative to accept insurance, not accepting insurance may send a series of metamessages that counseling is an elitist proposition. In a similar vein, the location of a practice or agency may also convey a metamessage about whether clients can arrive by public transport.

Ben decided to pursue therapy because the provider's online bio suggested he worked effectively with members of the LGBTQIA+ community. When Ben arrived at the provider's office, he felt reassured that his counseling experience would be positive. The provider displayed both heterosexual and same-sex couples in office artwork and brochures. He observed a safe-zone sticker and a collection of representative magazines, including copies of *The Advocate* and *Out*, publications geared specifically toward the gay community, which felt reassuring. During an early session with his provider, Ben experienced a disconnect as he described his attraction toward a young man he met at his local gym. It did not take Ben long to realize that although the accoutrements of acceptance appeared authentic given the office atmosphere, Ben experienced his provider's overtures as performative. Ben felt his provider overidentified with him by repeatedly referencing his cousin who was gay. As the reader might imagine, Ben interpreted these references as the provider's effort to demonstrate a false sense of mutuality due to his connections to someone who is gay. Ben did not sense that the provider had an abiding sense of empathy toward the LGBTQIA+ community or deep structural knowledge that would enhance his counseling experience. Although these overtures were the provider's way of demonstrating that he could not possibly be homophobic, Ben experienced his therapist as disingenuous and was put off because the provider had difficulty helping him explore concerns around sexuality. Shortly thereafter, Ben began his search for a new provider.

Metamessages are powerful symbols that demonstrate the provider's level of receptiveness to issues of social and cultural diversity. When determining whether counseling may in fact be safe, clients may place more credence in metamessages than verbal statements alone. As in Ben's case, many people from minoritized groups cannot rely solely on what providers say or do; they must also consider discrepancies between the provider's metamessage and actual behavior.

Intake Forms

Intake forms serve as another opportunity for providers to communicate their level of openness to addressing clients' REC concerns (Davis et al., 2018; Trevino et al., 2021). Essentially, intake forms help providers gather pertinent background information about the client, including but not limited to their reasons for pursuing counseling, prior counseling experience, age, race, ethnicity, religious/spiritual orientation, gender, gender identity, sexual orientation, marital status, medication, education, health, employment status, exercise, physical activity, diet and nutrition, sleep patterns, mental health history, family mental health history, substance use, significant relationships, satisfaction with life, stress levels, sense of safety, exposure to trauma, financial challenges, insurance details, and payment information. Embedding the collection of REC data into an intake form serves as a metamessage to clients that REC discussions are permissible within the counseling process. Additionally, this information helps the provider better understand clients' counseling needs, establish treatment goals, and develop treatment plans. Capturing REC information within intake forms normalizes, and paves the way for subsequent REC discussions.

Several scholars have advocated for the intentional inclusion of REC content within intake forms. For instance, Middleton et al. (2023) asserted that intake assessments should account for clients' intersectional encounters such as religion and the social determinants of health because they impact treatment. The social determinants of health include those structural factors that improve or diminish clients' level of health and well-being. For instance, the mental health of a low-wealth client who suffers from asthma and lives adjacent to factories that emit toxic fumes who cannot afford to move to more desirable areas of the city may be exacerbated by living conditions and the perceived lack of control over life's circumstances. Collins (2023) argued that given the volume of racial trauma encountered by clients from minoritized backgrounds, providers should inquire about clients' exposure to racial trauma. Such questions convey to clients that REC discussions are permissible during the counseling process and can operate as a starting point for building trust and the eventual discussion of the client's REC concerns. Far too much counseling practice ignores the contextual dimensions of REC or addresses REC ineffectively (Brawner et al., 2025; Depauw & Van Hiel, 2024).

Maureen obtained the intake report for her client and used that information to determine how she might proceed with the counseling process. The report indicated that the client sought counseling to discuss concerns about her health following a botched gynecological surgery that left her with serious medical complications. The client is a Latinx female, devout Catholic, mother, grandmother, and wife on Medicaid who speaks accented English and experiences chronic physical pain. Maureen plans to explore information contained in the intake report with her client in order to examine how the client's intersectional identities may contribute to her presenting concerns about debilitating pain levels. Although clients serve as historians over their own lived experiences, it is appropriate for providers to gauge possible topics for conversation. Inasmuch as the intake report provides clues about how the provider might proceed with the counseling process, completing the intake report can also serve as a cue to the client about the types of conversations that may be permissible in counseling. That is, the intake form may indicate to clients that REC discussions are appropriate. If we do not communicate to clients that it is acceptable to discuss varying aspects of their identity in counseling, clients may not know that such discussions are appropriate.

As stated above, broaching is not an event but a process that contains a series of steps that providers can enlist in order to prepare the client for the broaching experience. Broaching does not take place cold turkey. The provider sets the tone for broaching using a series of metacommunicative steps that prime the client that their intersectional identity domains serve as important content for the counseling process. This is especially important among clients for whom REC concerns are pertinent because it begins to personalize the counseling experience.

Verbal Invitational Skills

Inasmuch as nonverbal indicators function as metamessages that convey openness and acceptance to the client and set the stage for eventual broaching discussions, providers can also engage in more explicit overtures that reinforce the provider's willingness to validate and affirm the client and facilitate broaching discussions.

Small Talk

Joining includes the provider's effort to engage in small talk to help the client feel comfortable. For instance, providers may address the weather, the drive into the office, hobbies, musical tastes, pets, etc. Such discussions can help put the client at ease before delving into more substantive topics. The provider may compliment the client. From session to session, the small talk may become more personalized. For instance, if the client indicated in a prior session they were going to a concert, the provider may follow up in the subsequent session by inquiring about their concert experience. Personalized small talk helps clients feel like the provider was paying attention to them. Yalom (2013) emphasizes the importance of making the client matter to the provider. The provider's follow-up questions and comments may signal that the provider is completely and meaningfully engaged in the counseling process in ways that establish mutuality.

It is important to recognize that counseling is a Eurocentric enterprise that mirrors western cultural dictates that may be at odds with the cultural mores, values, and practices of people from nonwestern cultures. For instance, in many but not all cultures, small talk functions as a diplomatic nicety that fosters conditions for a productive counseling relationship. Many of my students of color as well as my more introverted students have informed me that small talk can feel uncomfortable, superficial, forced, and even exhausting. Several of my Asian students have told me that in their culture, small talk does not really exist and consequently requires them to make adjustments that are inconsistent with their cultural values and norms. For instance, in western culture, the individual serves as the psychosocial unit of measurement, so small talk may center around the individual. Conversely, in nonwestern cultures, the collective operates as the psychosocial unit of measurement. Asking people from more collectivist cultures how they are doing may feel alien, because in many of these cultures it would be more appropriate to ask how the family is doing (Sue et al., 2022). Essentially, emphasis centers on "we," not "I." Additionally many people characterize communication patterns in the United States as oriented toward verbosity and efforts to fill silence with excess chatter, whereas in many Asian countries, conversation is reserved for when dialogue is necessary.

As an African American female who is also introverted, I have had similar reactions. When I explain this dynamic to my students, I say that if I am in an integrated setting and someone asked me about a restaurant I visited, I might explain that the cuisine was superb, quenched my palate, that I really enjoyed the braised Brussels sprouts and caramelized onions, and that I hope to return to that restaurant soon. If my closest African American friends asked me about the identical dining experience, I might respond by saying, "Girl, mmh, mmh, mmh!" The statement may be accompanied by a facial expression that indicated the food was outstanding. In any case, both responses convey essentially the same sentiment – I enjoyed the meal immensely. Western culture is perceived by many to fill up conversation with chatter, whereas many nonwestern cultures are more prone to using economy of language. Because ethnic minorities do not constitute a monolith, providers must use their observational skills to determine how clients respond to small talk and make appropriate adjustments, by tailoring their small talk strategies to client preferences. In cases where clients appear uncomfortable with chatter, providers may opt to limit small talk. In light of the current, highly contentious and polarized political climate, providers are cautioned about discussing politics with clients as part of the small talk process.

Informed Consent

The informed consent process is an important preliminary phase of the counseling process that involves the provider's effort to orient clients to the counseling experience. Informed consent apprises the client of key counseling considerations such as agency or practice policies, the provider's credentials, state and federal laws, confidentiality and its limits, as well as detailed information about treatment. One often overlooked detail within the informed consent process involves the effort to engage in preliminary broaching efforts that encourage the client to discuss aspects of their REC identity. For instance, a provider may say something like,

> During our counseling sessions together, you are welcome to discuss mental health concerns, personal challenges, friendships, family relationships, life transitions, as well as concerns about culture, faith, race, social class, gender, or any other topic that may be important to you.

Without an explicit invitation, some clients for whom REC may be important believe that such discussions are off limits. Orienting clients to the counseling arena is important because some clients, especially those who have experienced counseling previously, understand how the counseling process unfolds. Conversely, other clients who have not engaged in prior counseling relationships may need more detailed information about how the counseling process unfolds.

When I was a school counselor, I would often explain to students what was involved in a counseling session and how it could help support them. Students who were new to the counseling process found this explanation very helpful. I had other students who had been in counseling for a period of time with providers in private practice who would say, "Oh, Mrs. Day-Vines, you don't need to explain the counseling process to me. I've been in counseling before, so I know that I'm supposed to tell you my problems and you're supposed to listen to me." Providing clients with details about the counseling process is critically important and can allay anxiety about topics appropriate for discussion. The informed consent process may be an appropriate time to explain to clients that REC discussions are suitable for counseling.

For instance, Erby and White (2020) offer helpful verbiage that normalizes the discussion of clients' REC concerns early in the counseling process. They suggest the following language:

> In our first session, we usually gather background information to get a 'snapshot' of where you are now so we can develop goals. I will ask about your family, significant relationships, health, work, past counseling, etc. I will also ask about your cultural background because I believe that is an important part of each person. This can include race, gender, sexual orientation, religion, or other things that might be important to you.

An important part of this illustrative example is the provider's explanation or rationale delineating why questions about REC are important to the counseling process. Also, the topics of discussion are not prescriptive but descriptive and can help clients think about other areas that they may want to share with the provider.

To illustrate, Yui is an international student who scheduled an appointment in the university counseling center because she is experiencing adjustment difficulties since her arrival in the United States. Unlike some of her international student peers who completed secondary school in the United States and who have a stronger frame of reference for American culture, Yui feels lost in her university, despite the fact that she appreciates the intellectual stimulation she is gaining from her studies. Yui has experienced difficulty acclimating to the weather, food, and U.S. culture, as well as the fact that she desperately misses her family. She is also feeling apprehensive about the polarized political climate and the treatment of immigrants in the United States.

During the informed consent process, the provider shared examples of problem situations that clients typically bring to counseling, as well as factors that contribute to challenges international students experience such as acculturative stress, what it means to be an international student in the United States, encounters with racism and discrimination, gender, religion, sexual orientation, college life, personal values, personal strengths, discrepancies between personal goals and family expectations, personal strengths, plans for the future, problem-solving approaches, etc. In light of the current political climate, the provider also disclosed that international students are starting to come forward of their own accord to share their sense of fear and trepidation about encounters with open hostility, detainment by immigration officers, anti-immigrant sentiment, and microaggressions both within and outside the classroom. The provider reassured Yui that she could structure the counseling sessions to meet her needs. Notably, Yui felt relieved that she could raise concerns that she had not even shared with members of her inner circle. Privately, Yui had hoped that she could address concerns the provider mentioned but would never have initiated such conversations without encouragement from the provider. In essence, the provider effectively communicated to Yui that if REC concerns are integral to her personal concerns, Yui should feel free to discuss them during the counseling process. Such an approach does not insist that clients discuss REC concerns but extends an invitation that clients may accept at some point during the counseling process when such topics become relevant for the client.

Davis et al. (2018) recommend that providers use the informed consent process to apprise clients that instances may arise when cultural ruptures may occur. They contend that such disclosures may help mitigate the damage that results from therapeutic impasses.

Validation Strategies

Validating the client's concerns serves as a facilitative counseling strategy that acknowledges the provider's understanding of client disclosures. This skill enhances the joining process by conveying acceptance and appreciation of the client; moreover, it helps build trust. This can be done in a number of ways. For instance, the provider might use active listening skills to help build empathy by communicating understanding of the client's concerns. With active listening skills, providers not only hear what clients say, but they also respond in ways that communicate understanding by using the basic listening sequence. This includes skills such as open and closed questions, encouragers, silence, paraphrases, and reflective statements that help clients feel heard and understood.

Summary statements that identify key client statements pull together the client's thoughts, feelings, and emotions. Attending skills demonstrate the provider is physically focused on the client by maintaining eye contact, leaning forward, demonstrating interest in the client's concerns, as well as verbal tracking to focus the session without changing subjects.

Sometimes my beginning students feel like active listening skills are unnecessary and have a hard time distinguishing them from parroting or mimicking the client in a robotic fashion. In these instances, students sometimes remain silent and miss key opportunities to capture and restate salient elements of the client's discussion without repeating what the client said verbatim. When this occurs, I ask them if they have ever been in a public place and heard a child call their mother repeatedly, saying, "Mommy, Mommy, Mommy." Usually, the class responds affirmatively, and I explain that most likely, the mother heard the child but did not communicate that understanding to the child. Consequently, the child calls the parent repeatedly because they may feel ignored or that their parent truly did not hear them. Similarly, clients will often repeat their concerns when providers do not convey their understanding of the client's experience through active listening. A considerable amount of research documents the fact that intentional use of these foundational counseling skills results in predictable client responses (Hill, 2020; Ivey et al., 2022). For instance, an open question will result in a more elaborated response from the client, while a closed question usually results in a brief, one-word, or short answer. Reflection of feeling statements usually lead to the client's discussion of their concerns at an affective level. These skills help the client feel heard and understood.

Identify Client Strengths

The identification of client strengths serves as an important component of the counseling process that helps build the therapeutic alliance. By the time many clients come to counseling, they have lost considerable amounts of objectivity. They feel demoralized and worry that their problems will not improve. Because clients may tend to overlook their strengths, the provider has an opportunity to restore objectivity by verbalizing critical client strengths, resources, and areas of resilience.

Several years ago, I conducted a demonstration tape for training purposes. I met with an older African American gentleman who had achieved sobriety following many years of active addiction that decimated his early life. In high school, he had been a star athlete and earned a full ride to a division 1 college. He received numerous accolades and seemed destined for a professional football career, until his drug addiction derailed his future. He subsequently lost his scholarship and, years later, the demise of his marriage and family life. In an effort to get on track, he entered an addiction treatment facility. During our mock counseling session, he described a pivotal moment in his sobriety. One evening after returning from an Alcoholics Anonymous meeting, he shared that he was watching a news broadcast about a murder that happened earlier that evening on the very street where he once sold drugs. In that moment, he made a firm commitment to himself to achieve sobriety and, as a consequence, started taking the program seriously. He confided to me that he couldn't understand why other patients struggled so hard to reach sobriety. I used a positive reframe to suggest that perhaps his success was related to the fact that he applied the skills and strict discipline he cultivated as an elite athlete to his recovery process. He nodded in agreement. In that moment, I used the positive asset search to acknowledge that he had a set of tools that aided in his recovery. This included a series of successes as an athlete, hours of practice, repetition of skill sets, membership on a winning football team, mastery of a skill set, the adulation of adoring fans, a heightened sense of confidence, an earnest desire to be drug-free, and his consistent journey toward sobriety. Given that clients battling addiction can often feel a sense of guilt, shame, and personal defeat, my intention was to draw on his strong sense of resilience and to acknowledge that he had a foundation his peers may not have had.

In a non-counseling example, I recall that as a little boy my nephew spent countless hours playing video games. He was so adept at video games that his father seldom beat him. One night when the entire family was together at my parents' house, my nephew competed against his father and my husband in a video game of *Madden NFL*. He defeated them repeatedly, until they lovingly told him that he could not go to bed until he lost – by then it was already 11:00 p.m. My husband eventually called in his younger brother as reinforcement, but my nephew continued to win. By midnight I went to bed, only to be awakened around 3:00 a.m. by an eruption of cheers and laughter. I rushed into the family room to see what was going on. In a dejected state, my nephew said, "Aunt Norma, I lost." I replied, "Carl, if it took three grown men whose combined age is at least 100- and more than five hours to defeat you, then you are not a loser you are a winner." My nephew equated a single defeat as representative of his overall performance and ability. He failed to see that he had competed successfully against adults for hours on end. It is critically important that we look for opportunities to help clients recognize their strengths, so they regain their sense of self-assurance. Sometimes we have to help clients re-story and redefine the flawed narratives they internalize in order to help them generate a new point of view. Incidentally, many of the skills we use in counseling prove helpful in our interpersonal relationships as well. As a caveat, there are instances when a positive asset search may be less effective. For for some clients, insincere praise may compromise trust between the provider and client. Individuals raised in cultures that emphasize modesty may struggle with praise because they do not want to be perceived as arrogant or engaging in self-aggrandizement. Additionally trauma survivors may experience praise as the precursor to manipulation or criticism.

Step 2: Assessment

A second component of the strategies framework involves the assessment phase (Day-Vines et al., 2021). During this phase of the broaching process, providers

Table 8.1 Components of the Assessment Phase

Multicultural case conceptualization	Provider's assessment of cultural dimensions that may impact the client's presenting concerns using approaches such as the RESPECTFUL model.
Racial identity functioning	Provider's consideration of the client's level of racial identity functioning and the impact on the client's counseling concerns.
Client readiness	Provider's assessment of the client's preparedness to engage in a broaching discussion.
Strength of therapeutic alliance	Provider's assessment that the relationship is healthy enough to proceed with a broaching discussion.
Provider self-efficacy	Provider's preparedness to execute a broaching encounter as evidenced by management of their own attitudes, biases, and assumptions; openness to engaging the client's REC concerns, counseling skill set, and belief that they can facilitate broaching strategies with fidelity.

gauge what is going on with the client that may both create barriers to their well-being and/or serve as sources of strength and resilience. To prepare for the broaching process, the provider engages in a series of cognitive processes that precede broaching statements in order to generate a holistic framing of the client's concerns by assessing five specific considerations. The cognitive processes involve (a) multicultural case conceptualization, (b) racial identity functioning, (c) client readiness to explore REC concerns, (d) the strength of the therapeutic relationship, and (e) provider self-efficacy. These six considerations help the provider determine which topic areas warrant more in-depth discussion and gauge when and how to proceed with the broaching process. Because these considerations incorporate clients' intersectional domains, providers reduce the likelihood of limiting clients to say their race, gender, or social class. Table 8.1 summarizes these considerations.

Multicultural Case Conceptualization

Multicultural case conceptualization involves the provider's effort to pay selective attention to the client's intersectional identity domains and the corresponding sources of power and oppression that are embedded in clients' presenting concerns. As discussed in Chapter 5, clients do not have single-axis concerns; instead, they have a full complement of intersectional concerns that may be rooted in interlocking systems of oppression that impinge on their sense of identity and well-being. These concerns warrant exploration during treatment. The multicultural case conceptualization framework provides an integrative approach to exploring clients' backgrounds.

When I am teaching, I refer to the provider's responsibility to engage in multicultural case conceptualization as WTHIGO. That means providers have a responsibility to determine "What the Heck Is Going On" with the client. Although there are several frameworks for examining a broad range of identity domains, I have selected the RESPECTFUL model to illustrate multicultural case conceptualization (D'Andrea & Daniels, 2001). This model contains ten specific considerations for attending to clients' intersectional concerns that permit the provider to better understand clients using a holistic framework that assesses both positive and oppressive forces that shape their realities and influence how they make meaning from their experiences. The RESPECTFUL model offers a template that providers may use to guide clients through broaching discussions in order to help them see themselves and their problem situations with more depth and complexity. When used as a mnemonic device, the RESPECTFUL model helps providers formulate a working hypothesis about the client's needs. Providers can use information gleaned from this model to better conceptualize the client's worldview (Davis et al., In the section that follows, Mei-ling, a second-generation Chinese American woman, is introduced. Her presenting concerns are conceptualized using the RESPECTFUL model to illustrate her intersectional identity domains and their relevance to the counseling process. Table 8.2 contains a synopsis of the RESPECTFUL model components and highlights how each dimension pertains to Mei-ling's presenting concerns. 2018).

Table 8.2 RESPECTFUL Counseling Model

RESPECTFUL Domain	*Characteristics*	*Relevance for Mei-ling*
Religious	Client's connection or disconnection to a religious and/or spiritual system; meaning systems	Raised Buddhist, but has chosen to become agnostic
Economic	Client's socioeconomic background and the way financial issues impact the client's sense of well-being, opportunity structures, and access to resources	Raised in a working-class home, but through education, preparing to enter the middle class
Sexual identity	Client's awareness of their gender, gender roles, gender identity, and sexual orientation	Identifies as a cisgender heterosexual woman
Psychological maturity	Client's ability to make reasonable decisions, delay gratification; regulate emotions, engage in perspective taking, believe in themselves, and control emotions; identity development	Experiences a sense of personal conflict over the cultural expectations demanded by her family, her sense of obligation to the collective, and the desire for her own autonomy.

(Continued)

Table 8.2 (Continued)

RESPECTFUL Domain	*Characteristics*	*Relevance for Mei-ling*
Ethnic-cultural-racial identity	Client's sense of connection and/or disconnection from people whose REC backgrounds are both similar to and/or different from their own	Maintains a healthy appreciation for both her Asian and American identity
Chronological development challenges	Client's recognition of development across the lifespan from infancy through adulthood; impact on the life course, including developmental and acquired disabilities	Meeting developmental targets as evidenced by her effort to solidify her racial, sexual, religious, and career identities
Trauma and other threats to one's well-being	Client's ability to manage stressful life events that may result in harm	Feels threatened by the current political climate in the United States
Family history and dynamics	Client's level of family functioning, family constellation, and the ability to identify strengths despite family organization and challenges	Second-generation immigrant who is working to reconcile the psychosocial challenges between first- and second-generation family members
Unique physical characteristics	Client's sense of physical beauty despite idealized characteristics, including physical disabilities	Early on internalized Eurocentric standards of beauty but is now gaining a healthy sense of self-acceptance and cultural pride.
Location of residence and language differences	Client's geographic origin and linguistic diversity	Bilingual; grew up in a monocultural community with fewer Asian influences outside of her immediate family

Religious/spiritual identity refers to the role religion and spirituality play in clients' lives. Providers can work with the client to determine whether religion and spirituality serve as a guiding force that shapes how clients make sense of their world. Further, they can examine whether and how religious principles, or a higher power, contribute to a belief system that influences how clients respond to phenomena. A provider engaged in multicultural case conceptualization would likely gather information about the value clients place on religion and spirituality and the extent to which religious norms and values shape their presenting concerns. It is reasonable to assume that some clients may not endorse a specific religious or spiritual grounding. In such cases, it may be helpful to explore how clients make meaning of life, as well as their inherent values and belief systems (Bishop, 2018).

Mei-ling, 20, a second-generation child of Chinese immigrants, was raised in a Buddhist household where religious cultural traditions were an important part of her upbringing. Now in her junior year of college, Mei-ling has become agnostic, distancing herself from the religious grounding in which she was reared. The provider's effort to explore the evolution of Mei-ling's religious beliefs, values, and experience seems important to discuss. The answers to questions such as what prompted Mei-ling's shift from Buddhism to agnosticism, the experience of entering a non-religious identity, possible encounters with ostracism or judgment from her community for leaving behind her religious traditions, Mei-ling's effort to establish boundaries with family and friends concerning her decisions about religion, and the meaning and significance of her new non-religious identity will ultimately help the provider work more effectively with Mei-ling; moreover, this discussion may likely deepen Mei-ling's level of self-understanding.

Economic and class backgrounds refer to the client's socioeconomic status and how financial resources and the meaning attached to social class status shape problem situations. Financial precarity may exacerbate distress levels. For instance, although many of Mei-ling's close friends hail from upper middle-class and/or affluent households, Mei-ling's parents are working-class people who toil long hours for owners of an Asian restaurant in her local community. Her father is a cook and her mother is a waitress. Mei-ling's parents took on enormous debt to finance her college education. Although her tuition and room and board are paid, she seldom has additional resources to take trips and enjoy leisure activities with her more materially privileged peers. Mei-ling feels like she is masquerading as someone who maintains the same privileges as her K peers. She harbors some shame and embarrassment that her parents are not as refined as her peers' parents. As a first-generation college student, Mei-ling has begun to experience a sense of social distance from her family, presumably because she is straddling two diametrically opposed worlds, the middle-class world she desperately strives to enter, and the working-class world she is in a rush to leave behind.

Alfred Lubrano's (2005) groundbreaking book, *Limbo: Blue-Collar Roots, White-Collar Dreams*, captures the internal conflict that can strain family relationships as individuals work to climb the social ladder. Relatedly, in her book, *Asian Americans in Class: Charting the Achievement Gap Among Korean American Youth*, Jamie Lew (2006) debunked the myth of the model minority as she compared and contrasted differing social, economic, and educational contexts of second-generation Korean immigrant students from both working- and middle-class backgrounds. Mei-ling's provider may explore Mei-ling's social class worldview and along with other salient identities (race, gender, family history). For instance, does Mei-ling experience internalized classism wherein she harbors negative feelings about trying to keep up with her peers who are more materially privileged than she is? To what extent does Mei-ling encounter emotional distress that results from straddling two social worlds and how do these feelings impact her family relationships and personal friendships? What is the relationship between Mei-ling's social class identity, gender, and race?

Sexual identity, according to the RESPECTFUL model, sexual identity refers to an individual's gender identity, gender roles, and sexual orientation. Mei-ling identifies as a cisgender heterosexual female who, although open to a dating relationship, has had difficulty finding the right partner. She is unwilling to compromise her values and feels exhausted by the hyper-sexualization she encounters as a young Asian woman on her college campus. Disturbingly, Mei-ling has experienced sexual harassment, but she has decided not to lodge a formal complaint against the perpetrator. In her groundbreaking book entitled *Patterns That Remain: A Guide to Healing for Asian Children of Immigrants*, Diane Stacey Arañez Litam (2025) described the demoralizing ways that many Asian women are seen and treated through pejorative stereotypes, aggressive sexual gestures, and taunts. She documented the mental health challenges that result from such unwanted sexual attention. Mei-ling's provider will need to provide emotional and psychological safety necessary to explore the consequences that result from unwanted sexual attention (e.g., anxiety, depression, loss of self-esteem). The provider may also explore the combined effects of racism and sexism, as well as the role of society in perpetuating and reinforcing various forms of sexual violence. Psycho-education seems appropriate to help Mei-ling cope and confront these situations and begin the healing process.

Psychological maturity encompasses one's ability to engage in age-appropriate behaviors, exhibit self-regulation, perspective taking, and self-control. As individuals develop psychological maturity, they shift from an egocentric or more self-centered orientation to an allocentric or other-centered way of interacting with their world (D'Andrea & Daniels, 2001). Although Mei-ling recognizes the enormous sacrifices her parents have made so that she can enjoy many of the comforts associated with American life, she harbors resentment about the control they exercise over her life, especially in terms of being a dutiful daughter; the pressure she experiences to achieve, make her family proud, avoid bringing shame on the family, marry within their cultural community, etc. The pressure her family exerts over her makes her feel that she lacks personal autonomy, which is important to her. At the same time, she harbors a sense of guilt and shame that she is not more appreciative of the sacrifices her parents have made for her. As Sahaj Kaur Kohli (2024) asserts in *What Will People Say?: Navigating Mental Health, Identity, Love, and Family Between Cultures*, clients like Mei-ling occupy two distinct cultural ethos that are at odds with one another. Clients often use counseling to reconcile cultural conflicts, especially when torn between the desire to honor family expectations and simultaneously work to meet their own personal needs. Although Mei-ling grapples with certain family dynamics, her provider is helping her approach her problem situations with growing levels of insight, personal awareness, perspective taking, and cultural norms that prohibit her from solely considering her own perspectives and viewpoints.

Ethnic-racial identity captures the client's sense of connection with or disconnection from people with whom they share the same racial designation, as well as their attitudes about people from other ethnic-racial groups. In the United States, race operates as an organizing principle that structures social hierarchies, the distribution of resources, the presence or absence of equitable treatment, and messages individuals internalize about their sense of worth and self-acceptance (Wilkerson, 2020). The racialization process holds considerable influence in the live and experiences of many clients from ethnic minority backgrounds. We will address racial identity separately in this chapter. In any case, Mei-ling has a healthy appreciation for both her Asian and American identity, although her parents accuse her of being entirely too American and abandoning her traditional Asian values. In order to better conceptualize her ethnic-racial identity, Mei-ling's provider asked her to describe how she identifies racially and/or ethnically, her degree of acceptance of her REC background, experiences with microaggressions, the intersection of racism and sexism, coping strategies, etc. Mei-ling appreciated her provider's effort to introduce issues about race into the counseling dyad. As many scholars have attested, without explicit acknowledgment of the way race intrudes upon clients' lives, many clients may withhold cultural content during treatment (Anandavalli et al., 2020; Drinane et al., 2018; Litam, 2025). As mentioned in earlier chapters, the provider wields the balance of power within the counseling relationship and therefore maintains a responsibility for initiating REC discussions during treatment (Choi et al., 2015). Ultimately, the client determines the extent to which they want to explore their ethnic-racial identity in session; however, the provider must at the very least pose a broaching question.

Chronological developmental challenges refer to age-related growth and developmental tasks and challenges that occur throughout the lifespan (e.g., infancy, childhood, adolescence, adulthood). Developmental tasks include physical, cognitive, and psychological changes that individuals undergo at predictable points throughout life. Successful negotiation of these tasks helps determine whether clients experience healthy self-esteem, lead productive lives, and/or experience personal satisfaction in life. As a young adult, Mei-ling is meeting developmental targets. For instance, physically, she has met developmental markers for her age group and has had few physical or health challenges.

Cognitively, Mei-ling thinks critically and analytically and she has achieved academic success. Psychologically she is working to balance her sense of independence from her family. As a young adult, Mei-ling is solidifying her racial, sexual, religious, political, and career identity in ways that will contribute to a fulfilling life course. Mei-ling is also working to gain emotional and financial independence from her parents, develop mature lasting relationships with her peers, and consider prospects for romantic relationships. During the counseling process, Mei-ling's provider has invited her to discuss how each of her identity dimensions intersect with one another in order to guard against oversimplifying or essentializing her experiences. As it stands now, Mei-ling is focused on her future, creating a career path for herself, and developing friendships that will help create balance in her life.

Threats to one's personal well-being refer to those inevitable encounters with stress that can disrupt normal development and a healthy sense of psychological well-being. Clients' coping mechanisms, self-esteem, social support, and personal power help them navigate tumultuous life events (D'Andrea & Daniels, 2001). Overwhelmingly stressful experiences interfere with psychological well-being. Mei-ling is coming of age in the United States during a very difficult point in history wherein the nation has become increasingly more polarized. Regular news accounts discuss growing animosity between competing political parties, the erosion of democratic norms, economic inequality, threats to women's reproductive rights, backlash against the LGBTQIA+ community, escalating racial tensions, anti-immigrant hostility, and in Mei-ling's specific case, persistent anti-Asian sentiment.

Although Mei-ling is a U.S. citizen, reports of growing authoritarianism in the country have left her on heightened alert about her sense of safety and security. Despite the fact that she is a citizen, she worries that Immigration and Customs Enforcement officials may harass and possibly detain her. Mei-ling has watched a disturbing number of media accounts about citizens being apprehended and, in some cases, deported. Although the vast majority of Asian deportees have roots in Southeast Asia and have been convicted previously of a crime, published reports have chronicled the deportation of undocumented Chinese migrants through removal flights (Gu, 2024; Wang, 2025). Mei-ling finds these reports unsettling, especially since her parents are undocumented. Essentially, she is experiencing vicarious trauma, or the internalization of stress that results from hearing about or witnessing violence versus directly experiencing violence. Despite the fact that she is a U.S. citizen, Mei-ling worries that she may be targeted indiscriminately. In recent months, Mei-ling has become hypervigilant, anticipating problematic situations that have resulted in her perpetual flight-or-fight mode. As a safety precaution, she has prepared herself to be stopped by police officers. When she leaves her apartment, Mei-ling carries legal documentation that attests to her legitimacy as a citizen. Mei-ling's personal observation of the stressors around her has given her cause for alarm. In order to support her, Mei-ling's provider works to build trust, validates her experiences, normalizes her reactions to the current political climate, uses grounding exercises to help manage bouts of anxiety, and has helped Mei-ling develop an emergency plan to secure her safety and connect with Asian organizations on campus and in the local town.

Family background history refers to dynamics associated with family functioning. One way of conceptualizing family dynamics involves consideration of family composition, such as whether the client is a member of a nuclear, single-parent, same-sex, blended, extended, adoptive-family unit, etc. Historically, people have used nuclear, two-parent (e.g., male-female) households as the standard against which other family systems are judged. Experts now understand that healthy family functioning can result from many different family constellations. The quality of family relationships has greater influence on healthy development and well-being than family constellation alone. Providers must explore the client's family functioning by inquiring about family dynamics such as social supports, strengths, stressors, coping strategies, resilience, and support. Additionally, they may want to explore family history and the impact of that history on client functioning.

Mei-ling's parents came to the United States to pursue social mobility. When they arrived, they were nearly penniless. They lived in a three-bedroom apartment with two other families to save costs. Her parents worked hard to move from their cramped living quarters to the more spacious single-family home her family now occupies. Mei-ling knows beyond a shadow of a doubt that her parents love her, but she senses their love is conditioned upon her academic and professional success. She gets annoyed when she hears her parents brag about her accomplishments and sometimes feels that they are more interested in her accomplishments and the pride she brings to the family than to her actual personhood. This sentiment leaves Mei-ling feeling wounded and unappreciated. Mei-ling disclosed to her provider that although she loves her parents dearly and recognizes that their love is genuine, she feels burdened by cultural expectations that she translate for her parents, accompany them to appointments, and follow what she perceives as stringent cultural expectations. She feels that the cultural practices that were sustained in China have far less relevance on her current lifestyle in the United States. Litam (2025) described the manner in which immigration status may impact attachment styles. More specifically, she notes that family challenges resulting from immigration histories, acculturative stress, survival needs, diasporic wounds etc., result in insecure attachment styles that interfere with healthy family functioning and personal development. Litam noted that caregivers may impose unrealistic expectations that overwhelm their offspring, as evidenced by hypervigilance, fear of disappointing family members, detachment from personal needs, and social distance from family members. Counseling provides an opportunity to heal many of these wounds.

Unique physical characteristics refer to how a client experiences standards of beauty that may be presented in ways that minimize and marginalize the client's sense of self. Society places undue pressure on women to meet rigid standards of beauty. For some clients, gaining self-acceptance is especially difficult to achieve. As children, these youngsters sometimes experience ridicule from peers because their physical appearance may not approximate Eurocentric notions of beauty, such as aquiline features, blond hair, or blue eyes. As a teenager, Mei-ling wished she were White and had blond hair and blue eyes because she believed that would make life easier. She avoided the sun at all costs, used copious amounts of sunscreen, researched ways to lose skin pigment, and experimented with skin-bleaching products, but stopped after learning that those products contained damaging ingredients. When she entered college, Mei-ling began spending time with more Asian peers and developed a greater sense of personal and cultural self-acceptance. Today when she looks back on her teenage years, Mei-ling appreciates how much she has evolved from a self-deprecating orientation to a healthier level of self-acceptance. She hopes to mentor other Asian teens who endorse unhealthy societal standards of beauty. Mei-ling's provider may want to explore how Mei-ling both adopted varying forms of internalized oppression and later unlearned the colonizing mindsets that allowed her to develop a healthy level of cultural pride. Additionally, the provider may want to examine any lingering sources of internalized oppression that Mei-ling may need to manage.

Location of residence and language differences include the client's geographic locale as well as issues of linguistic diversity. Mei-ling grew up in a suburban community outside a major urban center in the mid-Atlantic region of the United States. During her formative years, there were few other Asian families in her school and community. Consequently, Mei-ling socialized primarily with White students and gravitated toward Eurocentric standards of beauty that devalued her own culture. As a teenager, Mei-ling was embarrassed that her parents spoke very limited English and avoided public settings with them whenever possible. During her college years she pivoted and developed a renewed appreciation for her parents. Given that Mei-ling is developing a greater sense of cultural pride and personal self-acceptance, it may be important to discuss how living with few other Asian peers as role models may have contributed to earlier encounters with internalized oppression. Additionally, providers may explore how Mei-ling has worked to resolve earlier indifference toward her language of origin, discuss Mei-ling's efforts to forgive herself for rejecting her linguistic origins, examine the meaning she attaches to bilingualism, and discuss the importance of attributing her feelings of guilt and shame to sources of racialized oppression.

Essentially, multicultural case conceptualization is an important counseling component that involves the provider's consideration of multiple aspects of the client's identity. Providers can use the RESPECTFUL model to explore the complexity of clients' intersectional identities and corresponding sources of oppression in order to move toward greater levels of psychological well-being. This tool serves as a heuristic device that prevents providers from essentializing clients. Providers can consider the client's intersectional domains by exploring how issues of power and oppression shape clients' experiences.

The RESPECTFUL model can facilitate self-understanding by exploring the client's sources of strength, support, and resilience, as well as their encounters with both oppression and internalized oppression. Although dimensions of the RESPECTFUL model are presented in a linear fashion within the text, in actuality, they are overlapping and intersecting. That is, dimensions do not occur one by one; instead, they usually operate simultaneously. Exploration of the RESPECTFUL domains helps providers gain a more composite understanding of the client and can help pinpoint what topics are more salient and warrant more counseling attention, especially as it pertains to goal setting and treatment planning.

Growing up in a community where there were limited opportunities to interact with other Asians in ways that could promote healthy self-acceptance may have contributed to Mei-ling's internalized oppression, her longing to be White, and early rejection of her Asian culture. Attending a college where Mei-ling had opportunities to connect with Asian peers may have helped her gain a new perspective on her racial and cultural identity.

As the child of immigrants, Mei-ling likely experienced challenges that some of her Euro-American peers or Asian peers whose families have been in the United States longer may have already worked through. Mei-ling's parents are part of the immigrant generation, and she represents the second generation. Among immigrants, each generation has a different set of psychosocial tasks. For instance, Mei-ling's parents immigrated to the United States and assumed responsibility for settling in a new culture, obtaining work, reinforcing Asian culture, and rearing the children. They maintained close ties to their culture of origin. Because Mei-ling was inculcated within both Asian and American culture, she appreciates both cultures, which seems to have created tensions between herself and her parents who believe she has become too American. Mei-ling is straddling two cultural worlds and working to develop her own identity as it pertains to her new non-religious belief system, striving to attain middle-class social status, and the ambivalence she seems to experience as a first-gen college student. Mei-ling feels some shame for not accepting her parents, but she also respects all that her parents have done for her. Mei-ling has also experienced psychological distress because of the sexual harassment she experienced. This may also be an important topic of discussion for counseling.

Inasmuch as the RESPECTFUL model is a valuable tool for conceptualizing the client's presenting concerns, there are a number of caveats that providers must attend to. First, the model should not operate as a discrete set of identity domains that operate in isolation from one another. Instead, providers should integrate and synthesize these domains and recognize that clients' identities are not static but may continue to evolve. Second, even as providers gauge their client's level of functioning and positionality along each of these domains, it is incumbent among the provider to also consider their own attitudes, biases, and assumptions so that their idiosyncrasies do not interfere with the counseling process. This includes their work with clients who may differ from themselves, as well as toward clients with whom they share a number of commonalities, so as not to over-identify with clients (Bayne & Branco, 2018). Self-awareness functions as an important prerequisite for facilitating dimensions of the RESPECTFUL model.

The RESPECTFUL model helps providers shift from overly simplistic formulations that reduce clients to a single identity domain, such as race, and permits them to work collaboratively with clients to develop more robust conceptualizations about clients' REC concerns. Many clients have hidden REC discourses that are embedded within their presenting problems (Moodley & Kleiman, 2018). The provider's goal is to help clients uncover those hidden discourses.

Racial Identity Functioning

As we discussed in depth in Chapter 3, racial identity refers to how individuals perceive themselves and others as racial beings, as well as their perceptions on racial dynamics within society. Racial identity functioning operates on a continuum that advances from less complex, adaptive, and differentiated to more complex, adaptive, and differentiated functioning. Individuals with lower levels of racial identity commitment may adopt colorblind perspectives, minimize the significance of race, deny the existence of racism, and accept stereotypes about minoritized group members. In contrast, individuals with strong racial identity commitment levels exhibit positive in-group preferences and actively distance themselves from members of other racial groups. At times they maintain pejorative views toward people outside their racial group. Individuals functioning at the highest end of the racial identity continuum have more balanced racial identity perspectives, demonstrate a healthy appreciation for both their own and other racial groups, and tend to be less hostile and defensive and more willing to build meaningful relationships with people across racial boundaries.

Providers' level of racial identity functioning has important implications for their self-reported broaching behavior. For instance, school counselors operating at higher levels of racial identity functioning endorsed significantly fewer avoidant broaching behaviors and demonstrated a significantly greater commitment to social justice issues (Day-Vines et al., 2022). Helms and Cook (1999) asserted that providers operating at higher racial identity levels are better poised to support clients along the entirety of the racial identity spectrum. Sprinthall et al. (1997) concluded that clients benefit therapeutically when providers are more developmentally advanced than clients because they can stimulate more complex growth. Conversely, providers operating at lower racial identity levels feel less qualified to support clients who have more advanced levels of racial identity.

In their study, Thrower et al. (2020) interviewed graduate-level counseling supervisors who conducted lab sessions in a group counseling course to better understand their racial experiences managing group dynamics. Findings indicated that supervisors with lower levels of racial identity functioning reported feeling lost, confused, insecure, and underprepared at times when discussing issues of race with students. White supervisors described feelings of White guilt when raising concerns about race and representation. At times, supervisors of color struggled to manage their racial indifference toward White male students. Supervisors of color also exhibited more advanced racial identity schemas compared to their White counterparts.

Helms and Cook (1999) identified three core domains related to the racial identity social interaction model. This model describes provider-client alliances and emphasizes the impact of the provider's racial identity schema on the counseling process, namely, whether providers explore or ignore clients' racial concerns. They identified three specific schemas: (a) progressive, (b) regressive, and (c) parallel. Progressive providers have higher levels of racial identity functioning than their clients, which contributes to a more productive counseling dyad in that providers feel equipped to explore clients' REC concerns. Regressive counseling relationships result when the provider is less racially evolved than the client. Such provider-client relationships may hinder the discussion of clients' race-related concerns, contributing to relational discord and possibly leading to therapeutic ruptures. That is, clients may feel that the provider is poorly equipped to meet their REC concerns. Parallel interactions result when the provider and client have similar levels of racial identity functioning. Providers should engage in personal reflection about the specific nature of their counseling relationship, because they are better poised to address clients' REC concerns when their racial functioning is more advanced than their clients.

Drawing from the research of Helms and Cook (1999), Day-Vines et al. (2007) identified counseling considerations that providers should weigh as they determine how to proceed with clients with differing racial identity levels. Conceptualizing the client's level of racial identity development serves as an important first step that allows providers to both assess the client's level of identity functioning and subsequently meet clients where they are. It also reinforces the reality that people are not monolithic and may have varying approaches to expressing their level of racial identity schemas.

Day-Vines et al. (2007) theorized that clients operating at lower levels of racial identity functioning may decline the provider's invitation to explore racially, ethnically, and culturally contextualized meanings associated with their experiences and counseling concerns. These clients may adopt colorblind racial ideologies and, by doing so, struggle to recognize the salience of REC in their lives. In fact, they may identify other areas of salience apart from their racial identity. For instance, Sanjay is a biracial male whose father is South Asian and mother is White. Although he resembles both parents, phenotypically he looks Indian. His skin tone is more olive-complected, and he has naturally curly hair that he cuts close. He looks racially ambiguous but not White; however, most of his friends and acquaintances are White, and he becomes somewhat uncomfortable when issues of race emerge. Ordinarily, he responds by diverting conversations to race-neutral topics. He prefers to be called Jay, although that nickname unnerves his parents. He identifies more with his American heritage than his South Asian heritage.

Jay is a sophomore in college who rushed a fraternity but did not gain membership. Shortly after this experience he scheduled an appointment to meet with a provider in the university counseling center. He disclosed to his provider his utter disappointment about not receiving an invitation to join a fraternity, particularly the fraternity of his choice. He saw himself as an affable, outgoing, and stellar student. When prompted by his provider, Jay catalogued a number of possible reasons he was not offered a bid to his preferred fraternity. He reasoned that perhaps he did not stand out during rush social events or may have appeared socially awkward to fraternity members. He also shared that although his family was affluent, they did not come from old money, nor were members of his family fraternity members. Jay did not entertain the possibility that his rejection may be related to the history of segregation and discrimination in these organizations.

After Jay identified several possibilities for his rejection from the fraternity, the provider said very tentatively, "I wonder if there is at least a small possibility that your rejection may be attributed in part to your race and the long history of racially exclusive policies in fraternal organizations." Jay responded by asking the provider what she meant. The provider continued by adding that "some fraternities engage in activities that may discourage students of color from joining, such as racist themed parties. In 2020, college students started Instagram accounts documenting racist incidents that occurred on their campuses." Jay vehemently denied that he was rejected from fraternity life on the basis of his race. The provider did not contradict Jay but reasoned to herself that Jay's level of racial identity functioning may be low. The provider surmised that Jay maintained a colorblind racial ideology that would make it difficult for him to acknowledge how issues of race and representation may have impacted his prospects for admission to the fraternity of his choice. Rather than insist that racist incidents were prevalent in Greek letter college organizations, and that his rejection may be related to race, the provider said,

> The issue of race and Greek life may not seem plausible to you at this time; however, if there is ever a time where you feel that issues of race are relevant for you, I'm open to exploring that discussion with you.

The provider did not want to erode the counseling relationship by forcing Jay into discussions for which he was not prepared, because insistence on having such discussions might create a therapeutic rupture. It may also signal that the provider was more invested in demonstrating the prevalence of racism than accepting Jay's interpretation of events. As it stands now, race is not a salient identity for Jay. His career ambitions or his effort to gain social acceptance by his peers may hold more sway for him. Focusing on Jay's presumed internalized racism may be premature until Jay is more prepared for such discussions. When and if Jay feels prepared to discuss the role of race in his life, the provider will be available to facilitate those discussions.

Clients with a high level of racial identity commitment levels may exhibit a strong sense of connection and affiliation with their racial/ethnic cultural group. They may be deeply immersed in their cultural group and express anger and hostility toward individuals who do not share their strong racial/ethnic proclivities. They may express racial pride by immersing themselves in their culture, history, customs and may appear intense. Often, they express outrage toward unjust systems, engage in activism, and resent members of the dominant culture or individuals within their own racial/ethnic groups who do not share their viewpoints. Although some providers may be tempted to distance themselves from these clients, moving forward with a sense of cultural humility may help the client engage in healthier forms of self-expression.

Jorge is a Latinx man who has experienced what appeared to his provider as race-related stress. He was recently placed on a performance improvement plan at his job after lashing out at his supervisor. Human resources mandated personal counseling and anger management as a condition for continued employment. When Jorge first met with his provider, he presented as agitated and hostile, exhibiting behaviors that may be off-putting or intimidating to most providers. Jorge's provider observed that he had very provocative positions about race. Often providers express reluctance to engage these individuals in REC discussions because of the intensity of their self-expression. Rather than exhibiting fear and trepidation and avoiding the intensity of Jorge's emotions, the provider explored those factors and experiences that have contributed to Jorge's strong emotions. Although Jorge presented as strident and combative, the provider was not put off by Jorge's self-expression. In fact, the provider wanted to gather more information about factors that contributed to Jorge's frustration at work so as not to make unfounded assumptions. As it turns out, Jorge was placed on probation at work because he got into a disagreement with his supervisor. Jorge disclosed that the tension between them has been mounting for months. He noted that his supervisor would often distribute the workload unevenly, assigning Jorge to more difficult, labor-intensive tasks. Jorge is the only Latinx person in his department and feels a sense of isolation. His co-workers seldom invite him to lunch; he feels excluded from the information loop and has overheard jokes that have racial overtones. He senses that his supervisor is not only aware of the treatment he experienced from his co-workers but also condones his co-workers' behavior. Jorge filed a complaint with human resources concerning his perceptions that his supervisor is biased. This decision seems to have backfired because his supervisor has retaliated by micromanaging him in a way that feels patently unfair. Jorge confronted his supervisor rather aggressively and was written up. He now feels worried about the possible loss of employment. He is supporting his own immediate family and his sister's family. She has relied on Jorge to help supplement her family's income because her husband was deported recently due to his status as an undocumented immigrant.

During the counseling process, Jorge felt the opportunity to express the enormity of the stress he experienced was cathartic. The provider's sense of curiosity and empathy helped reduce Jorge's level of defensiveness. Jorge benefited from a full airing of his concerns, which cultivated trust and a sense of psychology safety. The sense of security his provider demonstrated allowed Jorge to be vulnerable and move forward in treatment. Jorge's provider was not put off by the intensity of his self-expression but instead recognized that his encounters with racial oppression justified the sense of pain, hurt, woundedness, and outrage he felt.

Table 8.3 Interactive Model of Broaching and Racial Identity Functioning

Interactive Model Broaching of Racial Identity Functioning		
Client's Racial Identity Functioning	*Client's Response to Provider's Broaching Effort*	*Counseling Considerations*
Low racial identity commitment levels	• May reject provider's invitation to broach • May have low salience attitudes about race	• Accept and explore the client's reaction to issues of race and representation • May help prepare the client to deal effectively with racialized encounters
Strong racial identity commitment levels	• May have strong reactions to provider's broaching efforts	• Do not personalize client reactions • Identify experiences that may have led to strong reactions • Develop interventions that help clients function more effectively
Balanced racial identity commitment levels	• May appreciate provider's willingness to explore how race shapes their presenting problems	• Broach using recommended guidelines

Source: Adapted from J. Helms' Interactive Racial Identity Model.

Providers may use the normal recommended broaching strategies for clients operating at the higher end of the broaching continuum who exhibit more balanced racial identity attitudes. Ideally, providers would be more evolved than their clients (e.g., progressive). In order to process clients' racial identity schemas effectively, providers need to exhibit progressive racial identity schemas (Thrower et al., 2020). Table 8.3 contains an interactive model for attending to clients' demonstrated level of racial identity functioning.

Client Readiness to Explore REC Concerns

Because broaching operates as a process or series of interconnected multicultural counseling skills and not an event or a singular, isolated moment within the counseling session, providers should assess the client's preparedness for more intimate conversations about their REC concerns. To begin, the provider should look for markers indicating the client's preparedness to engage in REC discussions. This includes gauging how effectively the joining process has unfolded and demonstration of warmth, empathy, and genuineness as important precursors to broaching discussions. Not only does the provider need to exhibit these attributes, more importantly, the client needs to experience the provider's behavior as authentic, especially since previous research documents the prevalence of negative relational dynamics (e.g., microaggressions) that disrupt the therapeutic process for minoritized clients in particular (Hook et al., 2016; Owen, 2014). Essentially, the client needs to feel psychologically safe and comfortable with the provider before an effective broaching discussion ensues.

Additionally, providers should consider the client's responsiveness to verbal and nonverbal invitational skills as well as markers associated with the RESPECTFUL model in order to develop a more holistic conceptualization of the client's needs that may serve as a springboard for facilitating deeper REC conversations. For instance, what importance does the client place on cultural values and viewpoints? Does the client appear comfortable talking about more intimate details of their life? Does the client exhibit visible signs of discomfort with the provider or respond to provider queries monosyllabically? Has the client discussed personal concerns in the context of any of the RESPECTFUL model components that warrant more in-depth discussion?

The provider should assess the extent to which the client appears attuned to REC concerns, has initiated REC discussions during treatment, seems poised to engage in such discussions, maintains a heightened level of social consciousness, or has a sense of curiosity about sociopolitical factors that may contribute to the presenting concern. The provider may consider where the client fits on the Interactive Model of Broaching and Racial Identity Functioning continuum (see Table 8.3). The client's level of racial identity functioning provides some insight into their readiness to discuss their REC concerns at a deeper emotional level.

Providers may gauge topics clients feel more and/or less comfortable discussing. That is, does the client perceive the provider as capable of recognizing their unique sociocultural, sociopolitical, and sociohistorical realities? This is not to say that the provider needs to agree with the client, or that the provider needs to have experienced the client's unique sociocultural experiences as a prerequisite for understanding, but they can benefit by having an empathic awareness of the client's concerns. Further, the client needs to perceive the provider as caring and compassionate toward their needs and circumstances.

The provider should look for additional markers indicating the client's preparedness to engage in REC discussions. Markers include assessment of the developing rapport between the provider and client. For instance, is the client responsive to the provider's effort to convey respect, empathic awareness, and understanding? The provider's ability to enter the client's unique perceptual world without judgment is an important indicator of readiness for a broaching event. Providers should also assess the extent to which they have created psychological safety for the client and, more importantly, whether the client experiences psychological safety within the counseling dyad.

Providers may use their personal impressions about the client's level of satisfaction with the counseling process to determine when and whether to proceed with a broaching discussion. Other factors that help determine client readiness for broaching discussions include the provider's impression that the client experiences therapeutic trust, demonstrates a willingness to be vulnerable, and senses that the provider is culturally attuned to client needs. Some clients may have a desire to discuss their REC concerns but may not address those concerns directly. Clients who imply or insinuate concerns about REC may be poised for a broaching event. Sometimes, their subtle references to cultural concerns may actually be an effort to test the provider and determine the provider's openness to discussing REC concerns. The provider should listen empathically and pay attention to the client's nonverbal cues, silences, gestures, movement, and posture. Recall Chapter 5, with Katrina, the single, gay Black female, from the Caribbean, with a physical disability. Although her presenting concerns seemed to suggest she wanted to process mounting frustration given her difficulty accessing work-related accommodations, she also intimated that she felt ostracized at work. Her deeper concern seemed to be the lack of belonging and the sense of isolation and alienation she experiences based on her race, gender, national origin, and linguistic diversity. Katrina may reason that providers who address her disability concerns effectively may also have the skills to address her intersectional experiences related to power and oppression. Incidentally, studies demonstrate that when clients have two or more salient identities, providers may struggle to demonstrate cultural understanding and consequently may miss opportunities to broach clients' cultural concerns (Anders et al., 2021).

These preliminary broaching steps can help provide assurances about whether to proceed with a broaching discussion. In fact, the provider's premature broaching behavior may serve as a turn-off to clients or may result in clients' emotional disengagement, such that they withhold critical cultural information because they experience the provider's comments and questions as intrusive, insensitive, and disingenuous. For many clients from minoritized backgrounds, moving forward with broaching discussions may feel risky. After all, in many minoritized communities, families strictly forbid the discussion of family matters outside the confines of the home. Exposing family dynamics to strangers is considered taboo and represents a form of family betrayal. Given this reality, providers must work diligently to gain the client's trust and respect by validating and affirming the client's experiences and showing deference to the client's culture.

Inasmuch as providers determine when a broaching discussion may be warranted, providers may also determine when broaching may be less appropriate such as when clients exhibit active psychotic symptoms, mania, or significant cognitive limitations that interfere with abstract thinking abilities (Day-Vines et al., 2021). In such cases, providers will usually postpone broaching discussions until clients have stabilized. In one notable exception, Pierre was remanded to an in-patient psychiatric facility that had a known history of mental health disparities among minoritized patients. In fact, local residents seldom used this particular hospital because of its history of medical and mental health abuses. Upon arrival, Pierre was placed in hand and foot restraints because he was agitated and lashing out at hospital personnel. He shouted at his psychiatrist that he did not think he would be treated fairly as an African American man within the hospital system. The psychiatrist did not contradict Pierre and instead acknowledged his awareness of the long history of mental health abuses perpetrated toward members of the African American community in particular. The doctor's acknowledgment of the patient's salient concerns about oppression helped alleviate some of the patient's initial agitation toward the doctor. Feeling validated, the patient was able to move forward with his psychiatric treatment.

Pierre: Let me go! Let me go! Y'all are trying to kill me. I know you are. You're putting poison in my veins. This hospital has killed lots of Black people. I know it. I have evidence. The devil told me so.

Psychiatrist: Pierre, I hear you. I recognize that in the past this hospital has engaged in mistreatment and medical abuses of Black patients that have resulted in tremendous harm. As your psychiatrist, I am committed to helping you heal and treating you with the utmost respect for your humanity and wellness.

Rather than respond defensively and refute Pierre's claims, the attending physician acknowledged Pierre's assertions, because Pierre was correct. Historically, the hospital had perpetrated medical abuses over its more than 100-year history. In fact, psychiatric abuses have been catalogued in documentaries, news articles, scholarly journals, books, and magazines (Hylton, 2024; Jones, 2000; Metzl, 2011; Pietila, 2018; Segrest, 2020; Summers, 2019). That admission astonished Pierre because he had fully expected the psychiatrist to gaslight him, deny the hospital's wrongdoing, and agitate him further. Much to Pierre's surprise, the psychiatrist validated Pierre's assertions. The psychiatrist knew that to do otherwise might be disingenuous, breed contempt, and foment even more distrust from the patient. Although hallucinations distorted Pierre's sense of reality, he seemed to have an accurate perceptual awareness of mental health disparities. Although the psychiatrist recognized the severity of Pierre's mental illness, he validated the aspects of Pierre's comments that were relevant by acknowledging the harm that patients with mental illness experience in psychiatric facilities. The psychiatrist's reassuring comments allowed Pierre to continue with treatment.

Strength of Therapeutic Alliance

The working alliance refers to agreements between providers and clients on goals, tasks, and the emotional bond. Cheng and Lo (2022) examined working alliances between a sample of social work case managers and clients and concluded that case managers' estimates of the working alliance were a significant predictor of client ratings of the working alliance, regardless of whether the case manager and client shared the same race. This study underscored the importance of mutuality and respect between the provider and client in developing a healthy therapeutic alliance.

Given that studies indicate providers fall prey to the Dunning–Kruger effect and overestimate their general and cultural knowledge concerning clients (Sadusky et al., 2024; Walfish et al., 2012), providers may want to gauge clients' perceptions of the counseling relationship throughout the counseling process, to avoid self-assessment bias. As described in Chapter 4, collecting feedback from clients using qualitative or empirically based measures that assess their experience within the counseling dyad seems important.

As discussed in Chapter 4, providers can use the intra-counseling broaching dimension to explore how the counseling relationship is unfolding. Gathering feedback about clients' experiences in therapy is an important step in determining the strength of the counseling relationship. Providers can inquire about whether clients feel heard or understood, valued, and supported before proceeding to more in-depth broaching discussions. The provider may also explore how the client's shared and different identity dimensions impact the counseling process. If the counseling relationship is sufficiently strong, as evidenced by the client's body language, investment in the counseling process, as well as willingness to talk at a deeper emotional level, the provider may proceed with the broaching process. If the therapeutic relationship is strained in some way, the provider may continue to both monitor and build the counseling relationship by inquiring about factors that may possibly inhibit the development of a stronger therapeutic relationship. In any case, the provider should proceed with warmth, curiosity, genuineness, and positive regard in order to help the client feel safe and supported. Chapter 10 addresses specific strategies for repairing therapeutic ruptures.

Provider Self-Efficacy

Self-efficacy refers to the provider's belief that they can facilitate the broaching process confidently, comfortably, and effectively, by helping clients making connections between their REC and presenting concerns. As the reader will recall from Chapter 2, the Multicultural and Social Justice Counseling Competencies (MSJCC; Ratts et al., 2016) provide guidelines for delivering culturally responsive and socially just counseling practice. The MSJCC framework emphasizes the complex interplay between the provider's social locations, or unique attributional characteristics such as race, gender, religion, sexual orientation, immigration status, linguistic diversity, and social class status, and the client's social locations. That is, providers and clients can have intersecting privileged and marginalized identity statuses that impact the counseling process. Incidentally, privileged individuals experience some form of social advantage and marginalized individuals experience some form of oppression. Successful counseling relationships rest heavily upon the provider's ability to manage the intersecting social locations that emerge within the counseling process.

To illustrate, Janet is a cisgender Native American clinical psychologist who is second-generation college-educated person. Her parents were both teachers. She experiences privilege on the basis of her education, professional accomplishments, and sexual orientation; conversely, she experiences marginalization on the basis of her race and gender. Janet is counseling a working-class White man who experiences privilege on the basis of his race and gender but encounters marginalization on the basis of his poor, working-class status. He grew up in poverty under enormous family challenges. He struggles with increasing amounts of depression and anxiety resulting from unresolved childhood sexual trauma.

As stated above, Janet understands that attending to the provider-client interaction will help strengthen the working alliance. As such, she attends to each of the steps of the joining and assessment components described above in order to forge a working alliance with her client and gain insights that will enable her to provide more effective and culturally responsive counseling care. As part of her effort to implement broaching strategies, Janet also attends to the MSJCC which identify four developmental domains that help providers exhibit culturally responsive counseling services: (a) self-awareness, (b) client worldview, (c) counseling relationship, and (d) counseling and advocacy interventions.

During treatment, Janet observed her client's indifference to the counseling process and made several overtures to help him feel more comfortable, to no avail. Instead of assigning blame to her client for the relational difficulties they experienced, she engaged in self-awareness. She decided to assess her own attitudes, biases, and assumptions and recognized that she felt annoyed and hurt about her client's lack of responsiveness to her overtures. She considered the possibility that their provider-client difficulties may be related to certain racial, gender, and class dynamics. She recognizes that previously, she has experienced resistance from White male clients in particular, which has left her questioning her skill set, and feeling hurt and annoyed. She contemplates the possibility that her frustration with previous clients may be seeping into her counseling efforts with her current client. In the past, she has experienced White men in particular as somewhat resistant to her help. Janet concedes that as a consequence, she experiences a form of both self-doubt and racial resentment over her client's condescending air. She considers her role in the relationship and asks herself whether she may be less warm and empathic due to prior negative encounters with White men who may object to working with women of color, and whether she is pre-emptively exerting more control in the counseling session in ways that may erode the working alliance. She also worries that the client may trigger prior traumas in ways that do not allow her to honor her own experiences with racial trauma, because she feels an ethical responsibility to attend to his psychic wounds. She feels her effort to maintain neutrality and demonstrate understanding toward her client dismisses her own personal angst.

Janet decided to seek supervision in order to consider her struggles and to avoid personalizing her client's behavior. During supervision, Janet strategized with her clinical supervisor to sort through her own ambivalence about working with her client. Her intended goal is to maintain her own authenticity while supporting her client. She explores how she can even raise a discussion about the tension in their relationship without the conversation spiraling out of control. How does she mask her anger toward her client? Would her client behave in the same manner with a man? Does the client's behavior dredge up unresolved concerns around race and intergenerational trauma? More specifically, stemming from historic incidents that are still somewhat raw for Janet such as the cumulative impact of the Indian Removal Act, Trail of Tears, Indian residential schools, murdered and missing Native women, construction of pipelines on sacred Native lands, as well as ongoing encounters with racism and discrimination. The supervision process helped Janet sort through her own difficulties and move forward strategically with her client.

Although Janet felt offended by her client's unwillingness to engage in treatment compliance, she also recognized that her client may struggle with receiving counseling services due to her race, class, and gender. She considered her client's worldview and reasoned that perhaps discussing unresolved trauma with a well-educated woman of color may make her client feel especially vulnerable and evoke feelings of shame, embarrassment, anger, and even emasculation. Janet also surmised that her client may struggle with concerns around race if he endorses a racial hierarchy that presumes his ideological superiority over people of color. Many, though certainly not all, Whites have been indoctrinated into a system of racial superiority that allows them to exert dominance against those they deem subordinate. In fact, philosopher Charles Mills (2022) enumerated what he defines as a racial contract that makes explicit, implicit ideas and tacit assumptions about the racial ordering that entitles some Whites to believe that they should have unlimited social advantages and that people of color should be consigned to social disadvantage. These guiding beliefs often operate under the guise of race neutrality (Bonilla-Silva, 2021). Perhaps former President Lyndon Johnson encapsulated this idea most vividly when he said, "If you can convince the lowest white man he's better than the best colored man, he won't notice you're picking his pocket. Hell, give him somebody to look down on, and he'll empty his pockets for you." This statement epitomizes the notion of differential privilege that guides assumptions about race.

In accordance with MSJCC (Ratts et al., 2016) guidelines, Janet considered the counseling relationship. She is working with her supervisor to self-monitor so that she takes responsibility for her thoughts and feelings and does not inadvertently undermine the counseling process. Together, they are processing how Janet's social locations and worldview interact with her client's social locations and worldview in ways that impact the counseling relationship. The supervisor has helped her strategize about ways to manage dynamics around power and privilege. Her increasing levels of self-awareness and openness to clinical supervision have had a positive impact on the counseling process. For now, Janet has decided to enter her own therapy so that she can continue to work through her own.

Counseling and advocacy interventions lie outside the scope of the individual counseling interventions (Ratts et al., 2016); however, Janet has impressed upon her employer the importance of helping clinicians in their agency develop tools for addressing the specific and unique needs for working with male sexual abuse survivors.

Broaching Readiness Model

Newton and Steele (2025) have developed the Broaching Readiness Model which overlaps with the MSJCC (see Chapter 2). Their model contains four specific skills that include (a) self-awareness or recognition of one's own feelings and thought processes, (b) cognitive reframing or management of dissonant thoughts by considering broaching as a helpful counseling intervention rather than an impediment to the counseling process, (c) discomfort tolerance reflection or managing strong emotions that emerge during the counseling process, and (d) education, which involves continuous professional development. Like the MSJCC, these dispositions and self-regulation tools function as prerequisites for broaching clients' REC concerns.

Multicultural Counseling Orientation

The provider must also determine their own readiness to facilitate a broaching conversation with confidence and facility. Limited levels of self-efficacy may upend the provider's broaching efforts. The self-efficacy requirement draws heavily on the Multicultural Counseling Orientation (MCO) framework, which shifts focus from a competence orientation and emphasizes cultural humility, or the provider's sense of curiosity about the client, ability to maintain an other-oriented stance, and realization that the provider is not all-knowing (Davis et al., 2018). Cultural comfort reflects the provider's ease of manner in engaging in broaching conversations, and cultural opportunities involve the provider's effort to actively engage in broaching discussions (Drinane et al., 2018; Hook et al., 2016; Perez-Rojas et al., 2019). Chapter 2 contains more detailed information about the MCO model.

Moon and Sandage (2019) asserted that the application of MCO may look different for providers of color compared to their White counterparts. They note that most counseling theories were developed primarily by and for White providers in ways that do not account for racial nuances. Many theories assume that its tenets are universal and consequently force providers of color to assimilate to a dominant stance. Moon and Sandage contend that when the race of the provider and client differ, White therapists may have to devote more attention to managing ethnocentric monoculturalism. In other words, they may have to divest themselves of attitudes and beliefs that suggest their own cultural values, viewpoints, and practices are inherently superior to those of others. Conversely, providers of color may have to manage countertransference resulting from varying forms of racial trauma. Moon and Sandage maintain that providers of color may struggle to exhibit cultural humility, namely, because cultural humility requires the provider to maintain a one-down position with a client. For people of color who already experience varying forms of racial and social subordination, leaning into cultural comfort, humility, and opportunities may result in a two-down position and contribute to additional forms of subordination that may lead to further subjugation of the self. Counselors who.

In Janet's case, cultural humility requires her to exhibit curiosity about the client's experience, reduce the power imbalance, and ensure she does not exhibit signs of superiority that may damage the counseling relationship, even as her client demonstrates indifference and hostility toward her. Janet's perception of her client's racialized behavior triggers intrusive thoughts around race and intergenerational trauma – more specifically, how dominant groups subjugated her people. Her effort to compartmentalize her feelings in order to manage the racial dynamics that emerge in the counseling process, means that she may ignore her own feelings. Clinical supervision provided an opportunity to examine the counseling relationship more holistically. For instance, she was able to disclose her concerns about her own emotional and physical safety within the counseling dyad. The heightened level of racial animus during the current political climate has given Janet pause. Supervision permitted Janet to explore deeper sociopolitical concerns that may intrude upon the counseling relationship. This conversation seemed to be an important prerequisite to broaching her client's REC concerns as it pertains to the counseling relationship, before delving further into the client's personal challenges around race, gender, class, and sexual trauma.

Burning Question

Norma, given Janet's strong visceral reaction toward her client, should she refer him to another provider?

Janet has taken some important steps by seeking supervision to help her strategize about working more effectively with her client. Given the level of personal and intergenerational trauma she has encountered, she made an important decision to seek her own therapy. In the event she continues to have strong visceral reactions to her client, and they are not able to resolve tensions within the counseling dyad, the ethically responsible next step would be to refer out to a new provider.

Summary

Joining involves the use of invitational nonverbal (e.g., policies, practices, intake forms) and verbal strategies (small talk, informed consent, client validation) that orient the client to the counseling process, help them feel safe, and communicate that REC discussions are appropriate within the context of counseling. Assessment strategies involve the provider's effort to conceptualize the client's cultural dimensions, inclusive of racial identity functioning, client readiness to explore REC concerns, the strength of the therapeutic alliance, and provider's self-efficacy or preparedness to broach the client's REC concerns.

In the chapter that follows, we identify steps that providers can use as they both prepare to deliver a broaching statement with the client and actually execute the broaching process.

References

Anandavalli, S., Harrichand, J.J.S., & Litam, S.D.A. (2020). Counseling international students in times of uncertainty: A critical feminist and bioecological approach. *Professional Counselor*, *10*, 365–375.

Anders, C., Kivlighan, D.M., Porter, E., Lee, D., & Owen, J. (2021). Attending to the intersectionality and saliency of clients' identities: A further investigation of therapists' multicultural orientation. *Journal of Counseling Psychology*, *68*(2), 139–148. https://doi-org.proxy1.library.jhu.edu/10.1037/cou0000447

Bayne, H. B., & Branco, S. F. (2018). A phenomenological inquiry into counselor of color broaching experiences. *Journal of Counseling & Development, 96*(1), 75–85. https://doi.org/10.1002/jcad.12179

Bishop, B. (2018). Advocating for atheist clients in the counseling profession. *Counseling and Values*, *63*, 17–30. https://doi.org/10.1002/cvj.12070

Bonilla-Silva, E. (2021). *Racism without racists: Color-Blind racism and the persistence of racial inequality in America*. Rowman and Littlefield.

Brawner, R., & Day-Vines, N.L. (2024). Invitational skills as a precursor to counselors' efforts to broach racial, ethnic, and cultural factors with clients. In K. Butler & A.S. Butler (Eds.). *Intersectionality: Becoming a culturally competent counselor*. (pp. 83–120). Cognella.

Brawner, R., Day-Vines, N.L., Gubara, S., Agorsor, C., Jackson, Z., Ran, T., & Caldwell, N. (2025). Perceptions of racial, ethnic, and cultural ruptures in counseling: A qualitative case study of a client from a minoritized background. *Journal of Multicultural Counseling and Development, 103*, 483-495. https://doi-org.proxy1.library.jhu.edu/10.1002/jcad.70004

Cheng, T.C., & Lo, C.C. (2022). Factors that contribute to strong working alliances between case managers and clients. *Journal of Social Work*, *22*(5), 1241–1254. https://doi-org.proxy1.library.jhu.edu/10.1177/14680173221083476

Choi, G., Mallinckrodt, B., & Richardson, J.D. (2015). Effect of international student counselors' broaching statements about cultural and language differences on participants' perceptions of counselors. *Journal of Multicultural Counseling and Development, 43*, 25–37. https://doi-org.proxy1.library.jhu.edu/10.1002/j.2161-1912.2015.00062.x

Collins, L.H. (2023). *Overlooked: Counselor insights for the unspoken issues in Black American life*. Rowman and Littlefield.

D'Andrea, M., & Daniels, J. (2001). RESPECTFUL counseling: An integrative model for counselors. In D. Pope-Davis & H. Coleman (Eds.), *The Intersection of Class, Culture, and Gender in Counseling* (pp. 417–466). Sage. https://doi.org/10.4135/9781452231846.n17

Davis, D.E., DeBlaere, C., Owen, J., Hook, J.N., Rivera, D.P., Choe, E., Van Tongeren, D.R., Worthington, E.L., Jr., & Placeres, V. (2018). The multicultural orientation framework: A narrative review. *Psychotherapy, 55*(1), 89–100. https://doi.org/10.1037/pst0000160

Day-Vines, N.L., Brodar, J.R., Hicks, D., Fernandez-Korto, E.B., Garcia, C., & Jones, K. (2022). An investigation of the relationship between school counselor trainees' broaching behavior and their racial identity attitudes. *Journal of Counseling and Development, 100*, 3–13. https://doi.org/10.1002/jcad.12406

Day-Vines, N.L., Cluxton-Keller, F., Agorsor, C., & Gubara, S. (2021). Strategies for broaching the subjects of race, ethnicity and culture. *Journal of Counseling and Development, 99*, 348–357. https://doi.org/10.1002/jcad.12380

Day-Vines, N.L., Wood, S., Grothaus, T., Craigen, L.,Holman, A., Dotson-Blake, K., & Douglass, M. (2007). Broaching the subjects of race, ethnicity, and culture during the counseling process. *Journal of Counseling and Development, 85*, 401–409. https://doi.org/10.1002/jcad.12069

Depauw, H., & Van Hiel, A. (2024). Uncovering patterns in perceived therapist behaviour: A xlatent profile analysis of broaching experiences among ethnic minority group member clients. *Clinical Psychology and Psychotherapy, 31*, e3067. https://doi.org/10.1002/cpp.3067

Drinane, J.M., Owen, J., & Tao, K.W. (2018). Cultural concealment and therapy outcomes. *Journal of Counseling Psychology, 65*, 239–246. https://doi.org/10.1037/cou0000246

Erby, A.N., & White, M.E. (2020). Broaching partially-shared identities: Critically interrogating power and intragroup dynamics in counseling practice with trans people of Color. *International Journal of Transgender Health, 23*(1–2), 122–132. https://doi-org.proxy1.library.jhu.edu/10.1080/26895269.2020.1838389

Fuertes, J.N., Mueller, L.N., Chauhan, R.V., Walker, J.A., & Ladany, N. (2002). An investigation of European American therapists' approach to counseling African American clients. *The Counseling Psychologist, 30*(5), 763–788. https://doi.org/10.1177/0011000002305007

Gu, B. (December 13, 2024). Chinese migrants in US illegally uneasy after fourth removal flight. *VOA News*. https://www.voanews.com/a/illegal-chinese-immigrants-uneasy-as-us-conducts-fourth-china-removal-flight-/7901128.html

Helms, J.E., & Cook, D.A. (1999). *Using race and culture in counseling and psychotherapy: Theory and process*. Allyn & Bacon.

Hill, C.E. (2020). *Helping skills: Facilitating exploration, insight, and action*. American Psychological Association.

Hook, J.N., Farrell, J.E., Davis, D.E., DeBlaere, C., Van Tongeren, D.R., & Utsey, S.O. (2016). Cultural humility and racial microaggressions in counseling. *Journal of Counseling Psychology, 63*(3), 269–277. https://doi.org/10.1037/cou0000114

Hylton, A. (2024). *Madness: Race and insanity in a Jim Crow asylum*. Legacy.
Ivey, A., Ivey, M., & Zalaquett. (2022). *Intentional interviewing and counseling: Facilitating client development in a multicultural society* (10th ed.). Cengage.
Jones C.P. (2000), Levels of racism: a theoretic framework and a gardener's tale. *American Journal of Public Health. 90*, 1212–1215.
Jones, C. (2022). The organ thieves: *The shocking story of the first heart transplant in the segregated south*. Gallery/Jeter.
Kohli, S.K. (2024). *But what will people say?: Navigating mental health, identity, love, and family between cultures*. Penguin Life.
Kuo, P.B., Rudecindo, B., Drinane, J.M., Tao, K., Epps, J.V., & Imel, Z.E. (2024). Cultural conversations in therapy: How often clients talk about their identities. *Psychiatric Services, 76*(2). https://doi-org.proxy1.library.jhu.edu/10.1176/appi.ps.2023026
Lew, J. (2006). *Asian Americans in class: Charting the achievement gap among Korean American youth*. Teachers College.
Litam, S.D.A. (2025). *Patterns that remain: A guide to healing for Asian children of immigrants*. Oxford University.
Lubrano, A. (2005). *Limbo: Blue-collar roots, white-collar dreams*. Wiley.
Metzl, J. (2011). *The protest psychosis: How schizophrenia became a Black disease*. Beacon.
Middleton, T.J., Toole, K.M., Culpepper, D., Hughes, D.C., Parsons-Christian, E., & Dollarhide, C. T. (2023). Decolonizing & decentering oppressive structures: Practical strategies for social justice in school and clinical counseling. *Journal of Counselor Leadership and Advocacy, 10*(2), 112–122. https://doi-org.proxy1.library.jhu.edu/10.1080/2326716X.2023.2237023
Mills, C. (2022). *The racial contract*. Cornell University.
Moodley, R., & Kleiman, S. (2018). Combating racism, racial discrimination, xenophobia, and related intolerance in counseling. In C. C. Lee (Ed.), Counseling for social justice (3rd ed., pp. 173–188). American Counseling Association Foundation.
Moon, S.H., & Sandage, S.J. (2019). Cultural humility for people of color: Critique of current theory and practice. *Journal of Psychology and Theology, 47*, 76–86.
Newton, C., & Steele, J.M. (2025). The broaching readiness framework: A path for psychologists to embrace cultural opportunities. *Counselling Psychology Quarterly, 38*, 1135–1152. https://doi-org.proxy1.library.jhu.edu/10.1080/09515070.2025.2458034
Owen, J., Tao, K.W., Imel, Z.E., Wampold, B.E., & Emil, R. (2014). Addressing racial and ethnic microaggressions in therapy. *Professional Psychology: Research and Practice, 45*, 283–290. https://doi.org/10.1037/a0037420
Pérez-Rojas, A.E., Bartholomew, T.T., Lockard, A.J., & González, J. M. (2019). Development and initial validation of the therapist cultural comfort scale. *Journal of Counseling Psychology, 66*, 534–549. https://doi.org/10.1037/cou0000344
Pietila, A. (2018). *The ghosts of Johns Hopkins: The life and legacy that shaped an American city*. Rowman and Littlefield.
Ratts, M.J., Singh, A.A., Nassar-McMillan, S., Butler, S.K., & McCullough, J.R. (2016). Multicultural and social justice counseling competencies: Guidelines for the counseling profession. *Journal of Multicultural Counseling and Development, 44*, 28–48. https://doi.org/10.1002/jmcd.12035
Sadusky, A., Yared, H., Patrick, P., & Berger, E. (2024). A systematic review of client's perspectives on the cultural and racial awareness and responsiveness of mental health

practitioners. *Culture and Psychology, 30*, 567–605. https://doi-org.proxy1.library.jhu.edu/10.1177/1354067X23115660

Schmidt, C. D. (2014). Integrating continuous client feedback into counselor education. *Journal of Counselor Preparation and Supervision, 6*(2). http://dx.doi.org/10.7729/62.1094

Segrest, M. (2020). *Administrations of lunacy: Racism and the haunting of American psychiatry at the Milledgeville asylum*. The New Press.

Sprinthall, R.C., Sprinthall, N.A., & Oja, S.N. (1997). *Educational Psychology: A developmental approach* (7th ed.). McGraw-Hill.

Sue, D.W., Sue, D., Neville, H.A., & Smith, L. (2022). *Counseling the culturally diverse: Theory and practice* (9th ed.). Wiley.

Summers, M. (2019). *Madness in the city of magnificent intentions: A history of race and mental illness in the nation's capital*. Oxford University.

Thrower, S.J., Helms, J.E., & Price, M. (2020). Racial dynamics in counselor training: The racial identity social interaction model. *Journal of Counselor Preparation and Supervision, 13*(1). https://doi.org/10.7729/131.1313

Trevino, A.Y., Tao, K.W., & Van Epps, J.J. (2021). Windows of cultural opportunity: A thematic analysis of how cultural conversations occur in psychotherapy. *Psychotherapy, 58*(2), 263–274. https://doi.org/10.1037/pst0000360

Walfish, S., McAlister, B., O'Donnell, P., & Lambert, M.J. (2012). An investigation of self-assessment bias in mental health providers. *Psychological Reports, 110*, 639–644. https://doi-org.proxy1.library.jhu.edu/10.2466/02.07.17.PR0.110.2.639-644

Wang, C. (September 29, 2025). Ice's deportations of south-east Asian refugees creating 'ripple effect' of trauma: 'I didn't get to say bye to my husband'. *The Guardian*. https://www.theguardian.com/us-news/2025/sep/29/ice-deportation-south-east-asians-vietnam-war

Wilkerson, I. (2020). *Caste: The origins of our discontents*. Random House.

Yalom, I. (2013). *The gift of therapy*. Harper Perennial.

Chapter 9

Preparation and Delivery Stage of Broaching Statement

As noted throughout this textbook, broaching is a process and not a singular event. More specifically, broaching is a planned, thoughtful, organized endeavor. From intake through to completion of counseling sessions, the provider orients the client to the fact that their REC concerns are integral to the counseling process. In the absence of intentionality, broaching efforts may result in cultural ruptures. This chapter covers strategies for formulating and executing sound broaching statements and addresses two specific skills: (a) preparation to articulate the broaching statement and (b) delivery of the actual broaching statement and subsequent discussion (Day-Vines et al., 2021).

Preparation Phase

In the previous chapter, we discussed preliminary steps that prepare providers to engage in broaching discussions with their clients. In particular, we covered the joining and assessment phases, which are prerequisites for the preparation stage. Joining refers to a strong relational foundation that is necessary for the broaching discussion to unfold. Throughout the counseling process, the provider builds and maintains a warm nurturing relationship with the client by establishing trust and therapeutic rapport. Not only does the provider build trust with the client, but the client must also experience the provider as authentic, genuine, and supportive. Development of a relational bond between the provider and client sets the stage for the broaching process.

During the assessment phase, the provider gathers information about the client by engaging in multicultural case conceptualization, determining the client's readiness to proceed with the broaching process, evaluating the strength of the therapeutic relationship, examining their own value orientations and the possible impact on the counseling relationship. Assuming providers feel confident continuing with the broaching process, they engage in the preparation stage. The preparation stage has three steps: (1) setting an intention, (2) formulating a preliminary broaching statement, and (3) identifying the particular form of oppression the client experiences (see Table 9.1).

DOI: 10.4324/9781003649311-9

Table 9.1 Preparation Phase

Step 1. Set an intention	Determine what aspects of the client's REC concerns warrant a broaching discussion; identify how broaching may help the client address their REC concerns
Step 2. Formulate broaching statement	Align intention with the integrated/ congruent aspects of the *Continuum of Broaching Behavior*, at least one domain of the MMBB (e.g., intra-counseling, intra-individual, Intra-REC, Inter-REC), as well as the RESPECTFUL model
Step 3. Identify specific forms of resilience and oppression	Label client strengths and encounters with oppression – engage in structural competence by processing sociopolitical realities for clients (e.g., sexism, homophobia, racism, ableism, classism, colorism)

Step 1: Setting an Intention

The first step of the preparation stage involves setting an intention. The intention is an internal cognitive process that precedes the actual broaching discussion. It is at this point that the provider determines what, when, and how they are going to broach, as well as why a particular broaching discussion may be helpful to the client. When setting an intention, the provider builds on information gleaned from the multicultural assessment stage to identify specific REC concerns that center the broaching conversation. Tools, such as the RESPECTFUL model described in Chapter 8 (D'Andrea & Daniels, 2001), help stimulate the provider's identification of specific REC content, allowing the provider to explore the full complement of intersectional concerns that impact the client's well-being and develop a more holistic sense of the client's broaching needs. As the client shares their presenting concerns, the provider may recognize connections between the client's personal concerns and underlying REC contexts that warrant further exploration. Moreover, the provider may have the sense that talking about REC aspects of the client's concern may lead to greater depth of self-awareness and enrich the therapeutic dialogue.

When Not to Broach

Providers with weak intentions may postpone their broaching efforts until they have had an opportunity to strengthen the counseling relationship, better understand the client's needs, or seek supervision. Additionally, the provider should consider their own preparedness to broach based on an examination of their own personal biases, attitudes, and assumptions so they do not interfere with the counseling process. As well, providers should consider their own preparedness and confidence in executing the broaching process. For instance, in Chapter 8, Janet, a Native American clinical psychologist, had a strong visceral reaction to her client, a White man who had experienced childhood sexual abuse. Janet was uncertain about why their therapeutic relationship had not fully crystallized and seriously considered her own intuitive reaction to her client's hostility and indifference toward her. Janet sought supervision to gain clarity about her feelings toward her client and strategies for salvaging the counseling relationship. In the end, Janet and her supervisor agreed that it may be better to table the broaching process until she had a better handle on her own inner thoughts and feelings and could determine whether to refer the client to another provider. Janet subsequently sought counseling because she had experienced challenges while working with White male clients in the past, which she attributed in part to their sexism and resentment over working with a highly educated woman of color. Engaging in counseling helped her realize that her strong reactions to her client may also be related to countertransference stemming from her sense of hurt that her counseling efforts were rejected, as well as her encounters with intergenerational trauma. As in the case of Janet, an important component of broaching is knowing when it may be important not to broach or when it may be more helpful to seek supervision and, if necessary, obtain personal counseling. In extreme cases it may be necessary to refer out.

Step 2: Formulate a Broaching Statement

In instances where providers have strong intentions and feel confident about moving forward with the broaching process, they may proceed to the second preparation step, which involves formulating a broaching statement. Ideally, the provider's intention should align with either the integrated/congruent or infusing category of the *Continuum of Broaching Behavior*, and at least one category of the Multidimensional Model of Broaching Behavior (MMBB). As the reader will recall from Chapter 3, the *integrated/congruent* category along the broaching continuum reflects the provider's ability to exhibit an ease of manner exploring the client's REC concerns in ways that help the client feel heard and understood. The provider generates facilitative responses in an effort to do the following:

- Think about client concerns in culture-specific ways
- Recognize and accept the cultural meaning clients attach to their experience
- Refrain from holding clients accountable for their encounters with varying forms of oppression
- Discuss REC concerns without losing empathy toward the client or developing a defensive posture
- Promote client empowerment

- Help clients identify healthy psychological resistance mechanisms for confronting oppressive forces
- Identify client sources of strength and resilience
- Demonstrate a marked degree of REC self-awareness
- Recognize the sociopolitical concerns that clients from minoritized groups confront
- Attach importance to culture-specific knowledge about groups
- Translate their awareness and knowledge of clients' REC concerns into culturally responsive broaching discussions and interventions without essentializing clients or seeing them as monolithic entities.

Integrated/Congruent providers can generate meaningful discussions with clients in each of the MMBB domains, in large measure because they have more than just a conceptual understanding of multicultural issues and because broaching functions as a salient aspect of their professional counseling behavior.

Infusing providers implement systems-level social justice interventions that eliminate structural barriers for clients. Their social justice advocacy interventions help eliminate structural barriers for clients and can occur with individual clients or in the context of group or community based initiatives.

In instances where the provider feels capable of moving forward in the broaching process, the provider advances to step 2. During step 2 of the preparation stage, the provider formulates a broaching statement and organizes their thoughts and comments in advance of delivering the actual broaching statement. Constructing broaching statements internally, and in advance of delivery, increases the likelihood that the provider will generate a clear, focused, and coherent statement and avoid sounding impulsive or out of touch with the client's concerns.

I notice that when my students start talking before they have organized their thoughts thoroughly, their broaching statements may sound incoherent and disjointed in ways that may confuse the client. Having already set an intention in step 1 (e.g., determining the reason broaching clients' REC concerns may be helpful, deciding what specific concerns to broach), providers can work toward constructing a preliminary broaching statement internally before actually verbalizing the broaching statement to the client. Essentially, broaching statements should be planned, thoughtful, and deliberate. They are not random or spontaneous. Unlike the popular sports brand, providers don't "Just Do It." They frame their thoughts carefully.

When formulating a broaching statement, the provider uses elements of the assessment phase described in Chapter 8, along with observations regarding the client's verbal and nonverbal behavior. This may include verbal statements the client makes that may be explicit or implicit, as well as nonverbal behavior such as facial expressions and lack of eye contact that may signal how the client feels internally.

The provider's understanding of cultural knowledge is an important variable in the delivery of culturally responsive care. The provider's decision to initiate discussions about the client's REC concerns may arise from something the client stated or implied during the counseling session that warrants further elaboration. The provider's inquiry about culture may also result from understanding differences between Western and non-Western cultural values or the understanding of the client's holistic social contexts. By exhibiting curiosity about the client's multidimensional concerns, the provider helps facilitate client self-understanding and permits the client to discuss their concerns beyond a surface level. Initiating broaching discussions may also stem from the provider's understandings of cultural nuances or values that warrant discussion.

During this step, providers identify one or more of the four MMBB domains (e.g., intra-counseling, intra-individual, intra-Racial, -Ethnic, -Cultural, and inter-racial, -ethnic, -cultural dimensions). As discussed in Chapter 4, the MMBB functions as a heuristic device for understanding and examining clients' REC-specific concerns. Providers broach *Intra-Counseling* dimensions in an effort to (a) convey that REC discussions are permissible within counseling, (b) invite clients to examine their concerns in a culture-specific manner, (c) use cultural immediacy to explore how shared and different identities between the provider and client impact the counseling process, and (d) reduce the power imbalance in an effort to increase the client's sense of trust and psychological safety.

Providers broach *Intra-Individual* dimensions to explore intersectional identity concerns that clients experience (e.g., race, gender, class, and sexual orientation). Providers broach *Intra-REC* dimensions to explore sources of both resilience and challenge that involve within-group experiences between people who share the same racial designation (e.g., family and community support, colorism, assimilation, and acculturation). The *Inter-REC* broaching dimension refers to encounters with racism and discrimination. Providers can use the RESPECTFUL model (D'Andrea & Daniels, 2001) to conceptualize the client more holistically by identifying multidimensional aspects of diversity that have important influences in clients' lives. Table 9.2 uses the case illustration of Mei-ling from Chapter 8 to describe connections between the MMBB and the RESPECTFUL model. Please note that the arrangement of MMBB dimensions and the RESPECTFUL model elements may differ depending upon client concerns. See Table 9.2.

Case Illustration

As the reader will recall, Chapter 8 contains a case illustration of Mei-ling, a second-generation, Chinese American cisgender college woman who feels conflicted about both her personal ideals and strivings and the expectation that she

Table 9.2 Step 2. Parallels between the MMBB Dimensions and RESPECTFUL Model

MMBB Dimension	*Purpose*	*Mei-ling's RESPECTFUL Dimensions to Address During MMBB Discussions*
Intra-counseling	Invite client to explore their REC concerns, reduce power imbalance, use of cultural immediacy to discuss the impact of shared and different identity domains between provider and client and the resulting impact on the client's counseling experience.	Exploration of provider-client relationship Invitation indicating that RESPECTFUL concerns are permissible in the context of counseling
Intra-individual	Explore the client's intersectional identity domains derived from the RESPECTFUL model.	**R**eligious – agnostic **E**conomic – working class **S**exual identity – cisgender heterosexual woman **E**thnic-cultural-racial identity – evolving appreciation of her Asian and American Identity **C**hronological development – meeting developmental targets (religious, sexual, career identity) **U**nique physical characteristics – growing sense of cultural pride **L**ocation of residence and language differences – grew up in a monocultural community with fewer influences outside of her immediate family
Intra-REC	Explore aspect of client concerns that arise within families and communities (colorism, classism, nationalism, immigration status, derived from the RESPECTFUL model).	**F**amily history and dynamics – intergenerational tensions between Mei-ling and her family **P**sychological maturity – conflict over cultural demands and desire for her own personal autonomy **E**conomic – working class – feelings of inadequacy based on perceived social class differences between self and peers
Inter-REC	Explore some aspect of racism and discrimination experienced by the client.	**T**rauma – experience with sexual harassment; current political climate **L**ocation of Residence and Language Differences – microaggressions about how well she speaks English

contribute dutifully to the needs of her family. As a second-generation immigrant of Chinese descent, she feels misunderstood by family members and experiences considerable stress given what she experiences as unreasonable expectations about loyalty and duty to family. She has experienced considerable strain regarding her parents' migration story. Mei-ling's parents are undocumented immigrants. Her father arrived in the United States on a tourist visa that subsequently expired, after which he began working as a cook in a Chinese restaurant. Mei-ling's mother joined her husband several years later, accompanied by her older brother. Once her parents settled into the United States with her older brother, Mei-ling was born. Sadly, she lives in the shadow of her family's hidden documentation status and feels burdened by the amount of support she provides her parents. Mei-ling is struggling to gain a sense of autonomy and individuate from her parents, as evidenced in part by her recent conversion to agnosticism. As a college student, she is pursuing higher education not only to satisfy her parents, but she is also hoping to leave her working-class suburban community and enter the ranks of the solidly middle class. Although Mei-ling is proud of her parents, she feels a tinge of embarrassment because her parents speak accented English and appear awkward in mainstream social settings. In marked contrast, Mei-ling perceives that her Asian American peers at college have parents who seem far more sophisticated and acculturated than her own parents. Her peers vacation regularly, have nice homes, parents with professional jobs, and the accoutrements of success. In her early teens, Mei-ling rejected her own Asian aesthetic, wishing instead that she could have blond hair and blue eyes. Since attending college, however, Mei-ling has developed a much healthier appreciation of her ethnic background. She has experienced sexual harassment and has felt objectified by some of the college men on campus. More recently, she has begun worrying about the political climate and, as a person of color, feels like she is under siege.

Providers using the RESPECTFUL model to engage in the multicultural case conceptualization would have a full complement of REC content to sort through with Mei-ling. To continue with the broaching process, the provider would need to determine which aspect of Mei-ling's concerns would be most meaningful. For instance, given the intensity of Mei-ling's desire to individuate from her family, the provider may prioritize discussion of intersectional identity domains and explore how issues of race, ethnicity, generational status, social class positionality, and religion shape her desire to distance herself from her working-class roots. Such a discussion would help Mei-ling explore her complex identity domains.

The provider's understanding of cultural knowledge is an important variable in the delivery of culturally responsive care. The decision to initiate discussions about Mei-ling's REC concerns may arise from something the client stated or implied during the counseling session that the provider deems worthy of further elaboration. The provider's inquiry about culture may also result from understanding differences between Western and non-Western cultural values or the understanding of the client's holistic social contexts. By exhibiting curiosity about the client's REC concerns, the provider facilitates client self-understanding and permits the client to discuss their concerns beyond a surface level. Initiating broaching discussions may also stem from the provider's understandings about cultural nuances or values that warrant discussion. Ideally, the provider will collaborate with Mei-ling to determine which broaching dimension(s) she wants to explore in more depth.

Step 3: Identify Client Resilience and Sources of Oppression

There are two components to step 3: (a) acknowledgment of client strengths and resources and (b) processing of the sources of oppression the client has encountered. Identifying client strengths and resources is important because, by the time many clients arrive in counseling, they have lost a considerable amount of objectivity. They often feel demoralized and, as a consequence, may find it helpful when providers reinforce their areas of strength and resilience. Enumerating strengths helps clients engage in cognitive reframing so that their circumstances exercise less control over their lives. Considering strengths and resources gives clients a sense of hope and possibility, reinforces their sense of dignity, builds efficacy and motivation in ways that humanize them, and leads to more effective problem resolution.

As a professor, I notice that my students are fairly adept at identifying client strengths; however, sometimes they struggle with this skill because they conflate client strengths with client challenges. For instance, I had a student who praised her client for being accommodating, but the client's presenting concern centered around disappointing others and prioritizing their needs at the expense of her own needs. Essentially, the student reinforced the client's difficulties by praising her for always being flexible. Although the student expressed optimism, optimism for the sake of being positive is unhelpful. The student could have tapped into other attributes such as the client's recognition that disappointing others has become draining, or that the client is astute at recognizing her own desire to pivot and exhibit more assertiveness in her friendships, or that she is becoming increasingly more decisive about wanting to find healthier approaches to navigating relationships. Provider optimism is a necessary albeit insufficient criterion for facilitating client growth. The provider must engage in an earnest appraisal of the client's effort to overcome adversity and identify healthy coping strategies the client has enlisted to manage personal challenges.

As part of the preparation process, providers may want to identify client strengths in advance of the counseling session. For example, given what Mei-ling's provider knows about her, the provider may highlight Mei-ling's effort to determine for herself her own values and personal belief systems, her decision to choose a nonreligious ideological path, the courage to honor her own internal compass and renegotiate her relationship with her parents, her growing self-acceptance and appreciation for her Asian American identity, her ability to form community with other Asian peers, as well as her commitment to education and career success. Articulation of client strengths can serve as a motivator to build resilience and promote client well-being; moreover, it shifts the focus from problems to possibilities.

The second component of step 3 requires the provider to label or make a mental note of the specific forms of distress (e.g., colorism, classism, sexism, racism) in collaboration with the client. The provider works with the client to understand the client's specific REC concerns. Relatedly, Metzl and Hansen (2014) emphasized the importance of providers demonstrating structural competence by naming the specific systemic sources of oppression that impact clients. Structural factors can include issues of racism, classism, homophobia, raciolinguistics, and ableism. Accurately naming structural barriers that clients encounter represents an important counseling consideration because these barriers often serve as root causes of clients' presenting problems. Zeroing in on structural factors reduces the likelihood that providers will blame clients for the specific challenges they encounter. Importantly, naming oppressive forces in clients' lives requires a marked degree of courage, fortitude, and perspicacity on the part of the provider, which, when done well, has the potential to stimulate catharsis and promote psychological liberation in clients. Incidentally, Hanna et al. (2000) defined "perspicacity" as the possession of strong perceptive abilities, the capacity of people from oppressed groups to see beyond the surface, and the deep awareness and wisdom to accurately interpret circumstances." They argue that people from oppressed groups have refined their perceptive abilities as a means of survival. In order to work effectively with clients, providers must also be able to navigate the client's racial, ethnic, and cultural terrain with a marked degree of perspicacity.

In addition to identifying structural factors that exacerbate clients' levels of psychological distress and general functioning, providers should also identify clients' sources of internal strength and resilience. As stated earlier, by the time a client enters counseling, they have lost a considerable amount of objectivity, and identification of client strengths can help to restore their sense of personal agency.

Inasmuch as Mei-ling's provider has catalogued a number of client strengths, the provider also recognizes that Mei-ling has experienced several forms of oppression that warrant more in-depth discussion. For instance, Mei-ling experiences classism stemming from her sense of shame and embarrassment about her family's working-class status and her desire to connect with middle- and upper-middle-class Asian peers. She feels like an imposter given that she portrays herself as someone who is of more means than she actually is. She is terrified of being illegally detained by immigration officials. Mei-ling is conflicted because of demands that she honor her parents in ways that preclude her from prioritizing her own individualism and worries that trying to discuss her concerns with her parents would be seen as disrespectful and ungrateful. Table 9.3 integrates the preparation steps and identifies sample broaching statements that the provider has formulated in advance of the delivery phase. These broaching statements help draw out Mei-ling's story in order to identify her specific REC concerns and better understand how she is impacted by her social circumstances.

Delivery Phase

Once providers have formulated a well-integrated broaching statement, they are ready to move forward with the delivery phase of the broaching process, which contains five components that require the provider to (1) communicate the broaching statement, (2) permit silence, (3) use reflective statements, (4) use the client's responses to discuss their concerns at a deeper level, and (5) gather more information about the client. See Table 9.3.

Step 1: Deliver the Broaching Statement

During step 1, the provider communicates a thoughtfully crafted broaching question or statement that was formulated during the preparation stage. It is during this phase that the client implements the preliminary steps of the strategies framework: (a) Joining, (b) Assessment or the use of conceptual tools to hypothesize about the client's REC concerns, and (c) Preparation or formulation of a specific broaching statement. The provider integrates these three steps and executes a broaching statement. See Table 9.4.

Step 2: Permit Silence

Once the provider has presented the broaching event, it is important to use silence and not follow up with unnecessary chatter. Following the broaching event, the provider uses silence and waits for the client to respond. Essentially, silence is a period of three to five seconds in which neither the provider nor the

Table 9.3 Delivery Phase

Delivery Phase	
Step 1	Communicate broaching statement
Step 2	Permit silence
Step 3	Use reflective statements
Step 4	Use client's responses to discuss relevant sociopolitical issues
Step 5	Gather more information – educate yourself

Table 9.4 Sample Broaching Statements – The Case of Mei-ling with RESPECTFUL Categories

MMBB Domain	*Broaching Statement Applied to Mei-ling*	*Purpose of Broaching Statement*
Intra-counseling Domain	We're both women; however, we're from different racial, ethnic, and cultural backgrounds, as well as different age cohorts. I'm wondering how you are experiencing the counseling process so far, given our differences in racial background and age? I ask because I want to tailor the counseling process to meet your needs because my intention is to be as helpful as I possibly can. If you have feedback that would assist me in making the counseling process more meaningful for you, please let me know.	• Acknowledges similarities and differences between the provider and client • Uses cultural immediacy to inquire about how those similarities and differences shape the client's counseling experience • Provides a rationale for the question • Invites the client to share feedback • Reduces the power imbalance by inviting the client for feedback
Intra-individual Domain	"What would you like me to know about you including race, culture, religion, lifestyle, socioeconomics, immigration, sexual preference, gender identity, or any other diversity topics?" (R. Levis as cited in Urdaneta, in press)	• Invites the client to identify the specific intersectional identity domains that are most salient without insisting that the client discuss a specific domain such as race • Provides a non-exhaustive list of identity domains that client may want to discuss
	What is it like for you navigating upper-middle-class social spaces as an Asian American female with working-class roots?	• Elicits more specific detail about issues related to social class impact the client • Addresses the intersections of race, ethnicity, gender, and social class status
	Tell me more about your decision to become agnostic and the impact on your family dynamics.	• Elicits more detailed discussion concerning the client's evolving religious identity • Recognizes that agnosticism may be inconsistent with Buddhist upbringing
	I get the sense that at times, you may feel like a fish out of water, navigating entry into the middle class, and as the first in your family to attend college	• Uses a metaphor to address the provider's perception that the client may feel awkward moving from her working-class roots to the middle class • Broaches tentatively so that the client may disagree or clarify the broaching statement

(*Continued*)

Table 9.4 (Continued)

MMBB Domain	*Broaching Statement Applied to Mei-ling*	*Purpose of Broaching Statement*
	Over the years, you have developed a healthy sense of self-acceptance regarding your Asian identity and a deepening appreciation for your own Asian aesthetic.	• Uses positive asset search to acknowledge client's commitment to her racial and ethnic identity and the growth that has transpired since her teenage years
Intra-REC Domain	It sounds like you feel torn between directing your own autonomous path forward and honoring traditional Asian family values. It's as if you are walking a cultural tightrope.	• Acknowledges the tension between personal desires and familial expectations/obligations • Uses metaphor to intensify meaning
	You have been raised with a cultural script that suggests as an Asian child of immigrants you should be indebted to your parents for all the sacrifices they have made, and although you have an abiding appreciation for your parents' sacrifices, you struggle with the expectation of filial piety because it feels somewhat overbearing to you and may even limit your sense of individuality. Is that correct? I get the sense that your feelings may not be open for discussion in your family. Is that your sense of what may going on? Provider may discuss these two questions separately.	• Acknowledges the cultural scripts that may make it difficult for Mei-ling to communicate with her parents about family dynamics • Verbalizes the tensions that may exist between Mei-ling and her parents that may limit her ability to have earnest conversations about her feelings because they may violate traditional Chinese family norms • Recognizes that the immigrant generation and the second generation have different psychosocial tasks that may lead to cultural misunderstandings • Checks with client for accuracy
Inter-REC Domain	Although you were born in the United States and you are a U.S. citizen, you experience a fair amount of anti-immigrant sentiment. It sounds like you are afraid of being illegally detained or deported given the current political climate.	• Acknowledges clients' fear and trepidation about current political climate for immigrants • Uses a reflective statement to identify Mei-ling's feelings about the current political climate

client talks (Hill, 2020). In counseling, five seconds can feel like an eternity. Yet, silence has multiple purposes that can differ from how we use it in our social worlds versus how we use it within the counseling dyad. In our personal worlds, silence can be used as an indicator that the speaker is at a loss for words, as a tool of manipulation, to demonstrate anger, etc. In counseling, a moment of silence functions as an empathic response that gives the client an opportunity to internalize and reflect on what the provider has said, without interruption (Hill, 2020). The provider's silence operates as an expression of noninterference that allows the session to proceed in an unhurried fashion in order for clients to reflect more deeply on their inner thoughts, feelings, and concerns; express emotional relief, construct meaning, and share personal disclosures (Cormier et al., 2016).

I find that when I'm teaching, students experience the most difficulty with silence. Sometimes they interrupt the client's train of thought by following up broaching statements with lecturing, advising, or a set of random questions that do not allow the client to reflect in a meaningful way about their inner experience. And so, when a beautifully crafted broaching statement is followed with something other than silence, the broaching momentum initially gained is subsequently lost. Instead, the provider should follow up a broaching statement with silence. I tell my students that typically the person that is most uncomfortable with silence will speak first. Because they are functioning in the counseling role, they should use silence deliberately and intentionally. I encourage my students to come to terms with the importance and therapeutic value of silence.

In class, I use a PowerPoint slide that contains the acronym, STFU, and I ask students to guess what the acronym represents. To date, no one has gotten it right. It stands for Stop That Faulty Ultracrepidarianism!!! Ultracrepidarianism refers to the habit of giving input on matters outside of one's own knowledge or expertise. It describes someone who confidently offers advice or critiques on subjects they know very little about. Additionally, I show a video clip of CNN news anchor, Anderson Cooper, interviewing filmmaker, and journalist Cameron Crowe. Crowe describes an interview with musician Kris Kristofferson. During the interview, Crowe asked Kristofferson whether he got lonely on the road. Kris Kristofferson did not respond immediately, and Crowe panicked, worrying that he may have asked an inappropriate question. Although Crowe presumed the silence reflected a possible rupture, in actuality, Kristofferson used the period of silence to think deeply about and respond honestly to Crowe's question. In counseling we refer to Kristofferson's use of silence as a working silence.

Silence operates as an opportunity for both the client and provider to engage in unhurried reflection. This is particularly important during broaching discussions because we live in a society where we have relatively few opportunities to engage in meaningful conversations about REC, and people do not have a template for facilitating such conversations (Trevino et al., 2021).

In instances where the silence becomes uncomfortable, unproductive or a lot has been said that has not yet been processed, the provider is encouraged to break the silence. For example, the provider could say something like, "We've covered a lot of territory in this session. I would like to pause for a moment and invite you to share what is coming up for you based on our current discussion."

Step 3: Use a Reflective Statement

Following a period of silence, the provider integrates and synthesizes their broaching statements and questions with foundational and advanced counseling skills. These skills include attending behavior, minimal encouragers, reflection of content, reflection of feelings, reflection of meaning, and interpretation skills. Each of these skills communicates that the provider is listening and helps the client feel heard and understood. Minimal encouragers are brief verbal statements like mm-hmm, yes, go on, continue that demonstrate the provider's engagement in what the client is saying and help the client continue talking. Attending behavior refers to the provider's effort to pay attention to the verbal and nonverbal behavior that the client displays. It also involves the provider's orientation toward the client, which is indicated by leaning forward, maintaining eye contact, having a relaxed body posture, and having a calm and measured tone of voice, as well as an effort to match the client's grammatical style and pace. Matching the client's grammatical style indicates that providers mirror the client's discourse style to reflect similar pacing, level of formality, and complexity of sentence structure. This skill is very different from imitating the client, which may be perceived as a form of ridicule, internalized as offensive, and experienced as a type of raciolinguistic microaggression. Incidentally, raciolinguistics refers to the evaluation of an individual on the basis of their race and discourse style due to the presumption that the individual's communication style lacks prestige. Individuals experience language oppression in the same way they experience racism and discrimination (Ortega et al., 2022).

Reflection of Content/Feeling

Reflection of content is a form of active listening where the provider restates or paraphrases the client's comments using a concise statement that reiterates what the client has said by highlighting key points. A reflection of content focuses on facts associated with the client's statements. In the case of Mei-ling, the provider may say, "Your parents expect you to accompany them to appointments so that you can interpret for them." In marked contrast, a reflection of feeling highlights the emotions associated with the client's concerns (e.g., mad, sad, glad, afraid). Mei-ling's provider may say, "You feel emotionally drained because your parents rely so heavily on you to help them navigate their appointments," in an effort to draw out the client's underlying felt-level experience and promote catharsis. An appropriate reflection of feeling matches the client's level of intensity (Hill, 2020). For instance, stating that Mei-ling is devastated that her parents rely on her may be an overstatement. The overstatement of feelings may signal to clients that the provider is not listening or may be projecting emotional states onto the client. In instances where the provider may not be entirely accurate, the client will likely clarify their feelings in ways that improve understanding for both the provider and client. If the provider is apprehensive about using reflection of content, in lieu of a question, they may probe for thoughts by saying something like, "Mei-ling, tell me more about how you have been impacted by having to provide your parents with support."

Reflection of Meaning

Reflection of meaning is an insight-oriented skill that moves beyond what the client has stated explicitly and elicits meaning associated with the client's experience (Ivey et al., 2022). Mei-ling's provider may elicit meaning by asking her to reflect more deeply on prior statements that she has made. For instance, the provider may use reflection of meaning to elicit a deeper discussion by saying something like,

> Culturally it seems you feel a deep sense of obligation to assist your parents in navigating social systems in the United States, even though personally you find it difficult to provide this level of support at this stage in your life.

In instances where the provider feels less comfortable structuring a reflection of meaning statement but wants to explore client concerns beyond surface-level topics, the provider may ask an open question for meaning by saying something like, "Culturally, what does it mean for you to invest a considerable amount of your personal time and energy into helping your parents navigate U.S. culture?" By posing an open question for meaning, the provider uses a less directive counseling approach and does not make assumptions about the client's motivations. Mei-ling's client can explore her experience in the way she chooses.

Interpretation

Interpretation involves the provider's intent to make connections between comments the client has stated or implied in order to identify a new meaning that perhaps the client had not previously considered (Hill, 2020). Essentially, the provider helps promote insight by helping the client identify patterns in thoughts, feelings, and behavior. The provider may say something like,

> I get the sense that you feel emotionally drained not only because your parents rely on you so heavily to help them navigate their life in the United States, but also because your investment in their well-being syphons time and energy from your own pursuits.

This interpretation makes connections between the client's stated sense of obligation to her parents and her commitment to social mobility. Following an interpretation, the provider will use silence to allow the client to process her inner thoughts and feelings. Following a period of silence, the provider will respond using the basic listening sequence. In the event the provider's interpretation is inaccurate, the client will likely counter with a more accurate statement that provides clarity for both the provider and client. In instances where the provider may be uncertain or even tentative about Mei-ling's dilemma, they may want to ask an open question for interpretation that relies heavily on the client's subjective insights and personal narratives, rather than offering an interpretation. In such instances, the provider may pose the following question: "What are some underlying factors that contribute to your frustration about how much your parents expect of you?" This question prompts the client to elaborate on their own subjective beliefs about the underlying issues.

Summary Statement

Providers use summary statements to review what has transpired during the course of the counseling session. The summary provides a concise overview of the client's thoughts, feelings, and behaviors and helps communicate to clients that the provider heard them accurately. Summary statements may occur at the beginning of a session to provide a synopsis of what transpired in the previous session, and to prepare the client to transition into the current session. Summaries may also occur when a client has talked for a protracted period of time during the session in order to help maintain focus. Frequently, providers use summaries at the end of a session to recap what transpired during the counseling session. Summary statements allow clients to hear what they sound like, clarify thoughts, and chart progress. Mei-ling's provider offered a summary statement at the conclusion of the session and said,

> Today we discussed how it is becoming increasingly more challenging for you to support your parents. You are torn between honoring traditional Chinese cultural values around duty to family that have been instilled in you and your growing need for more independence. You are also worried that tending to family obligations may interfere with your personal and professional goals and you find it difficult to communicate your feelings to your parents because your family may perceive you as ungrateful, entitled, and far too American. Does that sound accurate?

The check-in allows the client to agree or disagree with the provider's summary statement.

Throughout the broaching process, the provider should exhibit multicultural orientation, which was discussed in Chapter 2 and refers to the provider's commitment to a way of being present with the client in order to strengthen relational dynamics. Multicultural orientation involves (a) cultural humility or a deep and abiding sense of curiosity and recognition that the provider may not know everything, (b) cultural comfort or an ease of manner communicating with the client, and (c) availing oneself of cultural opportunities by engaging in broaching behavior. These skills are important as providers integrate and synthesize the broaching behaviors and have been linked to stronger alliances and greater client satisfaction.

Step 4: Discussion of Sociopolitical Issues

As stated in the opening chapter of this book, we reside in a society that has encountered tremendous difficulty discussing the elephant in the room – Race, Ethnicity, and Culture. Because counseling is a microcosm of society and what unfolds in our social world is often mirrored within the counseling dyad, many providers experience significant difficulty facilitating REC discussions with clients. In this sense, the counseling dyad bears close resemblance to society at large. Providers' difficulty initiating or responding to the client's REC concerns contributes to cultural concealment, or the tendency for clients to withhold pertinent information about REC, cultural ruptures, less favorable counseling outcomes, and premature termination (Brawner et al., 2025; Day-Vines et al., 2024; Depauw et al., 2024; Drinane et al., 2018; Fuertes et al., 2002; Lukowitsky et al., 2024; Zhang & Burkard, 2008).

The challenges providers experience delving into clients' REC concerns are closely tied to the training and preparation they received. Multicultural counseling approaches have evolved considerably since my graduate studies more than 30 years ago when we operated under the auspices of the groundbreaking Multicultural Counseling Competencies (MCC, Sue et al., 1992). These competencies were designed to make counseling more inclusive and disrupt Eurocentric assumptions embedded within the counseling profession. At the time of my training, I was instructed to cultivate a marked degree of self-awareness so that I could recognize and mitigate my own biases and develop a nonracist identity; maintain a functional knowledge base about the challenges and worldview of clients from marginalized groups; use culturally appropriate assessment tools; identify individual and institutional intervention strategies that are consistent with clients' cultural values and experiences; remain abreast of the theoretical and empirical literature concerning the mental health of various racial and ethnic groups, get involved with clients at the community level; and pursue continuous training and seek consultation. Notably, multicultural counseling coursework was not infused throughout the counseling curriculum; rather, it was relegated to a single course. When I first started teaching, students reported that when diversity issues came up in other classes, faculty would say that you'll discuss that when you get to diversity.

Although the original MCCs stated the importance of engaging in a variety of verbal and nonverbal helping responses (Sue et al., 1992), comparatively less attention was focused on specific more clinically oriented counseling skills for facilitating meaningful REC conversations with clients. At the time of my training, MCC was considered avant-garde and pushed professional boundaries that had not previously been attempted. The authors were prescient in noting that scholars and practitioners should continue to build on the foundation, the competencies established. Indeed, such advancements have occurred, but proponents of multiculturalism have had to vie for legitimacy.

In fact, in my own training, I was not instructed to engage in the explicit naming or labeling of sociopolitical issues around REC as central to the counseling process, presumably because naming sociopolitical issues could be construed as directing the client in ways that imposed the provider's will and robbed clients of their sense of agency. Yet we know now, however, that if we do not invite clients to discuss their sociopolitical concerns, clients may conceal their underlying reasons for seeking counseling. Avoiding such discussions helps maintain social hierarchies and the system of marginalization and subordination that contributes to heightened levels of psychological distress in clients.

It is precisely because women have been empowered to say unapologetically, "Me too," both within and outside counseling settings, that greater efforts are being made to hold predators to account for their nefarious behavior and that women are experiencing catharsis and gradually healing. Yet, all too often, expressing sociopolitical issues has been regarded as subversive. "Black lives Matter," diversity-equity-and-inclusion, critical race theory initiatives have been categorized as divisive indoctrination, and proponents of these ideologies are considered to maintain a radical obsession with oppression that unfairly villainizes Whites, in particular (Washington et al., 2023). Yet, a growing corpus of scholarship indicates that increasingly clients are experiencing multiple intersecting forms of racial and social distress that cannot be addressed adequately without attending to their sociopolitical contexts.

Exposure to traumatic incidents renders clients fearful and hypervigilant. Take, for example, families who live in constant fear that immigration and customs enforcement officers may ransack their homes in search of undocumented individuals who are eligible for deportation; trans individuals who live with the threat of physical and emotional violence; the more than 500,000 Black women who were forced out of the labor force since 2025; the growing number of missing and murdered indigenous women on Native American reservations; the poor and working-class families facing exorbitant health insurance costs given abrupt shifts in healthcare policy. Clients seek counseling in order to mitigate the psychological costs of these calamities, which are inherently intersectional in nature – shaped not by situational factors, but by the manner in which structural forces intersect with race, gender, class, sexual orientation, etc., to impinge on their experience. The threat of these consequences evokes a fear and trepidation that rattles the nervous system making, it difficult for individuals to maintain psychological homeostasis. Consequently, clients are in need of opportunities to have these conversations, and graduate training programs must equip providers to address the contextual dimensions of REC on their sense of well-being.

Williams (2026) used a training intervention with graduate students completing a social and cultural diversity course to help them become more proficient with their broaching behavior. During the early part of semester, students were asked to devise broaching statements in response to counseling vignettes. Afterward, they were given specific instructions and guided practice using four criteria: (a) develop a statement that directly acknowledged race, (b) validate the client's experience, (c) move beyond surface-level reflective statements, and (d) develop explicit statements that name race or some form of systemic discrimination clearly, concisely, and confidently.

At the pre-test level, one student responded to a broaching scenario in the following manner, "I hear that you're frustrated and upset." Although this statement captured the client's affective state, it did not satisfy criteria for an effective broaching statement. Following several weeks of didactic instruction and guided practice, the student's final response to the same scenario evolved: "I hear that it's frustrating and hurtful to feel ignored as a Black man in this workplace." The follow-up statement not only validated the client's affective experience but also addressed directly, concisely, and confidently, the role of race, gender, and systemic oppression. By semester's end, the majority of students in the study demonstrated a similar ability to meet the broaching parameters set by the researcher.

There is a famous African proverb that says, "as long as the lions have no historians, the tale of the hunt will glorify the hunter." This quote means that individuals who occupy subordinate statuses in society will have their voices persistently silenced unless they are afforded opportunities to name and contextualize the oppression they face. Within this analogy, providers function as facilitators who help create psychologically safe spaces that permit clients to engage in open, uninterrupted discussions about their sociopolitical realities. It is important to note that providers differ greatly in their perceptions about whether to label clients' sociopolitical concerns. The manner in which the provider proceeds should be contingent upon the needs of the client.

Step 5: Gather More Information

Step 5 occurs outside the confines of counseling and requires the provider to gather more detailed information about the client's background. A few years ago, I conducted a broaching presentation, and an audience member commented that I seemed to have a wealth of knowledge about many different cultural groups. That is true because I have been teaching for nearly 30 years; I read voraciously and travel extensively, which gives me great insight into a variety of different cultural groups. I also have the benefit of teaching students from across the country and around the globe who have enhanced my understanding of various cultural groups. My students' disclosures give me a unique window into their cultural worlds. The audience member suggested that it was not possible to accrue detailed information about each specific cultural group with whom providers work. I agree partially; however, I believe that after formal training has ended, providers continue their professional development by increasing their knowledge base about the populations with whom they work/or more frequently. This includes reading, attending cultural events, expanding social groups beyond one's own cultural groups, leaning into group differences, reading, volunteering, attending cultural events, connecting with people who are different from us, as well as enlisting cultural informants or people who understand the central properties of mainstream American culture and a minoritized group, expanding one's cultural repertoire, etc. Although providers may not learn detailed information about every distinct cultural group, they build their repertoire of skills by recognizing patterns in the way groups are treated and respond to stress.

For me, travel has been a key source of learning and understanding the world outside my little bubble. I listen to talk show host Karen Hunter on SiriusXM Radio. One day on my way home from work, she admonished her listeners to travel not just to soak up the sun's rays and ski down the highest slopes but to develop deeper knowledge and understanding about the world around us. That comment resonated with me as a counselor educator. Venturing beyond tourist dives has been quite informative. Maintaining curiosity about the world around us is critical. Importantly, maintaining curiosity about the clients before us is equally as critical. Much of my cultural knowledge has been imparted by clients and students who talk openly about their own inner experiences and cultural values.

Burning Question

Norma, you Defined Broaching as Instances in Which Providers Initiate or Respond to Clients' REC Concerns. Does the Broaching Process Unfold Differently Based on Whether the Provider Initiates or Responds to REC Content?

Broaching refers to the provider's effort to either *initiate* or *respond* to cultural content that emerges during the counseling process (Day-Vines et al., 2018). When providers initiate broaching discussions, they invite the client to discuss how culture influences their presenting concerns. Providers often initiate broaching discussions because they recognize that the client's worldview may inform how the client interprets life experiences, especially when those values differ from mainstream cultures. Sometimes clients raise REC concerns before the provider does. The broaching process will unfold similarly whether the provider or client initiates the discussion. When the client raises REC concerns,

Table 9.5 Initiating vs. Responding to a Broaching Statement

	Initiating Broaching	*Responding to Broaching*
Who introduces broaching content	Provider invites the client to consider the relationship between presenting concern and REC	Client introduces a discussion about REC proactively
Provider's role	Provider opens the door to a discussion about REC	Provider walks through the door the client has opened
Rationale	Provider develops a more holistic understanding of the client's social contexts and recognition of how culture and history shape client experience	Client describes impact of concerns to provider
Sample Statement	Provider: "What is it like for you as an international student who is navigating immense amounts of anti-immigrant sentiment?"	Client: "Every time I see a police officer, I worry that I am going to be stopped and harassed by an ICE agent"
Purpose	Communicates to client that REC discussions are appropriate for counseling	Client communicates how anti-immigrant sentiments impact their sense of safety
Risk if omitted	Client may be reluctant to share cultural concerns in the future	Client may be reluctant to share cultural concerns in the future

the provider will follow steps 2–5 of the delivery phase. That is, the provider will listen, pause to reflect on the client's stated concerns (step 2), use a reflective statement to integrate and synthesize the client's broaching statements with foundational and advanced counseling skills (step 3), address the client's sociopolitical concerns as appropriate (step 4), and engage in continued learning about the client's background (step 5). Table 9.5 compares and contrasts provider and client initiation of broaching discussions.

Burning Question

Norma, I Think I Asked This Question in An Earlier Chapter, But I Want To Ask Again. What If I Broach and My Client Isn't Interested in Discussing Their REC Concerns?

Do not fret. The client may decline an opportunity to discuss REC concerns in that moment because they do not regard broaching as relevant to their presenting concerns. This may result because the client (a) does not have conscious awareness about the embeddedness of REC in their problems; (b) may feel that REC is not relevant to their concerns; and (c) lack a deep enough sense of trust with the provider or preparedness to engage in a broaching discussion.

In Chapter 3, we used a restaurant analogy and noted that if a waiter asked the customer if they wanted steak sauce and the customer said, "No thank you," the waiter wouldn't panic and feel that they had made a drastic mistake; they would use that information as diagnostic information to understand that steak sauce was not important to the customer in that moment. The waiter would be open also to the possibility that at some later point the customer may want steak sauce, and they can revisit that request when it is more relevant. Similarly in a counseling context, the provider may introduce a broaching statement and determine the relevance of that statement to the client. If the client is not ready in that moment to engage in a broaching discussion, the provider may revisit the broaching discussion at a later time when it seems more relevant to the client.

The final section of this chapter presents a broaching dialogue between Mei-ling and her provider. Although there are multiple focal points that the provider can draw from, the dialogue centers specifically on the Family History and Dynamics component of the RESPECTFUL model (D'Andrea & Daniels, 2001). In this segment, Mei-ling laments the intergenerational tensions she experiences with her family. The provider uses the Intra-REC and intra-counseling dimensions of the MMBB. The transcript contains process comments that help the reader recognize specific counseling skills and the corresponding rationale (Table 9.6).

Guo et al. (2022) conducted a study of intergenerational conflict among Chinese immigrant families in the United States. Findings demonstrated that younger respondents, those with higher levels of education compared to their parents, and those who had less investment in filial obligation reported more family conflict. The growing tensions that Mei-ling currently experiences may have to do with acculturation differences between herself and her family members. As a U.S. citizen, she has likely had more freedoms and opportunities to immerse herself in mainstream American culture in ways that have not been available to her parents and brothers. In subsequent sessions, the provider used psychoeducation to help Mei-ling recognize that each immigrant generation has different psychosocial tasks. The provider explained that the immigrant generation helps the family get settled and often maintains cultural norms and values. Compared to members of the immigrant generation, the second-generation maneuvers with greater ease in the host culture and experiences a much more rapid rate of acculturation. They have a healthy appreciation of their culture of origin as well as the new American culture. These differences may contribute to some of the tensions Mei-ling is currently experiencing. As Mei-ling recognized this pattern in her own experience, her provider helped her develop communication skills that

Table 9.6 Dialogue with Mei-ling

Dialogue	*Process Comments*
Provider: Mei-ling, in our last session, you shared some family concerns. You noted that you are very devoted to your family, but right now, you feel torn between honoring traditional Asian family values and directing your own autonomous path forward. It's as if you are walking a cultural tightrope. You have been raised with a cultural script that suggests as the child of Chinese immigrants you should be indebted to your parents for all the sacrifices they have made. And even as you have an abiding appreciation for your parents' sacrifices, you struggle with the expectation of filial piety because it feels somewhat overbearing to you and may even limit your sense of individuality. It sounds that this concern is not open for discussion in your family and you're worried that if you bring it up things will devolve. Is that your sense of what's going on?	The provider opens the session with a summary statement to recap the primary concerns Mei-ling addressed in the previous session. The delivery is direct, concise, and stated confidently. The provider uses a metaphor to convey and intensify meaning (e.g., cultural tightrope). Afterwards, the provider checks in with the client to check for accuracy and give Mei-ling to clarify the summary. The provider's synopsis demonstrates an understanding of the client's collectivist worldview and the expectation that children of immigrants have an obligation to take care of their parents. The provider is addressing the Intra-REC broaching dimension of the MMBB dimension by exploring family dynamics. Afterwards, the provider checks in with Mei-ling to determine accuracy.
Mei-ling: Yes, exactly. You are correct. I love my parents dearly and I am proud of all they have accomplished. They risked a lot to get here, and they are risking even more as they work to stay here. You see, my parents came to the United States with my brother before I was born. Their visas expired and they have lived under the radar and in constant fear of deportation ever since. Because I was born here, I am a citizen and so I have spent my entire life navigating health, education, social services, and financial systems for them, completing forms, and serving as an interpreter. Because they spend the majority of their time in the restaurant, they have not really had an opportunity to learn English. I go to college 45-minutes away from home, and at any given moment, my parents may call and ask me to come home and help with something. I feel like it's my time now – to be me and to be free.	The provider has created a sense of psychological safety and Mei-ling feels heard and understood. As a consequence, she talks at a deeper emotional level about her family dynamics. The fact that she has divulged her parents' documentation status suggests that she trusts her provider. Mei-ling's disclosure suggests that she has spent the majority of her life in a caretaking role for her parents, even while she is away at college.

(*Continued*)

Table 9.6 (Continued)

Dialogue	*Process Comments*
These demands are beginning to take their toll on me. Asian families are not like American families in the sense that children tell their parents what they will and won't do. There are clear boundaries, so even bringing my concerns up in conversations would be seen as rude, disrespectful, and hurtful. I don't want to seem ungrateful.	
Provider: You have a strong sense of loyalty toward your family, but you feel trapped by family expectations. You've assumed adult roles as caretaker for family members and now you're beginning to feel taken advantage of.	The provider uses the positive asset search to validate the Mei-ling's commitment to her family while simultaneously acknowledging the accompanying strain on family dynamics. The provider also acknowledges the emotional toll that the family tension is taking on her.
Mei-ling: Pretty much, yes (*sighs*). Not only that, but there's also tension in our family because we are in a mixed status household. I am the only one in my family who is a U.S. citizen. At times my family has accused me of being tài měiguó le. That means too American and that I am abandoning my traditional Chinese values. I have acclimated to U.S. culture at a much faster rate than the rest of the family because I've been in school, extracurricular activities, and now college with American people. It hurts when they say that, because I see myself as very Chinese.	As a result of feeling heard and understood, Mei-ling provides further elaboration about her experience by sharing how gaps in the family's acculturative process have strained family dynamics. Geopolitical tensions between China and the United States are playing out in your household.
Provider: I get the sense that at times, you feel like an outsider in your own home.	Provider reflects meaning by noting the sense of isolation and alienation Mei-ling experiences from family members.

(*Continued*)

Table 9.6 (Continued)

Dialogue	*Process Comments*
Mei-ling: Absolutely. I do. My brother calls me a banana. Do you know what that means?	Mei-ling is wondering whether she will have to educate the provider.
Provider: I do. A banana is a derogatory term used to describe someone who is not seen as Asian enough. It's a way of othering you. We have a similar term in the African American community referred to as oreo. It describes someone Black who acts so White they are not recognizably Black. I was referred in that way when I was growing up.	The provider establishes credibility by communicating understanding sentiments that are used to indicate someone is too westernized. The provider also uses a self-disclosure to communicate her shared understanding of Mei-ling's dilemma and to help her feel less alone.
Mei-ling: Laughs. Oh wow! So, you know personally what it means to be othered.	Mei-ling is pleasantly surprised that the provider understands what it means to be othered.
Provider: Absolutely! Pauses. You feel really misunderstood by your family members because they assume you are abandoning your traditional Chinese cultural values.	The provider reflects feeling in order to normalize Mei-ling's experience.
Mei-ling: Yes, I often do feel misunderstood. They think I'm acting superior, and I feel I can't do enough to demonstrate my commitment to my family and culture. Even though my family is proud of my academic accomplishments, and it gives them status and bragging rights among their peers, they also accuse me of not being loyal enough.	Mei-ling elaborates about the level of intergenerational conflict she experiences. Because Mei-ling has had opportunities her family has not had, they expect more of her. It seems the family sees Mei-ling drifting away from traditional Chinese values.
Provider: The tension is wearing on you. You feel rejected by your family, and I imagine that hurts.	The provider uses reflection of meaning to convey that feeling misunderstood leaves Mei-ling with a sense of woundedness.

(*Continued*)

Table 9.6 (Continued)

Dialogue	*Process Comments*
Mei-ling: Yes, sometimes I feel like an outcast in my own family. It's gotten to the point that I do not share some of the exciting things I'm experiencing away at college because I'm afraid it would fuel shame and resentment.	Mei-ling is apprehensive about being more transparent with her family about her personal world.
Provider: The growing tensions have created a social distance between you and your family. You've mentioned that living in a mixed documentation status family has contributed to some of the challenges you're experiencing. I wonder if being a member of an immigrant family has resulted in different levels of adjustment that contribute to family strain.	
Mei-ling: I hate to admit this, but I think my family resents the opportunities I have and my prospects for the future. It's not so much that they are jealous, but my success is a reminder that they are pretty much stuck in their current circumstances. Yes, my parents had hopes of coming to this country and getting educated, but they ran out of money and the only option they had was to work in a restaurant. My mother is a waitress, and my father is a cook. I try not to personalize their actions toward me because I know that their dashed dreams have crushed them to some extent. I am the embodiment of their unrealized aspirations. Even though they are proud of me, they worry that they will lose me. They feel that somehow, I will abandon them. They want me to carry on cultural traditions that feel out of touch for me.	Mei-ling discloses more intimate details of her family life. She does not blame them, but recognizes how structural factors have shaped outcomes for her family members.
Provider: These cultural expectations feel burdensome to you.	The provider uses reflection of feeling to validate Mei-ling's sentiments.

(*Continued*)

Table 9.6 (Continued)

Dialogue	*Process Comments*
Mei-ling: I would agree. I feel silenced.	
Provider: I'm wondering – tell me if this fits for you - whether your decision to become agnostic is one way asserting your independence and creating at least some symbolic distance between yourself and your family.	The provider uses an interpretation that tries to connect the pressure that Mei-ling feels. The interpretation is tentative which allows Mei-ling to disagree or clarify the interpretation.
Mei-ling: Wow. I haven't looked at my situation in that way. My religion is actually one of the few choices I have control over.	Mei-ling is pondering the reality that she may be exercising the few choices she actually has and will likely spend time following the session pondering the provider's interpretation.
Provider: Before we close today, I want to thank you, for being vulnerable with me about your family circumstances. I feel honored that you felt comfortable enough to share this with me.	The provider validates the Mei-ling for sharing intimidate details of her life.
Mei-ling: I'm so glad to finally have a provider that seems to get me and understand what it means to be the child of immigrants. I've had providers that have seemed oblivious about Asian culture. I appreciate you very much.	
Provider: Before we close, I would like to acknowledge that we're both females, but we're from different cultures and age cohorts, and I wonder how that has impacted your experience in counseling.	The provider broaches intra-counseling dimensions to ascertain how their different sociodemographic characteristics impacted the counseling process.
Mei-ling: Well to be honest, I was hoping to have a Chinese provider, or at least an Asian provider. When I first met you, I wondered if I could really be authentic. You made it okay for me to talk about my culture unapologetically.	Mei-ling feels that sociodemographic differences did not impact the quality of the counseling relationship.

would reduce the family conflict by establishing healthy boundaries, developing more effective communication patterns, and balancing her personal values with her family's traditional values.

This dialogue reinforces the fact that broaching is a process and not an event. After the provider's summary statement that taps into the main content of the previous session, Mei-ling talks at length about her experience. In turn, the provider uses elements of the basic listing sequence to validate Mei-ling's emotions she attaches to her personal challenges using advanced counseling skills such as reflection of meaning and interpretation. These skills allow Mei-ling to talk in more depth about her concerns.

Gundel et al. (2020) conducted a case study to examine multicultural counseling processes between an African American, Muslim woman client who sought counseling and a White woman psychologist following the death of the client's father. Each participant was asked about their experiences addressing culture during the counseling process. The client reported that she both expected and valued the opportunity to explore her intersectional identities related to race, religion, and gender. Consistent with guidelines prescribed by Gundel et al. (2020), Mei-ling's provider worked to understand her background without imposing cultural assumptions based on her cultural background and demographic characteristics. In future sessions, the provider may use the same broaching processes to explore how gender shapes Mei-ling's specific concerns. This same sequence of counseling processes may have differed if culture had assumed limited salience for Mei-ling.

Summary

The preparation phase of the broaching strategies model contains three steps. First, the provider decides what broaching concerns warrant discussion. Second, the provider operates from the integrated/congruent category of the *Continuum of Broaching Behavior*, and at least one domain of the MMBB (e.g., intra-counseling, intra-individual, Intra-REC, Inter-REC). The provider may use the RESPECTFUL model to determine what aspect of the client's sociocultural and sociopolitical experience to highlight.

During the delivery phase of the broaching process, the provider communicates the broaching statement, uses silence, followed by the basic listening sequence. The provider also discusses the client's relevant sociocultural and sociopolitical as warranted. Outside of the counseling dyad, the provider educates themself about the client's cultural background.

References

Brawner, R., Day-Vines, N.L., Gubara, S., Agorsor, C., Jackson, Z., & Ran, T., & Caldwell, N. (2025). Perceptions of racial, ethnic, and cultural ruptures in counseling: A qualitative case study of a client from a minoritized background. *Journal of Counseling and Development, 103*, 484–495. https://doi-org.proxy1.library.jhu.edu/10.1002/jcad.70004

Cormier, S., Nurius, P.S., & Osborn, C.J. (2016). *Interviewing and change strategies for helpers.* Nelson Education.

D'Andrea, M., & Daniels, J. (2001). RESPECTFUL counseling: An integrative model for counselors. In D. Pope-Davis & H. Coleman (Eds.), *The intersection of class, culture, and gender in counseling.* (p. 417–466). Sage. https://doi.org/10.4135/9781452231846.n17

Day-Vines, N.L., Booker Ammah, B., Steen, S., & Arnold, K.M. (2018). Getting comfortable with discomfort: Preparing counselor trainees to broach racial, ethnic, and cultural factors with clients during counseling. *International Journal for the Advancement of Counselling, 40*(2), 89–104. https://doi.org/10.1007/s10447-017-9308-9

Day-Vines, N.L., Cluxton-Keller, F., Agorsor, C., & Gubara, S. (2021). Strategies for broaching the subjects of race, ethnicity and culture. *Journal of Counseling and Development*, 99, 348–357. https://doi.org/10.1002/jcad.12380

Day-Vines, N.L., Zhang, J., Cluxton-Keller, F., Hicks, D., Jones, C.T., Spann, T., Daga, D., & Agorsor, C., (2024). An investigation of the construct validation of the broaching attitudes and behavior scale – clients. *Journal of Multicultural Counseling and Development.* https://doi-org.proxy1.library.jhu.edu/10.1002/jmcd.12300

Depauw, H., & Van Hiel, A. (2024). Uncovering patterns in perceived therapist behaviour: A xlatent profile analysis of broaching experiences among ethnic minority group member clients. *Clinical Psychology and Psychotherapy*, 31, e3067. https://doi.org/10.1002/cpp.3067

Drinane, J.M., Owen, J., & Tao, K.W. (2018). Cultural concealment and therapy outcomes. *Journal of Counseling Psychology, 65*, 239–246. https://doi.org/10.1037/cou0000246

Fuertes, J.N., Mueller, L.N., Chauhan, R.V., Walker, J.A., & Ladany, N. (2002). An investigation of European American therapists' approach to counseling African American clients. *The Counseling Psychologist, 30*(5), 763–788. https://doi.org/10.1177/0011000002305007

Gundel, B.E., Bartholomew, T.T., & Scheel, M.J. (2020). Culture and care: An illustration of multicultural processes in a counseling dyad. *Practice Innovations, 5*(1), 19–31. https://doi.org/10.1037/pri0000104

Guo, M., Lemke, A., & Dong, X. (2022). Sources of intergenerational conflict in Chinese immigrant families in the United States. *Journal of Family Issues., 43*(9), 2275–2294. https://doi.org/10.1177/0192513X211030724

Hanna, F.J., Talley, W.B., & Guindon, M.H. (2000). The power of perception: Toward a model of cultural oppression and liberation. *Journal of Counseling and Development, 78*, 430–441. https://doi.org/10.1002/j.1556-6676.2000.tb01926.x

Hill, C.E. (2020). *Helping skills: Facilitating exploration, insight, and action.* American Psychological Association.

Ivey, A., Ivey, M., & Zalaquett, C.P. (2022). *Intentional interviewing and counseling: Facilitating client development in a multicultural society* (10th ed.). Cengage.

Lukowitsky, M.R., Winseman, J.S., Feld, E, Kam, S.M., & Balkoski, V.I. (2024). Patients' perceptions of their therapist: Effects of race, culture, and cultural competency on the working alliance. *American Journal of Psychotherapy.* https://doi.org/10.1176/appi.psychotherapy.20230056

Metzl, J.M., & Hansen, H. (2014). Structural competency: Theorizing a new medical engagement with stigma and inequality. *Social Science and Medicine, 103*, 126–13. https://doi.org/10.1016/j.socscimed.2013.06.032

Ortega, P., Martínez, G., Alemán, M.A., Zapién-Hidalgo, A., & Shin, T.M. (2022). Recognizing and dismantling raciolinguistic hierarchies in Latinx health. *AMA Journal of Ethics, 24*(4), E296–E304. https://doi.org/10.1001/amajethics.2022.296

Sue, D.W., Arredondo, P., & McDavis, R.J. (1992). Multicultural counseling competencies and standards: A call to the profession. *Journal of Multicultural Counseling and Development, 20*(2), 64–88. https://doi.org/10.1002/j.2161-1912.1992.tb00563.x

Trevino, A.Y., Tao, K.W., & Van Epps, J.J. (2021). Windows of cultural opportunity: A thematic analysis of how cultural conversations occur in psychotherapy. *Psychotherapy, 58*(2), 263–274. https://doi.org/10.1037/pst0000360

Washington, A. R., Williams, J. M., & Byrd, J. A. (2023). Exposing blindspots and the hidden curriculum within counselor supervision models. *Counselor Education and Supervision, 62*, 149–156. https://doi-org.proxy1.library.jhu.edu/10.1002/ceas.12260

Williams, J. (2026). Broaching race, ethnicity, and culture: Examining counselor trainees' growth through experiential training. *Journal of Multicultural Counseling and Development, 54*(2), 55–66. https://doi-org.proxy1.library.jhu.edu/10.1002/jmcd.70014

Zhang, N., & Burkard, A. (2008). Client and counselor discussions of racial and ethnic differences in counselling: An exploratory investigation. *Journal of Multicultural Counselling and Development, 36*, 77–87. https://doi.org/10.1002/j.2161-1912.2008.tb00072.x

Chapter 10

Cultural Ruptures

When I teach about ruptures, I usually start by asking students to raise their hand if they ever had a friendship or relationship that ended prematurely because they reached an impasse or some type of disagreement that was not properly resolved. Usually, most hands go up including my own. Next, I ask students to explain what contributed to the impasse and how they managed the conflict. Usually, students talk about the hubris or pride that prevented them from exhibiting humility and acknowledging their contribution to the conflict. Upon further discussion, students often admit the difficulty they experience with vulnerability and owning mistakes when conflicts arise. Some students concede that it is easier to abandon certain relationships than to engage in the emotional labor necessary to resolve the impasse. We then talk about the messages and role models class members experienced as children that may have shaped their conflict resolution styles. A surprising number of students concede that they did not have the best role models during their upbringing to help them navigate relational challenges. Consequently, they often struggle to address relational breaches during adulthood. As the class continues, we discuss the fact that counseling is a microcosm of society. Whether a function of interpersonal difficulties or geopolitical clashes among nations, conflict is inevitable.

Therapeutic ruptures refer to a breakdown in the therapeutic tasks, goals, and alliance between the provider and client. Scholars estimate that ruptures occur in 50–70% of counseling sessions, and they identify two predominant types of ruptures: withdrawal and confrontation (Muran et al., 2010). A withdrawal marker involves emotional disengagement from the counseling process, as evidenced by the client's silence, monosyllabic responses, topic shifts, as well as overcompliance or efforts to appease the provider. Confrontation markers, on the other hand, represent a more direct challenge or expression of dissatisfaction with the provider regarding interpersonal dynamics. A spate of previous research has demonstrated the relationship between ruptures, premature termination, resentment, and a weak therapeutic alliance (Homan et al., 2024; Safran & Muran, 2006).

DOI: 10.4324/9781003649311-10

Saoirse is an Irish American female who pursued counseling to address the depression she experienced as a result of a recent breakup with her long-term boyfriend. They dated for more than five years and discussed marriage, career, and family plans. Their future seemed bright and exciting; however, Saoirse was devastated when her boyfriend decided he was not ready for marriage. Although she found the counseling sessions comforting, she was annoyed that as late as her fifth counseling session, the provider continued to mispronounce her name, despite the fact that each week Saoirse corrected her provider. During their most recent meeting, the provider mispronounced Saoirse's name again. Upon hearing the mispronunciation, Saoirse became annoyed but remained patient. She responded by sounding out her name phonetically (SER-sha) and explaining the meaning and significance of her name, which means freedom based on the Irish fight for independence during the 1920s when her grandparents migrated to the United States. Instead of affirming the symbolic significance of Saoirse's name, the provider became tickled and said, "Thanks, I have it now. You have almost every vowel in your name," and then chuckled. Saoirse bristled because she did not find the comment helpful or funny. At a period in her life when she felt especially vulnerable, Saoirse felt unseen and humiliated by her provider, similar to the sense of personal violation she experienced by her boyfriend. Needless to say, Saoirse did not return for services, nor did she bother to discuss her concerns with her provider. Although the provider may not have intended to offend Saoirse, the issue is not the intent, but the impact of the provider's insensitive comments.

As the above scenario suggests, the counseling concern lies not with the rupture itself but how Saoirse's provider chose to manage the incident. Unlike the real world, in counseling, we have an ethical obligation to resolve ruptures that emerge during treatment in order to safeguard the client's well-being and facilitate healing. Power dynamics between the provider and client are usually asymmetrical. Because the provider wields the balance of power in the counseling relationship, it is incumbent upon the provider to reduce the power imbalance through a rupture resolution process. In other words, ruptures will inevitably arise inadvertently, and providers must mitigate them in culturally responsive ways (Chang et al., 2020).

Scholars have devoted far less attention to cultural ruptures that result from therapeutic impasses occurring within diverse provider-client dyads (Chang et al., 2020). Cultural ruptures result when clients perceive that providers have ignored or minimized salient aspects of their REC identity (Lee & Horvath, 2014), much like the rupture with Saoirse. Microaggressions reflect a specific type of cultural rupture that occurs in diverse provider-client dyads that result from slights and indignities clients experience on the basis of their minoritized status (e.g., race, ethnicity, gender, sexual orientation, religion, disability, and national origin). Previous research indicates that between 50 and 80% of ethnic minority clients have reported experiencing at least one microaggression during treatment (Hook et al., 2016; Owen et al., 2011). Avoidance of REC concerns during treatment has emerged as the predominant form of microaggression, followed by stereotypes, denial of cultural biases, and minimizing the importance of cultural issues during treatment (Hook et al., 2016). In the above scenario, the provider insulted Saoirse by making light of the pronunciation of her name and its spelling and seemed to lack awareness about the hurt her comment inflicted. In many cultures, names have symbolic significance and connect clients to their community, identity, and sense of belonging across generations. Unresolved microaggressions contribute to a sense of personal violation. Additively, scholars have linked microaggressions to depression, anxiety, and psychological distress (Rudecindo et al., 2024; Sue & Spanierman, 2020).

Recall in Chapter 3, during the discussion of the *Continuum of Broaching Behavior*, as Hernando, the gay Latino man who struggled with whether to come out to his family and worked with an avoidant provider who minimized his concerns about coming out. The avoidant provider stated that Latino families were not the only families to object to gay family members. Hernando felt dismissed and, in response, defended his stance about the significance of sexuality in Latino families. He emphasized the enormous stigma that his family may have to endure if he decided to come out. In that same chapter, the continuing/incongruent provider engaged in microaggressive behavior when he assumed that Hernando was an immigrant, when in fact Hernando was born in the United States. In each case, the provider minimized Hernando's concerns and seemed to lack awareness about the impact of the hurtful comments on Hernando.

Despite the fact that ruptures may be unintentional on the part of the provider, clients often experience these behaviors as offensive, malicious, upsetting, and hurtful. So much so that they may not return for follow-up sessions.

In a recent manuscript, my colleagues and I conducted a case study of a female Somali-Dutch American immigrant who sought counseling services to address escalating symptoms of depression and anxiety that stemmed from her tumultuous migration and resettlement process in the United States during her childhood, at the height of 9/11 (Brawner et al., 2025). Although the client intended to explore how her migration experience contributed to her ongoing trauma, the provider regarded the client's trauma as separate and distinct from the oppressive forces she faced. The client tried to convey to her provider that her depressive symptomology was a function of the trauma she encountered, including her acculturation process as a child, which was hampered by her limited ability to speak English, encounters with anti-Muslim sentiment, and the fact that phenotypically, she appeared African American. As an adult, she wanted to revisit some of her childhood traumas in therapy. Much to the client's dismay, the provider ignored her REC concerns altogether, opting instead to focus exclusively on the client's diagnosis of depression. Conceptualization of the client's presenting issues as a single-axis concern neglected the extent to which multiple, intersecting sources of oppression shaped the client's tumultuous orientation into U.S. culture. By only considering the client's diagnosis, the provider failed to explore the client's REC concerns holistically.

The client in our study did not merely experience one oppression but endured multiple sources of oppression and marginalization that were compounded. The provider's inability to address the client's nuanced concerns resulted in an unfortunate microaggressive rupture that ended in premature termination. Focusing exclusively on diagnoses without attention to the sociocultural, sociopolitical, and sociohistorical concerns that contributed to the client's distress is narrow in scope and reductionistic. The provider may have been able to offer better care for the client had she recognized the interaction between the client's race, gender, religion, immigration status, language, etc. Further, had the provider recognized the hierarchies related to privilege and marginalization that shaped the client's mental health functioning, as well as the power dynamics governing the provider-client relationship, the provider and client may have made more clinical progress. Responsiveness to the multidimensionality of the client's varied oppressions cannot be understated. Ignoring those concerns exacerbated the client's rupture experience.

Compared to White clients, ethnic minority clients have higher rates of unilateral termination that scholars have linked, in large measure, to cultural miscommunication (Kearney et al., 2005; Owen et al., 2014, 2012). Unilateral termination differs from other forms of termination wherein the provider and client come to a mutual agreement about the need to terminate, perhaps because counseling goals have been achieved or for other more mutually agreed-upon reasons. In unilateral termination, the client summarily ends the counseling session without notifying the provider.

When ruptures occur during treatment, providers have an opportunity to salvage the relationship. Findings from previous research indicate that rupture-repair episodes or situations in which the provider addresses the conflict or impasse were positively associated with improvements in the therapeutic alliance and greater retention. For instance, Yeo and Torres-Harding (2021) found that when the provider worked collaboratively with the client to resolve a rupture, the therapeutic bond was strengthened.

Chang et al. (2020) developed a critical-cultural-relational approach to resolving ruptures comprised of three specific components: (a) critical self-awareness – recognition of a priori biases that providers may have; (b) wise affect, or the provider's effort to self-regulate by responding appropriately to negative interactions by demonstrating compassion, interconnectedness, and mindfulness in order to manage anxiety related to the rupture itself; and (c) anti-oppressive interpersonal engagement, which refers to the avoidance of hierarchical power relationships and the ability to engage in perspective taking.

Chang et al. (2020) devised a six-step approach to resolving ruptures. During step 1, the provider recognizes the rupture marker by paying attention to verbal and nonverbal cues indicating a shift in the client's affect or level of engagement in the counseling session. For instance, Saoirse's provider might have taken cues when she grimaced and neglected to laugh at comments about her name. Additively, the fact that Saoirse did not find humor in the provider's comments might signal that she experienced the comments as offensive. Additionally, Saoirse provided contextual information about the symbolic significance of her name that the provider seemed to ignore. Once the provider observed that the interpersonal interaction shifted, the provider may move to step 2, which necessitates determination of how issues of power, oppression, privilege, and identity have contributed to the rupture. For instance, the provider might have considered that in the United States there is often a tendency to "other" people who do not have Anglicized names. It is possible that Saoirse has spent her life dreading how people respond to her name, listening to insensitive remarks, the taunts of her peers as a child, and efforts to have her generate a nickname that makes people more comfortable. In any case, these expectations are oppressive and, when perpetrated by the provider, invoke an unfair power dynamic. In the event, the provider recognized her faux pas during the session, the provider may have moved to step 3 and taken responsibility for addressing the rupture in the moment. This would involve the provider's effort to acknowledge the inappropriateness of her comment. Acknowledgment of mistakes is a necessary albeit insufficient criterion for working through a rupture. By only apologizing, the provider engages in a unidirectional discussion that does not permit the client to respond or engage in some level of self-expression. Moving to step 4, the provider invites the client to express their feelings and reactions about the rupture, in ways that allow the client to engage in self-expression. It is important for the provider to both listen nondefensively and internalize exactly how the client was impacted by the rupture. It is through this exchange that mutual understanding and the restoration of trust can occur. The provider may also invite the client to explore what it was like to engage in a conversation about the rupture experience.

So many relationships end unnecessarily because the involved parties do not have the skills and the tools to engage in an earnest discussion about their sense of personal violation. As a consequence, many relationships end prematurely rather because neither party has engaged in the work necessary to preserve what may otherwise operate as a worthwhile relationship. For instance, Saoirse's provider may elicit a discussion about what the client experienced as the rupture, how it felt to experience the rupture, whether the rupture event triggered related encounters with oppression and marginalization, how the client felt about the counseling relationship, a discussion about the damage that ensued, and whether the counseling relationship can withstand the rupture. Although this may be difficult for the provider to hear, the client is essentially putting a mirror up to the provider, so the provider gets a better sense of the magnitude of the rupture.

Table 10.1 Chang et al.'s (2021) Rupture Resolution Stages

1	Attend to the rupture marker – pay attention to verbal and nonverbal indicators that there is tension in the relationship.
2	Analyze the rupture – consider the extent to which power, privilege, identity, culture, and structural factors impact the counseling relationship. Provider's awareness of countertransference reactions.
3	Explore the meaning of the rupture – provider processes the rupture with the client in a culturally humble manner by acknowledging contributions to the rupture and minimizing defensiveness.
4	Explore the avoidance – address the client's feelings, reactions, and fears concerning the rupture event.
5	Affirm the relationship – validate the client for sharing their concerns. Provider remains accountable.
6	Repair the rupture – validate the client's efforts at assertiveness and ability to challenge oppressive structures that have a negative impact on the client and that reinforce issues of inequality in society.

During stage 5, the provider validates and affirms the client for sharing their experience. The provider may acknowledge the courage required to have an earnest conversation about a rupture. In stage 6, the provider helps the client extend the effort of self-assertion to other related instances. The opportunity to dialogue about the rupture may serve multiple purposes. It may help restore the counseling relationship. Additionally, it may provide a model and framework for helping the client address similar relational strains outside the counseling relationship, especially as it pertains to encounters with power, control, and marginalization. See Table 10.1 for a synopsis of Chang et al.'s model.

In the case illustration that follows, the provider has been working with LaKeisha, a 27-year-old African American woman who recently graduated from law school. She landed a tony position in a law firm as a junior associate. She is finally earning the money she envisioned, but she is working long hours and struggles with work-life balance. Although there are other African American attorneys in her firm, she feels out of place because several of them are second- and third-generation attorneys. She should be proud that she passed the bar exam on her first try, but she still feels out of place and at times inadequate, primarily because she's the first in her family to attend college and law school. She's been seeing her provider for a few months now, and her sessions are going well. LaKeisha is feeling a little more confident, so she has been experimenting with hairstyles. Last week she wore individual braids. This week she has a wavy afro. As she enters the counseling office, the provider greets her warmly and rubs her hand across LaKeisha's coiled tresses. Lakeisha winced and appeared visibly annoyed. The provider recognized LaKeisha's reaction and addressed her sudden shift in demeanor.

Provider: It's good to see you again this week (*as she opens the door and ushers LaKeisha into the office*). As always, your hair looks lovely. Your afro frames your face nicely (*as she reaches to touch LaKeisha's hair*). And it's so soft (*surprised*).

LaKeisha: (*shrugs away from the provider*). What do you mean it's so soft?

Provider: Well, umm! I don't know. It's pretty. I like it (*rhetorical incoherence*).

LaKeisha: Remains quiet and takes a seat – visibly annoyed

Provider: How have things been since last week?

LaKeisha: Fine (*responds monosyllabically, unlike her usual engaging interpersonal style*).

Provider: As I'm reflecting on the exchange we had a few minutes ago when you entered the office, I realize that you may have been put off when I touched your hair, and I instantly recognized that I crossed a boundary. I probably was a little too familiar with you. I invoked a power dynamic that offended you.

LaKeisha: Yes, I believe you did.

Provider: I'm so sorry that I took the liberty of touching your hair. I did not intend to offend you. I take full responsibility for my actions.

LaKeisha: I'm sure your intention was not to offend me.

Provider: But I did. I'm sure my actions drudged up a lot of uncomfortable emotions for you.

LaKeisha: For me, it felt like an invasion of my personal space. Although it seems harmless, it's something I've had to deal with a lot. As a young attorney, I know I have the right to wear my hear in an afro, given the Crown Act. Are you familiar with the crown act?

Provider: No, I can't say that I am.

LaKeisha: The crown act is legislation enacted in 25 states that bans race-based discrimination against, braids, twists, locs, afros, and other hairstyles. In my own journey as an attorney, this is something that I have deliberated about a lot. Will I be taken seriously, viewed as militant, unprofessional, excused from certain cases, excluded from certain events? The list goes on. Being scrutinized because of my hairstyle is stressful. I'm trying to be myself in an organization that sees me as invisible. I vacillate between invisibility and hypervisibility. It's stressful. I am one of the top producers at work, so my co-workers and supervisors do not say much about my hairstyle. I'm resisting the notion that I can only be taken seriously if I assimilate and straighten my hair. I'm through using harsh chemicals on my hair to gain the approval of people who no matter how much I contort myself will find a reason to reject me.

Provider: If you feel comfortable, please describe what our interaction brought up for you, especially given some of the stressors you have dealt with around your hair?

LaKeisha: Well, you also said my hair was soft, as if you expected it to be coarse or unmanageable. That really seemed like the stereotypical statements people make about Black hair. It's offensive, especially given the cultural significance of natural Black hair and the fact that many of us are proud of our natural hair. Touching my hair without permission also felt like an infringement on my personal space. Historically, African Americans have been violated physically and lacked the right to establish boundaries without harsh consequences.

Provider: As someone who is White, I realize I made assumptions about your hair that were hurtful. It was problematic for me to believe that it was okay to touch your hair.

LaKeisha: I appreciate you acknowledging that you were in the wrong by touching my hair. Most people would have ignored my reactions.

Provider: I respect and value the courage it took you to talk honestly and openly about how you experienced this encounter. I hope that in the future, if I do or say something inappropriate you feel like you can confront me.

LaKeisha: Definitely.

During this scenario, the provider followed each of Chang et al.'s (2020) rupture-repair strategies. The provider opened the session by complimenting LaKeisha's new hairstyle as a means of exchanging pleasantries and engaging in small talk. Soon after, she went a step too far by touching LaKeisha's hair and commenting that it felt soft, as if surprised. The provider recognized the rupture marker because LaKeisha shrugged, moved away, and became monosyllabic. Based on their conversation, it seems like the provider had little awareness of how her actions invoked a form of social dominance that consigned LaKeisha to a subordinate status, except for the fact that she questioned the provider about what she meant by "soft hair." The provider responded with what Bonilla-Silva (2021) characterizes as rhetorical incoherence, the discomfort that results when racial issues arise and speakers become uncomfortable and resort to communicating using disorganized and incomprehensible speech patterns. The provider rambled when LaKeisha confronted her.

Fortunately, the provider seemed to recognize that LaKeisha experienced her comments and gestures as upsetting. Although it might have been easy to ignore the rupture and maintain a colorblind stance, the provider recognized her blunder and used a form of cultural immediacy to elicit feedback from LaKeisha about the relational dynamics. The provider used the next part of the counseling session to gain clinical insights about the depth of the rupture. The provider admitted wrongdoing, apologized, and confided that she did not intend to be offensive and accurately surmised that her actions made LaKeisha uncomfortable. LaKeisha agreed and shared that the provider's actions were hurtful and connected them to an ongoing pattern of having her hair scrutinized by others. She even talked about hair from a sociopolitical standpoint by inquiring about the provider's familiarity with the Crown Act. The provider exhibited humility by acknowledging her lack of awareness about the legislation. The context LaKeisha shared extended the provider's understanding about the depth of the pain she caused.

The provider maintained a nondefensive posture, remained open to LaKeisha's experience, and invited Lakeisha to share how the exchange impacted her. LaKeisha noted that she was particularly offended by the provider's incredulity that her hair was soft, which suggested that the provider harbored stereotypes about Black hair. Further, LaKeisha shared that she felt personally violated because the provider touched her hair without permission. That experience drudged up unpleasant memories about the reality that historically, African Americans were not permitted to object to boundary violations without the threat of harsh, usually violent repercussions. As the session drew to a close, the provider again admitted to wrongdoing, accepted responsibility for her behavior, and acknowledged the harm she caused. LaKeisha accepted her apology, and the provider encouraged LaKeisha to confront her if another rupture occurred. The provider praised the courage it took for LaKeisha to talk openly about the incident.

Much has been written about respectability politics in the African American community, wherein African Americans are expected to conform to rigid, idealized standards around acceptable behavior, comportment, and standards of beauty in order to achieve approval in mainstream society (Cooper, 2018; Higginbotham, 1994). The irony is that typically no amount of contorting will garner the intended praise, adulation, and authentic inclusion in dominant groups. In her groundbreaking text, *Sister Citizen: Shame, Stereotypes, and Black Women in America,* Melissa Harris-Perry (2011) theorizes about the politics of Black womanhood. She used an analogy to demonstrate that Black women exist in a crooked room, drawing on a seminal study in which subjects were placed in a crooked room and asked to adjust themselves until they were perpendicular to the room. Some subjects were able to straighten themselves despite being mired in a crooked room, while other subjects contorted themselves by tilting their bodies to an unbelievable 35-degree angle while claiming they were perfectly aligned with tilted objects. Harris-Perry asserted that Black women must align themselves in crooked rooms as they confront the warped images about themselves and their humanity.

LaKeisha's effort to wear her hair in an afro may suggest that she is working to reject the politics of respectability and align herself in crooked spaces. Ironically, the counseling office became a crooked space for LaKeisha. Future counseling sessions may explore how LaKeisha navigates this dynamic not only in her choice of self-presentation but also in how she manages as a first-generation attorney, especially given social class differences between herself and her more affluent African American peers. It may be helpful to understand how and whether LaKeisha connects with other associates in the firm, feels a sense of belonging, has an experienced mentor or peer mentorship, and engages in self-care and social support networks. Given that she is a first-gen college graduate and attorney, the provider may also discuss LaKeisha's relationship with her nuclear and extended family, as social mobility can intensify social distance between family members (Lubrano, 2005). It may be that LaKeisha is operating in multiple crooked spaces that warrant re-alignment.

During the session, it became clear that there were several rupture markers to which the provider was oblivious. For instance, the provider's belief that touching LaKeisha's hair was acceptable, or her seeming surprised about how soft LaKeisha's hair was, the lack of awareness about the inter-racial and intra-racial tensions regarding hair texture within the African American community, the politics of respectability, as well as the social stratification that occurs within African American communities (Cooper, 2018; Graham, 1999; Robinson, 2011). The provider's humility salvaged the relationship, but the provider's desire to understand her client's reality must be accompanied by greater self-understanding or critical self-awareness, as well as more concrete information. The provider can benefit from developing greater foundational knowledge about the African American community, especially if she has a large or growing African American caseload. The fact that LaKeisha had to educate the provider about important aspects of the African American experience may also be construed as a microaggression. LaKeisha noted that she must contort herself in many spaces in order to manage microaggressions, but having to contort herself within the counseling seems burdensome. A growing body of evidence indicates the health consequences associated with hypervigilance (Lee & Hicken, 2016). The provider may also benefit by engaging in professional development training, seeking supervision, and pursuing personal counseling as necessary.

Burning Question

Norma, I'm not really sure why it's so important for providers to apologize for mistakes. Sometimes it seems self-deprecating.

I believe that acknowledging our limitations is an important expression of integrity. Although we can pretend to have superior moral awareness, whether acknowledged or not, clients will be able to see through this. Years ago, I was teaching my daughter how to drive. On our way home from church, we stopped at the grocery store. I was in the parking lot and a car attempted to head out in front of me. As I gripped the steering wheel tightly, I looked at my daughter and said sternly, "I will not let her get in front of me." It's not that I mind yielding the right of way to other drivers, I resented the person's sense of entitlement when they did not have the right of way. At the very least, I expected the other driver to use a gesture that signaled she was asking if she could get in front of me. I responded by positioning my car so she could not get in front of me. Immediately afterward, I looked at my daughter and I apologized. I said, "Jaelyn, I am so embarrassed. I'm trying to teach you how to drive, but I'm driving aggressively, and we just left church." She accepted my apology, but then she continued by saying, "Exactly! You run around the house quoting scriptures talking about, 'but the fruit of the spirit is love, joy, peace, patience, kindness goodness, gentleness, and self-control." In that moment I realized that my apology was insufficient. I acknowledged my aggressive driving, but my daughter responded to my hypocrisy – the discrepancy between my values and behavior. The scripture, for me, was not a moral mandate to be imposed on others, but an ethical touchstone – one I had failed to embody.

Similarly, clients will often see how short we fall from the values and identities we profess. We may express commitment to empathy, humility, and cultural responsiveness yet act in ways that undermine those commitments. James Baldwin (1962) observed, "I can't believe what you say, because I see what you do." Remaining congruent, then requires more than verbal acknowledgment or performative repair. It calls for critical self-awareness and openly and meaningfully acknowledging our fallibility when our actions fall short of our ideals. This is an important pathway to repairing ruptures, restoring trust, helping clients heal, and symptom improvement.

Summary

Therapeutic ruptures refer to a breakdown in trust between the provider and client. Scholars estimate that ruptures occur in one-half to more than a third of counseling sessions. Cultural ruptures result from cultural tensions within diverse provider-client dyads. When not managed appropriately, ruptures contribute to less favorable counseling outcomes and premature termination. Chang et al. (2020) developed a critical-cultural-relational approach to managing and resolving ruptures that involves critical self-awareness, wise affect or emotional regulation, and an anti-oppressive interpersonal style.

References

Baldwin, J. (1962, January 14). As much truth as one can bear. *The New York Times Book Review*, 1, 26–27.

Bonilla-Silva, E. (2021). Racism without racists: Color-Blind racism and the persistence of racial inequality in America. *Rowman and Littlefield.*

Brawner, R., Day-Vines, N.L., Gubara, S., Agorsor, C., Jackson, Z., Ran, T., & Caldwell, N. (2025). Perceptions of racial, ethnic, and cultural ruptures in counseling: A qualitative case study of a client from a minoritized background. *Journal of Counseling and Development, 103,* 484–495. https://doi-org.proxy1.library.jhu.edu/10.1002/jcad.70004

Chang, D.F., Dunn, J.J., & Omidi, M. (2020). A critical-cultural-relational approach to rupture resolution: A case illustration with a cross-racial dyad. *Journal of Clinical Psychology*, 77(2), 369–383. https://doi.org/10.1002/jclp.23080

Cooper, B. (2018). *Eloquent rage: A Black feminist discovers her superpower.* St. Martin's Press.

Graham, L.O. (1999). *Our kind of people: Inside America's Black upper class.* Harper Collins.

Harris-Perry, M. (2011). *Sister citizen: Shame, stereotypes, and Black women in America.* Yale University.

Higginbotham, E.B. (1994). *Righteous discontent: The women's movement in the Black Baptist church, 1880–1920.* Harvard University Press.

Homan, J.B., Talbott, M.M., & Holliday, M. (2024). Clients' reasons for dropping out of therapy: A qualitative study. *Counselling and Psychotherapy Research*, 25, e12882. https://doi-org.proxy1.library.jhu.edu/10.1002/capr.12882

Hook, J.N., Farrell, J.E., Davis, D.E., DeBlaere, C., Van Tongeren, D.R., & Utsey, S.O. (2016). Cultural humility and racial microaggressions in counseling. *Journal of Counseling Psychology*, 63(3), 269–277. https://doi.org/10.1037/cou0000114

Kearney, L.K., Draper, M., & Baron, A. (2005). Counseling utilization by ethnic minority college students. *Cultural Diversity & Ethnic Minority Psychology*, 11, 272–285. https://doi.org/10.1037/1099–9809.11.3.272

Lee, H., & Hicken, M.T. (2016). Death by a thousand cuts: The health implications of Black respectability politics. *Souls, 18*(2–4), 421–445. https://doi-org.proxy1.library.jhu.edu/10.1080/10999949.2016.1230828

Lee, E., & Horvath, A.O. (2014). How a therapist responds to cultural versus noncultural dialogue in cross-cultural clinical practice. *Journal of Social Work Practice*, 28(2), 193–217. https://doi-org.proxy1.library.jhu.edu/10.1080/02650533.2013.821104

Lubrano, A. (2005). *Limbo: Blue-collar roots, white-collar dreams.* Wiley.

Muran, J.C., Safran, J.D., & Eubanks-Carter, C. (2010). Developing therapist abilities to negotiate alliance ruptures. In J.C. Muran & J.P. Barber (Eds.), *The therapeutic alliance: An evidence-based guide to practice.* (pp. 320–340). Guilford.

Owen, J., Imel, Z.E., Adelson, J., & Rodolfa, E. (2012). No-show: Therapist racial/ethnic disparities in client unilateral termination. *Journal of Counseling Psychology, 59*, 314–320. https://doi.org.proxy1.library.jhu.edu/10.1037/a0027091

Owen, J., Tao, K.W., Imel, Z.E., Wampold, B.E., & Emil, R. (2014). Addressing racial and ethnic microaggressions in therapy. *Professional.*

Owen, J.J., Tao, K., Leach, M.M., & Rodolfa, E. (2011). Clients' perceptions of their psychotherapists' multicultural orientation. *Psychotherapy (Chicago, Ill.), 48*(3), 274–282. https://doi.org/10.1037/a0022065

Robinson, E. (2011). *Disintegration: The splintering of Black America.* Anchor.

Rudecindo, B., Imel, Z.E., Kuo, P.B., Smith, W.A., & Tao, K.W. (2024). Impact of racial microaggressions in psychotherapy vignettes with African American clients:

An experimental analogue design. *Journal of Counseling Psychology*, *71*, 203–214. https://doi.org/10.1037/cou0000742

Safran, J.D., & Muran, J.C. (2006). Has the concept of the alliance outlived its usefulness? *Psychotherapy*, 43, 286–291.

Sue, D.W., & Spanierman, L. (2020). *Microaggressions in everyday life* (2nd ed.). Wiley.

Yeo, E., & Torres-Harding, S.R. (2021). Rupture resolution strategies and the impact of rupture on the working alliance after racial microaggressions in therapy. *Psychotherapy*, 58, 460–471. https://doi.org/10.1037/pst0000372

Appendix A

Broaching Attitudes and Behavior Scale (BABS)

Broaching Attitudes and Behavior Scale (BABS)

This survey examines the extent to which providers discuss or *broach* the subject of race, ethnicity, and culture with their clients of color during the counseling process. Essentially, *broaching* refers to the provider's effort to determine the extent to which race, ethnicity, and culture may be related to the client's presenting problem. Using the Likert scale below, please circle the response that best describes your behavior.

Strongly Disagree	Disagree	Neither Agree/ Nor Disagree	Agree	Strongly Agree
[1]	[2]	[3]	[4]	[5]

1	Broaching racial and cultural factors represents the client's effort to avoid taking responsibility for her or his actions.	1	2	3	4	5
2	I experience a sense of awkwardness when I address racial and cultural factors during the counseling process.	1	2	3	4	5
3	I need a broader range of counseling strategies in order to broach racial and cultural factors more effectively with my clients of color.	1	2	3	4	5
4	The client's race doesn't matter because good counseling is good counseling.	1	2	3	4	5
5	I am not sure that broaching is an effective counseling strategy.	1	2	3	4	5

Broaching Attitudes and Behavior Scale (BABS)

Strongly Disagree	Disagree	Neither Agree/ Nor Disagree	Agree	Strongly Agree
[1]	[2]	[3]	[4]	[5]

6	When I am working with a person of color, I broach issues of race and ethnicity several times throughout the course of the counseling relationship.	1	2	3	4	5
7	I initiate discussions that help my clients understand that their problems may be connected to a larger set of system issues such as race and culture.	1	2	3	4	5
8	I have integrated the concept of broaching into my professional identity.	1	2	3	4	5
9	I feel uncertain about my ability to broach cultural factors with clients of color.	1	2	3	4	5
10	As a counselor, I am personally committed to the eradication of all forms of oppression.	1	2	3	4	5
11	Disagreeing with racial discrimination is not enough because counselors must be willing to engage in advocacy and systemic change efforts.	1	2	3	4	5
12	If a client is the victim of overt or institutional racism, I act as a change agent and advocate for that client.	1	2	3	4	5
13	Sometimes I have difficulty identifying facilitative responses once the client begins to talk about racial and cultural issues.	1	2	3	4	5
14	Sometimes I have difficulty translating my broaching efforts into culturally responsive counseling interventions.	1	2	3	4	5

Broaching Attitudes and Behavior Scale (BABS)

Strongly Disagree	Disagree	Neither Agree/ Nor Disagree	Agree	Strongly Agree
[1]	[2]	[3]	[4]	[5]

15	Given the time-limited nature of counseling, broaching is not appropriate for short-term problem-solving.	1	2	3	4	5
16	As a counselor, I am socially/politically committed to the eradication of all forms of oppression.	1	2	3	4	5
17	I believe that the counselor should only broach racial and cultural factors when the client initiates such discussions.	1	2	3	4	5
18	I generally broach racial and cultural factors throughout my counseling sessions with clients.	1	2	3	4	5
19	I encourage my clients to make culture-specific interpretations of their counseling concerns.	1	2	3	4	5
20	Counselors should appreciate the daily experiences and challenges of clients who are culturally diverse.	1	2	3	4	5

Scoring Procedures

Sum the items for each subscale and divide the number of items within the subscale. Respondents obtain a separate score for each subscale. The subscale with the highest score represents greater endorsement of a particular broaching category and the respondent's predominant mode of functioning. Given the complexity of the counseling process, counselors can operate in more than one broaching category simultaneously.

Scale	**Items**
Avoidant	1, 4, 15, 17,
Continuing/Incongruent	2, 3, 9, 13, 14,
Integrated Congruent	5 – reverse score, 6, 7, 8, 18, 19
Infusing	10, 11, 12, 16, 20

Glossary

Acculturative stress the strain that results from adapting to a new cultural environment.

Anticipatory grief the mourning that occurs for individuals before an expected loss.

Avoidant broaching behavior broaching behavior in which the provider ignores or minimizes the client's race, ethnicity, and culture (REC) concerns.

Broaching refers to the provider's effort to initiate or respond to discussions about the way issues related to race, ethnicity, and culture influence the client's presenting concerns.

Continuing/Incongruent broaching behavior broaching behavior in which the provider broaches awkwardly, mechanically, and ineffectively.

Continuum of Broaching Behavior a conceptual framework that describes the orientations that providers can assume as they determine whether and how to examine clients' REC concerns.

Countertransference situations in which the provider's unresolved concerns impact their reactions to the client. Those reactions include positive and negative responses such as overidentification with clients, as well as microaggressions directed toward the client, whether or not they are intentional.

Cultural humility the provider's sense of curiosity about the client and willingness to admit mistakes and the limits of their knowledge.

Cultural immediacy the provider's proactive and timely exploration of the relationship dynamics that are shaped by the social identities and power relations of both the provider and client.

Culture the shared set of attitudes, values, beliefs, norms, patterned ways of behaving, and symbol systems that provides groups with a sense of social meaning and a way of living and operating in the world.

Emic cultural understanding that reflects the specific and unique meanings, values, and viewpoints that group members assign to their own culture.

Ethnicity the shared cultural heritage that includes language, geography, religion, nationality, cuisine, ancestry, politics, and a sense of group solidarity.

Etic cultural understanding that reflects universal standards, values, and viewpoints across cultures without attention to cultural means groups assign to their own culture.

Healthcare disparities individuals from marginalized groups experience preventable differences in health outcomes due to social, economic, and environmental disadvantages that result in unequal access to treatment, higher disease rates, and shorter life expectancies.

Infusing broaching behaviors broaching behaviors in which providers implement social justice and advocacy interventions to remove structural barriers that affect clients' mental health.

Integrated/Congruent broaching behaviors a dimension of the multidimensional model of broaching behavior that involves effective broaching behaviors in which the provider addresses clients' REC concerns meaningfully, comfortably, and effectively.

Inter-REC broaching dimensions a dimension of the multidimensional model of broaching behavior that involves discussion of clients' encounters with racism and discrimination.

Intra-Counseling broaching dimensions a dimension of the multidimensional model of broaching behavior involving the discussion of interpersonal processes between the provider and client to both invite the client to discuss their REC concerns and address how shared and different identity domains between the provider and client impact the counseling relationship.

Intra-Individual broaching dimensions the provider's holistic consideration of the confluence of identity dimensions that are embedded within the client's presenting concerns.

Intra-REC broaching dimensions a dimension of the multidimensional model of broaching behavior involving the client's connection or disconnection with people from their own REC communities.

LGBTQIA+ refers to sexual minorities who are lesbian, gay, bisexual, transgender, or queer.

Minoritized a verb describing groups of people who have experienced oppression, marginalization, discrimination, and inequality by a dominant or more powerful group.

Mixed-status families families in which some members are documented and other members are undocumented in ways that may create strain on the family system.

Multicultural Orientation the provider's demonstration of cultural humility, cultural comfort, and the ability to engage in broaching discussions reflects an overall way of being with the client.

Multidimensional Model of Broaching Behavior (MMBB) conceptual tool that describes four specific broaching contexts that providers explore with clients: Intra-counseling, Intra-individual, Intra-Racial, -Ethnic, -Cultural, and Inter-Racial, -Ethnic, -Cultural dimensions.

Nativism tendency to protect the interests of native-born individuals versus the interests of immigrants.

Oppression an umbrella term that refers to multiple forms of domination and control such as racism, sexism, classism, homophobia, religious intolerance, raciolinguistics.

Race a classification schema that originally organized people on the basis of their phenotypic characteristics (skin color, hair texture, facial features); however, race is now considered a social construct that stratifies people on the basis of their phenotypic characteristics and consigns minoritized individuals to subordinate status and treatment.

Raciolinguistics the devaluing of an individual on the basis of their race and language due to assumptions that the individual's communication style lacks prestige.

Racism the systematic process of enlisting institutional resources, not only to support and promote a belief in the inferiority of groups on the basis of skin color but also to deny opportunities to one group and subsequently grant them to a preferred group.

Rupture a breakdown in the therapeutic process that results from miscommunication, microaggressions, negative perceptions about the counseling process, and/or a weak connection between the provider and client.

Rupture-repair situations in which the provider works to mend the counseling conflict.

Social Determinants of Health non-medical factors that impact health, well-being, and quality of life such as housing, nutrition, education, access to health care, and social policies (e.g., immigration).

Social locations unique attributional characteristics such as race, ethnicity, gender, religion, immigration status, sexual orientation, and linguistic diversity that effect provider-client interactions.

Toxic positivity expectation that clients exude a positive mindset despite the experience of emotional pain that negates the client's experiential reality by discouraging justifiably negative emotions.

Index

Note: **Bold** page numbers refer to tables and *italic* page numbers refer to figures.

For Product Safety Concerns and Information please contact our EU representative GPSR@taylorandfrancis.com
Taylor & Francis Verlag GmbH, Kaufingerstraße 24, 80331 München, Germany

www.ingramcontent.com/pod-product-compliance
Ingram Content Group UK Ltd.
Pitfield, Milton Keynes, MK11 3LW, UK
UKHW022351190926
475702UK00015B/2229

9781041092827